# SCIENCE ESSENTIALS
## SOLAR SYSTEM

# GRADES 1-3

AMERICAN EDUCATION PUBLISHING™

Columbus, Ohio

School Specialty
Publishing

Copyright © 2003 School Specialty Publishing. Published by American Education Publishing™, an imprint of School Specialty Publishing, a member of the School Specialty Family.

Printed in the United States of America. All rights reserved. Except as permitted under the United States Copyright Act, no part of this publication may be reproduced or distributed in any form or by any means, or stored in a database or retrieval system, without prior written permission from the publisher, unless otherwise indicated.

Send all inquiries to:
School Specialty Publishing
8720 Orion Place
Columbus, OH 43240-2111

ISBN 0-7696-6047-9

2 3 4 5 6 7 QPD 13 12 11 10 09

Science Essentials
# SOLAR SYSTEM

## Table of Contents

# Table of Contents

# THE SOLAR SYSTEM

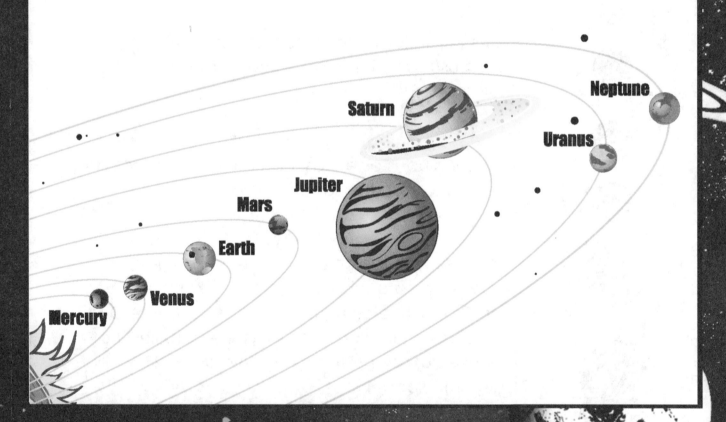

Saturn · Neptune · Uranus · Jupiter · Mars · Earth · Venus · Mercury

A solar system is more than a sun and its planets — it's anything and everything that revolves around a star!

Our solar system gets its name from the Sun. *Solar* means "of the Sun."

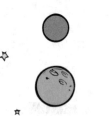

Our solar system is made up of our local star, the Sun, plus the nine major planets that orbit it and their moons.

It also includes asteroids, comets, and the gas and dust particles in the space between them!

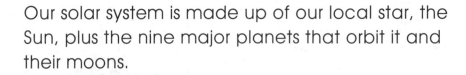

The outermost region of the solar system is thought to be an area occupied by what is known as an **Oort Cloud**. Stretching far off into space, the Oort Cloud is a collection of orbiting ice particles that extends our solar system 4 light-years, or 23.6 trillion miles, into space!

All the planets in our solar system move around the Sun in the same direction. The solar system itself rotates around the Milky Way!

# Space

Space is what separates one thing from another. When objects are close together, there is not much space between them. When they are far apart, there is a lot of space. The space between planets is called **interplanetary space**. The space between stars is **interstellar space**. The space between galaxies is **intergalactic space**. There is more space between stars than between planets. Space is everywhere. Look around, and you will see that there is space between you and other people and objects. There is a lot of space in the universe. Space is not empty. It can be filled with air. Air is made of different gases. Earth's air is made of mainly nitrogen, oxygen, and carbon dioxide. The air on other planets is made of gases, but some are poisonous for human beings to breathe.

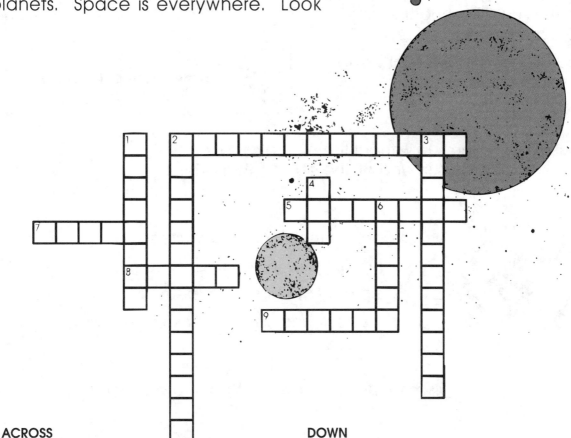

**ACROSS**
2. Space between galaxies
5. A gas that is found in air
7. There is more____between the stars than between the planets.
8. The system we live in (first word)
9. _____dioxide is a gas.

**DOWN**
1. There is a lot of space in the____.
2. The space between planets
3. The space between stars
4. It is made of different gases.
6. Another gas that is part of Earth's air

## The Solar System

Our solar system is made up of the sun and all the objects that go around, or orbit, the sun.

The sun is the only star in our solar system. It gives heat and light to the eight planets in the solar system. The planets and their moons all orbit the sun.

The time it takes for each planet to orbit the sun is called a year. A year on Earth is 365 days. Planets closer to the sun have shorter years. Their orbit is shorter. Planets farther from the sun take longer to orbit, so their years are longer.

Asteroids, comets and meteors are also part of our solar system.

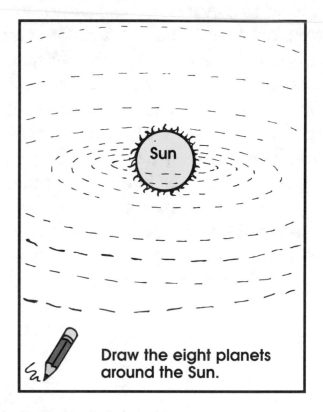

Draw the eight planets around the Sun.

**Underline:**

The solar system is:     the sun without the nine planets.
                         the sun and all the objects that orbit it.

**Check:**

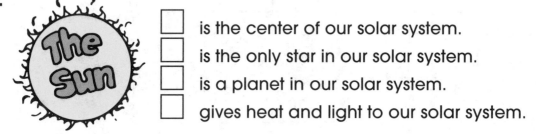

☐ is the center of our solar system.

☐ is the only star in our solar system.

☐ is a planet in our solar system.

☐ gives heat and light to our solar system.

**Write:**

A _____ is the time it takes for a planet to orbit the sun.
    month     year

**Match:**

Planets closer to the sun . . .          have a longer year.
Planets farther from the sun . . .       have a shorter year.

# What's in Our Solar System?

An **astronomer**, or scientist who studies the universe, might make this list if you asked her what is in our solar system.

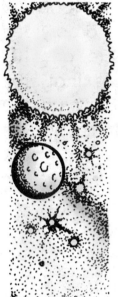

- one **star**, or hot glowing ball of gases, called the Sun

- all the planets' moons

- small chunks of rock or ice called **meteoroids**

- lots of empty space

- eight worlds called **planets** that travel around the Sun

- chunks of rock and metal called **asteroids**

- frozen balls of dirty ice called **comets**

Now write a definition for each of these words.

1. astronomer _____

_____

2. star _____

_____

3. planets _____

_____

4. asteroids _____

_____

5. meteoroids _____

_____

6. comets _____

_____

# Solar System

Solar means anything having to do with the Sun or something that uses or operates with energy from the Sun. Our solar system consists of the nine known planets, their moons, asteroids, meteoroids, and comets orbiting the Sun. A **meteoroid** is a small piece of rock or metal traveling through space. A **meteor** is the name of a meteoroid that falls to Earth, producing a streak of light in the sky. A **comet** is a mass of ice and rock that orbits the Sun. **Asteroids** are large pieces of rock and metal that are mostly found between Mars and Jupiter. There are 101 known moons, or satellites, that orbit the planets. The Sun is by far the biggest and heaviest celestial body in our solar system.

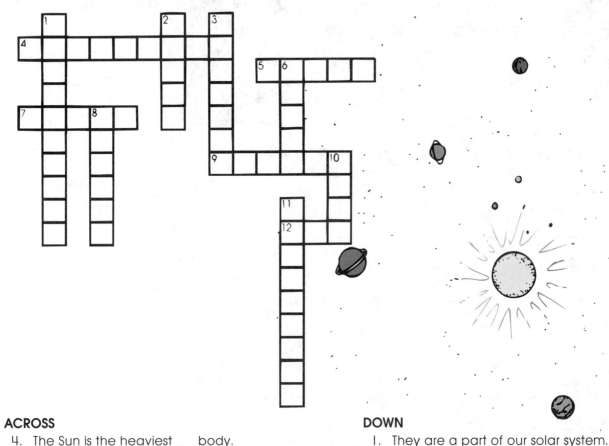

**ACROSS**

4. The Sun is the heaviest____body.
5. Pertaining to the Sun
7. A mass of ice and rock that orbits the Sun
9. Earth is part of the solar____.
12. Earth orbits the____.

**DOWN**

1. They are a part of our solar system.
2. Number of planets in our solar system
3. Earth and Mars are____.
6. To repeatedly move around a star or planet in the same path
8. Earth uses____from the Sun.
10. Earth's closest neighbor
11. They are large pieces of rock and metal.

The Solar System

# Space Words

Find the space words in the puzzle below.  The words go across and down.
Use the Word Bank to help you, and circle the words as you find them.

## Word Bank

| | | | |
|---|---|---|---|
| Moon | Shuttle | Land | Orbit |
| Flight | Comet | Astronaut | Star |
| Rocket | Planet | Space | Sun |

```
S   S   O   R   B   I   T   M   A

G   U   R   L   A   N   D   C   S

W   N   R   A   F   P   L   O   T

S   H   U   T   T   L   E   M   R

T   X   N   S   P   A   C   E   O

A   F   M   O   O   N   T   T   N

R   V   E   B   A   E   U   T   A

F   L   I   G   H   T   P   R   U

L   F   R   O   C   K   E   T   T
```

# Solar System Scramble

Unscramble the name of each numbered object below. Write the name on the correct line below.

**Word Bank**

| | | | |
|---|---|---|---|
| Neptune | Asteroids | Mars | Earth |
| Jupiter | Sun | Saturn | Uranus |
| | Venus | Mercury | |

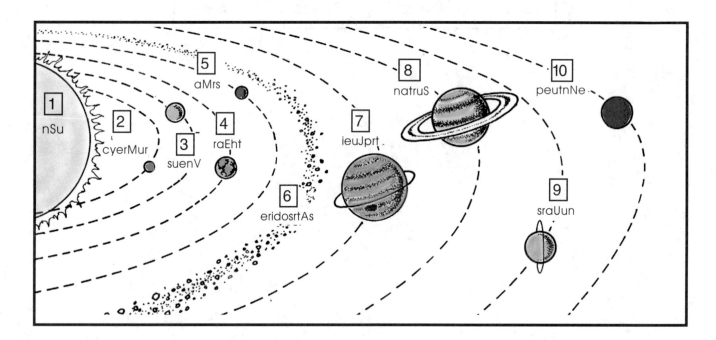

1. _____    5. _____    9. _____

2. _____    6. _____    10. _____

3. _____    7. _____

4. _____    8. _____

# A Strip of Space

Compare the positions of the planets from the Sun.

1. Color:

- the Sun yellow
- Mercury brown
- Venus yellow

- Earth green
- Mars red
- Jupiter orange

- Saturn yellow
- Uranus and Neptune blue

2. Cut out the four strips below.

3. Glue:

- strip 2 to the right end of strip 1
- strip 3 to the right end of strip 2
- strip 4 to the right end of strip 3

(Distances are to approximate scale.)

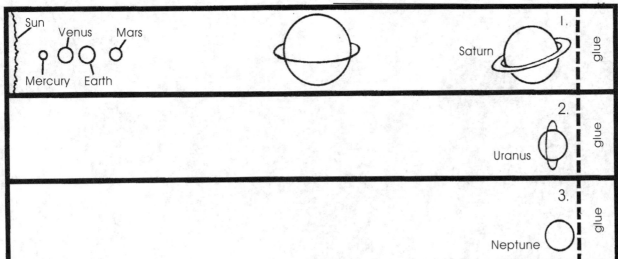

# Your Solar Family

Our solar system is like a family with the Sun being the parent. The planets are like children orbiting around the Sun. The planets and the Sun make up a family.

Planets **revolve**, or move, around the Sun. When a planet starts at one place, goes all the way around the Sun, and ends up back at the same place, we call that one **revolution**.

While each planet is revolving or orbiting the Sun, it is also doing something else. It is spinning like a top. We call this **rotation**.

## Your "Solar" Family

1. Use a piece of white paper, a pencil, crayons, and a glass.
2. Let's compare your family to the Sun's family! Put the glass in the center of the paper. Trace around the glass to draw a circle. Inside the circle, you may draw the face of your mom, dad, or grandparent as in the example.
3. Now, around the outside of the paper, draw more faces to show all the children in your family.

# Found in Space

Read each riddle. Then write the answer using one of the scrambled words from the Word Bank.

## Word Bank

| | | |
|---|---|---|
| tlfoa | nuS | htlesut |
| srast | rEath | nruSat |
| rMas | erscrat | |

1. This huge star lights the day. __ __ __

2. These shine at night. __ __ __ __ __

3. These are on the Moon. __ __ __ __ __ __ __

4. This is our home planet. __ __ __ __ __

5. This flies into space. __ __ __ __ __ __ __

6. This planet is red. __ __ __ __

7. This planet has rings. __ __ __ __ __ __

8. Astronauts do this in space. __ __ __ __ __

# Studying the Solar System

## Game Directions

**To Play:**

1.   Carefully cut out the cards on page 19.

2.   Mix them up and place them face down in a pile next to the game board on page 18.

3.   Each player takes a card, answers the equation on it, and then uses that answer to mark a number on the game board. If the players draw a card and the number is not on the game board, they may draw another card.

4.   The first player to cover all of the numbers on the planets wins!

# Studying the Solar System

**Object:** To cover all the planets in the solar system

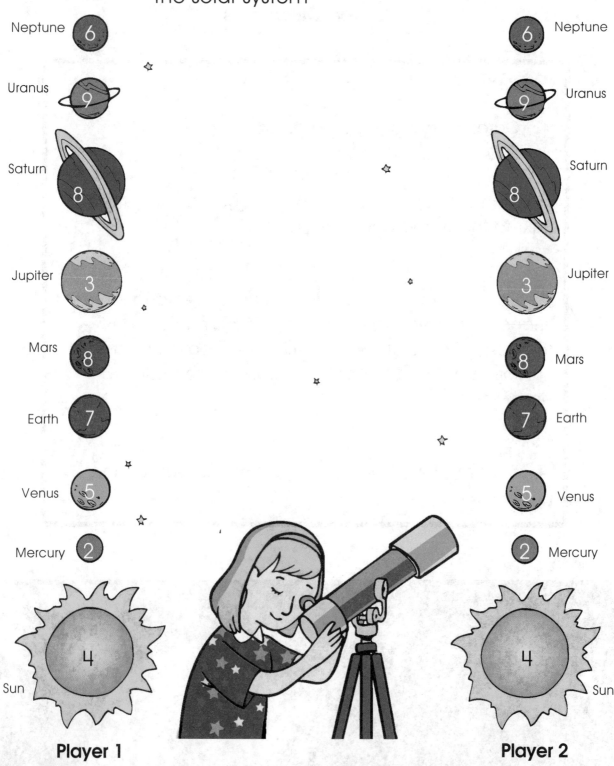

Player 1

Player 2

# Studying the Solar System Game Cards

| | | | | | |
|---|---|---|---|---|---|
| 5 + 0 | 1 + 1 | 7 + 1 | 5 + 2 | 5 + 3 | 5 + 5 |
| 4 + 0 | 10 + 0 | 6 + 1 | 4 + 2 | 4 + 3 | 6 + 4 |
| 3 + 0 | 9 + 0 | 5 + 1 | 3 + 2 | 3 + 3 | 5 + 4 |
| 2 + 0 | 8 + 0 | 4 + 1 | 2 + 2 | 8 + 2 | 4 + 4 |
| 1 + 0 | 7 + 0 | 3 + 1 | 9 + 1 | 7 + 2 | 7 + 3 |
| 0 + 0 | 6 + 0 | 2 + 1 | 8 + 1 | 6 + 2 | 6 + 3 |

# Beyond Our Solar System

Astronomers know that much lies beyond our solar system. In fact, in the drawing on this page our solar system is just a tiny speck in a larger group of objects in space. This larger group is called the **Milky Way galaxy**. The Milky Way is made up of all the stars you can see in the night sky and many more beyond those. It also contains large clouds made of gas and dust. But that's not all! Beyond our Milky Way, astronomers have seen millions of other galaxies. Each of these has billions of stars. Astronomers call space and everything in it the **universe**.

Our Solar System

1. What is the name of our galaxy? _____

2. What have astronomers seen beyond our galaxy? _____

_____

3. What is the universe? _____

_____

4. Which contains the largest group of objects—the solar system, the

   universe, or the Milky Way? _____

5. What two kinds of objects does the Milky Way contain? _____

_____

# Where in the World Is...

What is your global address? It's more than your street, city, state, and ZIP code.

What would your address be if you wanted to get a letter from a friend living in outer space?

Use an atlas, encyclopedia, science book, or other source to complete your global address.

## Inter-Galactic Address Book

Name _____

Street _____

County or Parish _____

State or Province _____

Country _____

Continent _____

Hemisphere _____

Planet _____

Galaxy _____

Draw an **X** to mark the approximate place where you live.

# A Space Riddle

Find a word in the Word Bank that matches each clue below.  Write the word on the blanks.

## Word Bank

| | | | |
|---|---|---|---|
| atmosphere | axis | revolve | planets |
| rings | star | orbit | astronomer |
| astronaut | rotate | craters | |

1. person who travels in space __ __ __ __ __ __ __ __ __

2. deep holes __ __ __ __ __ __ __

3. eight worlds __ __ __ __ __ __ __

4. to spin __ __ __ __ __ __

5. to travel around __ __ __ __ __ __ __

6. scientist who studies the objects in space

__ __ __ __ __ __ __ __ __ __

7. imaginary line through the center of a planet __ __ __ __

8. a planet's path around the Sun __ __ __ __ __

9. ball of hot glowing gases __ __ __ __

10. Saturn, Jupiter, and Uranus have these __ __ __ __ __

11. a blanket of gases __ __ __ __ __ __ __ __ __ __

Answer this riddle!  Write the circled letters on the blanks below.

### *What is another name for our solar system?*

__ __ __ __ __ __ __ __ __ __ __ __ __ __ __ __
8   I   4    II   3   9   2   5     7   6     10   II   9   2   5

# States of Matter

*Can a solid become a gas?*

**Background:**
Everything in the universe, from the smallest ant to the largest star, is made of **matter**. Matter comes in three states, or forms: solid, liquid, and gas.

**What You'll Need:**
- three ice cubes
- zip-top sandwich bag
- microwave-safe dish
- microwave oven

**What to Do:**
1. Put the ice cubes into the sandwich bag. Seal the bag.

2. Place the bag on a microwave-safe dish. Put the dish inside the microwave oven.

3. Ask an adult to help you heat the bag for 90 seconds at high power. If the ice isn't completely melted, heat the bag for another 30 seconds. The ice will form water.

4. Now heat the bag for another 30 seconds. What happens? Why?

5. Let the bag cool completely before removing it from the microwave.

## What Happened:

In this experiment, matter changed its state, or form. Solid ice became liquid water, then a gas called water vapor. This happened because the molecules, or particles, of matter where heated up. The molecules of matter are always moving around. In a solid, like ice, the molecules are close together and move very slowly. When a solid is heated, the molecules move farther apart. The solid becomes a liquid. When a liquid is heated, the molecules move even faster and farther apart, becoming a gas. Your bag puffed up because the water became water vapor. The gas molecules moved farther apart, filling more space in the bag. Matter can also change its state in the other direction. When a gas is cooled enough, it can become a liquid, then a solid.

## One Step Further:

When you finish the experiment, put the bag in the freezer. Check it after three or four hours. What happens to the bag? Why?

## Questions:

1. Is your body made of matter?
2. If you leave a chocolate bar out in the hot sun, it melts. Why does this happen?
3. Can you name a solid? A liquid? A gas?
4. What's the name of the red-hot liquid that pours out of a volcano? What does this liquid form when it cools?
5. In science fiction stories, spaceships sometimes use "matter" or "antimatter" as fuel for their engines. When matter and antimatter collide, they release tremendous energy. Make up a science fiction story that contains the words *matter* and *antimatter*.

25

# Mystery Picture

Use the clues below to find the mystery picture! Read each sentence and then cross out the picture that does not belong. Which picture is left?

1. It is not Earth.

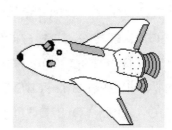

2. It is not an astronaut.

3. It is not a space shuttle.

4. It is not the Sun.

5. It is not a satellite.

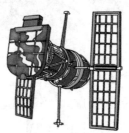

6. It is not a rocket ship.

7. It is not a telescope.

What is the mystery picture?

# Make Your Own Solar System

Our solar system has one Sun, eight planets, asteroids, comets, and moons. Ours is a sun-centered or **heliocentric** solar system, since our Sun is at the center.

Create your own heliocentric solar system!

**New Solar System Discovered!**

1. Use a large piece of black construction paper as your background.
2. Cut out the Sun to fit in the middle of the page. Will your Sun be yellow or another color?
3. Color the things you want in your solar system. Do your planets have craters? Are they blue or green? Maybe they are pink? Do they have volcanos? Are they smooth as ice? It's your solar system!
4. Cut out the shapes you want and glue them around your Sun or use them as patterns to make more.

What is the name of your new solar system?

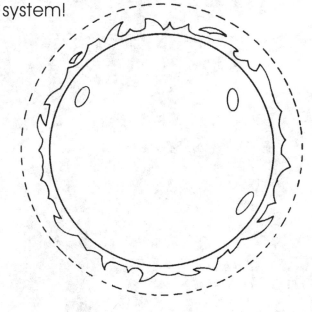

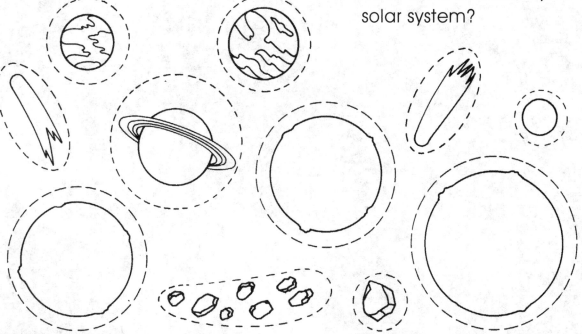

# The Universe

The universe contains everything you could see, or touch, or measure that exists, no matter how close or how far away. All the galaxies and the space between them are part of the universe. All the stars and planets in the galaxies are part of the universe. Some of the planets are much larger than Earth, some are smaller. Almost all the stars are big.

The Sun is a star. Did you know that more than a million planets the size of Earth would fit into the Sun? The Sun is only a medium-sized star. There are stars much larger than the Sun in the universe. Even though there are large planets and giant stars in the universe, there is more space than anything else.

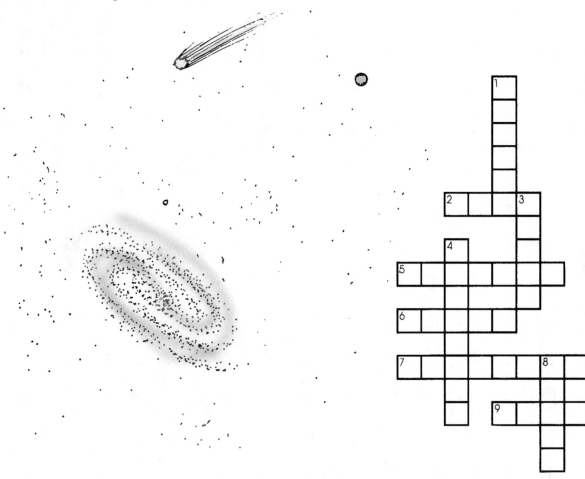

**ACROSS**

2. There is____space that anything else in the universe.
5. Earth, Mars, and Venus are all____.
6. Size of some planets
7. It includes all the galaxies and the space between galaxies.
9. The Sun is one.

**DOWN**

1. Size of some planets in comparison to Earth
3. The planet we live on
4. The universe includes all the____ and space between them.
8. Empty area

# Hunt for It!

Now that you know more about the solar system, see if you can find the hidden words from the Word Bank in the puzzle below. Circle the words as you find them.

## Word Bank

| | | | |
|---|---|---|---|
| Planet | Meteor | Oort Cloud | Sun |
| Asteroid | Space | Milky Way | Solar System |
| Comet | Galaxy | Astronomer | Universe |

```
M  E  T  E  O  R  Q  G  W  E  R  T  Y  S  U  N
S  D  T  F  G  F  R  A  P  L  I  K  M  N  N  S
A  C  Z  B  N  M  I  L  K  Y  W  A  Y  W  I  S
S  B  N  M  O  P  R  A  W  E  R  S  P  R  V  N
T  X  N  O  A  T  Y  X  W  G  H  P  A  W  E  A
R  A  S  T  R  R  T  Y  P  O  R  S  C  R  R  S
O  R  T  O  E  A  E  P  L  J  R  G  O  O  S  D
N  S  S  O  L  A  R  S  Y  S  T  E  M  S  E  F
O  L  K  R  J  H  G  F  S  D  D  R  E  R  S  G
M  F  G  T  S  D  E  R  S  L  K  T  T  P  O  H
E  T  R  C  S  T  O  P  P  I  O  S  D  O  P  J
R  A  S  L  D  F  S  G  A  P  P  L  A  N  E  T
T  Y  R  O  E  W  F  S  C  D  S  A  G  H  R  K
S  A  Q  U  W  A  S  T  E  R  O  I  D  E  R  L
Z  X  C  D  V  B  N  M  L  K  J  H  G  F  D  P
```

# The Planets

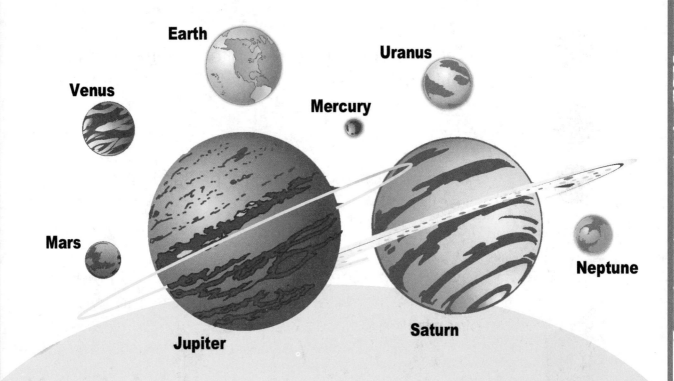

# Fascinating Facts About the Planets

No two planets in our solar system are exactly alike. However, the planets can be divided into two categories, terrestrial or gas giants.

The four inner planets — Mercury, Venus, Earth, and Mars — all have rocky surfaces.

The four outer planets — Jupiter, Saturn, Uranus, and Neptune — are gas giants. These planets also have orbiting rings.

All the planets move around the Sun in the same direction.

Seven of the nine planets rotate, or spin, in the same direction. Venus and Uranus are the two planets that spin the opposite way!

The planets were all named after Greek or Roman gods.

# The Planets in Our Solar System

Mercury, Venus, Earth, Mars, Jupiter, Saturn, Uranus, and Neptune are the eight planets in our solar system!

The solar system is made up of these eight planets and their moons. The system also includes all of the dwarf planets, asteroids, meteors, and comets that revolve, or orbit, the Sun.

## Can You Remember?

Would you like to be able to recite all of the planets in order from the Sun? It is easier than you think! Try using the **mnemonic device** below. A pneumonic device is a learning tool that can help you memorize important information. To create a mnemonic device, you take the first letter of each word in the series you are trying to memorize and create a funny phrase or saying with the letters. For instance, a common pneumonic device used to memorize the planets is:

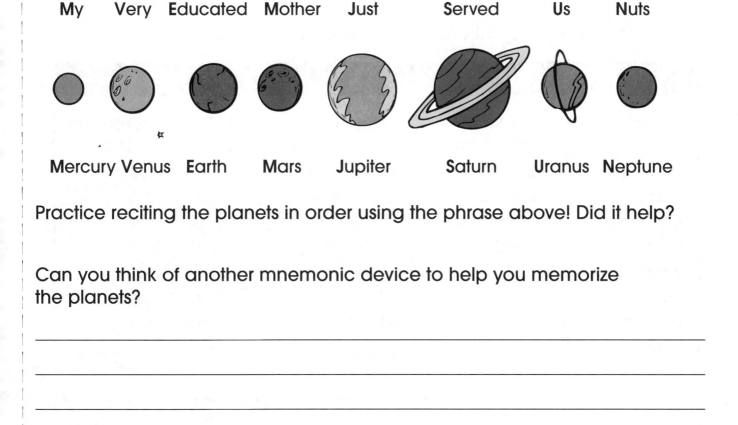

| My | Very | Educated | Mother | Just | Served | Us | Nuts |

| Mercury | Venus | Earth | Mars | Jupiter | Saturn | Uranus | Neptune |

Practice reciting the planets in order using the phrase above! Did it help?

Can you think of another mnemonic device to help you memorize the planets?

_____

_____

_____

# Rock, Liquid, or Gas?

There are two kinds of planets. Mercury, Venus, Earth, and Mars are in the inner solar system and are "terrestrial" planets, meaning they are rocky and dense. In the outer solar system, the planets Jupiter, Saturn, Uranus, and Neptune are made mostly of liquids and gases. These gaseous planets also have rings around them. Saturn has the largest, brightest rings around it. The rings are not solid. They are made up of chunks of rock and frozen materials.

Pluto, a dwarf planet, is made mostly of ice and frozen gases and is the smallest of the planets. Pluto doesn't spend all of its time being farther from the Sun than the planets. Planets orbit in elliptical, round or oval, paths, and Pluto orbits for part of the time inside Neptune's orbit.

**Saturn and its rings**

The chart below shows that each planet has its own personality.

| PLANET FACTS | | | |
|---|---|---|---|
| **Planet** | **Color Seen From Earth** | **Diameter** | **Earth Time to Orbit Sun (Length of a Year)** |
| Mercury | orange | 3,031 miles | 88 days |
| Venus | yellow | 7,521 miles | 225 days |
| Earth | blue & white | 7,927 miles | 365 days |
| Mars | red | 4,197 miles | 687 days |
| Jupiter | yellow | 88,733 miles | 12 Earth years |
| Saturn | yellow | 74,898 miles | 29 Earth years |
| Uranus | green | 31,600 miles | 84 Earth years |
| Neptune | yellow | 30,200 miles | 164.8 Earth years |

# ABC Planets

Unscramble the names of the eight planets in our solar system. Then write the names of the planets in ABC order.

1. _____

2. _____

3. _____

4. _____

5. _____

6. _____

7. _____

8. _____

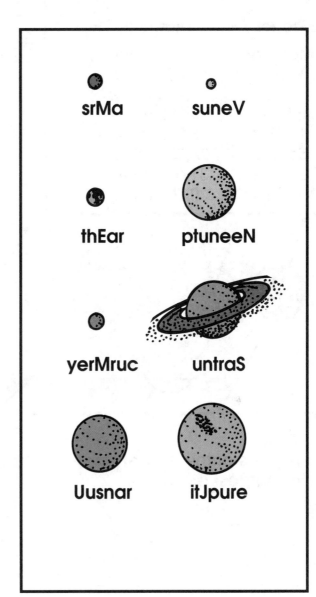

srMa          suneV

thEar          ptuneeN

yerMruc          untraS

Uusnar          itJpure

# How Big?

Planets vary greatly in size. Look at the list of planets and their diameters rounded to the nearest hundred miles.

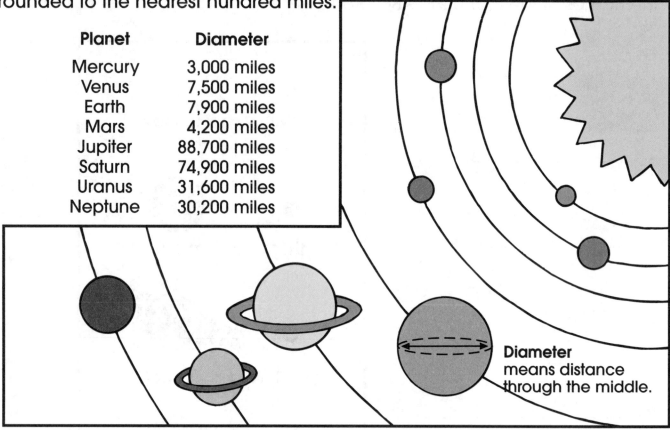

| Planet | Diameter |
|--------|----------|
| Mercury | 3,000 miles |
| Venus | 7,500 miles |
| Earth | 7,900 miles |
| Mars | 4,200 miles |
| Jupiter | 88,700 miles |
| Saturn | 74,900 miles |
| Uranus | 31,600 miles |
| Neptune | 30,200 miles |

**Diameter** means distance through the middle.

Write the names of the planets in order by size, starting with the planet that has the **largest** diameter.

1._____

2._____

3._____

4._____

5._____

6._____

7._____

8._____

# Nine Planets Orbit Our Sun

Cut out the eight planets below and paste them in their correct order from the Sun.

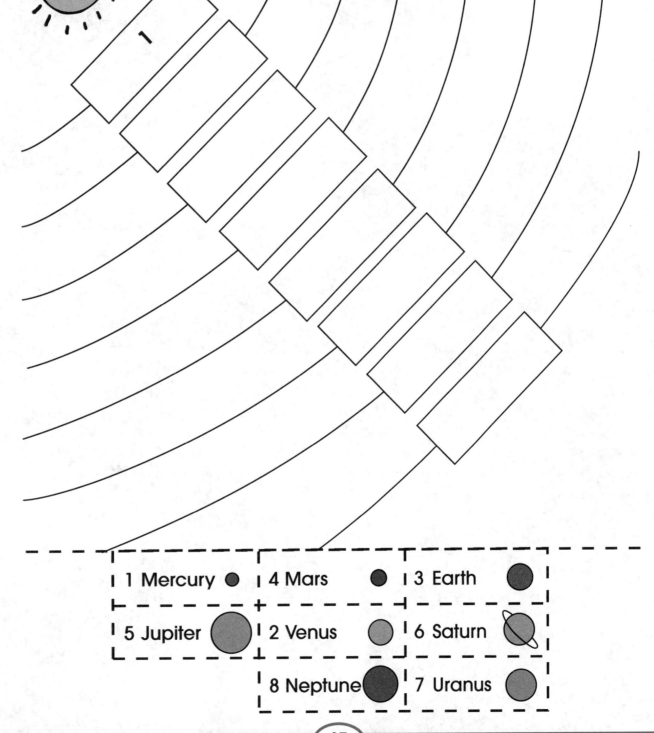

1 Mercury ● | 4 Mars ● | 3 Earth ●

5 Jupiter ● | 2 Venus ● | 6 Saturn ●

8 Neptune ● | 7 Uranus ●

# The Planets Are Moving!

Each of the planets in our solar system **revolves**, or travels, around the Sun. The planets circle the Sun along paths called **orbits**. Because the planets are at different distances from the Sun, each one takes a different length of time to revolve once.

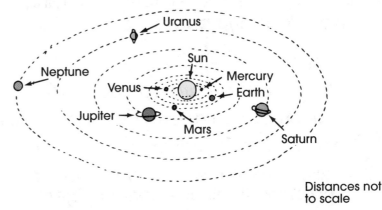

Distances not to scale

1. What word means *travels around*?
   _____

2. What are the planets' paths around the Sun called?
   _____

3. Why do the planets take different lengths of time to revolve around the Sun? _____
   _____

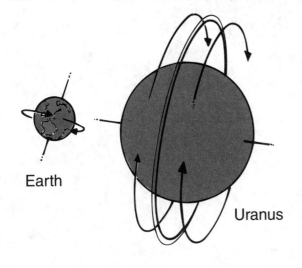

Earth

Uranus

Each planet in our solar system **rotates**, or spins, around a line through its center. This imaginary line is called an **axis**. It takes each planet a different length of time to rotate once.

4. Each planet _____ around a line through its center.

5. This imaginary line is called an _____.

6. *Rotates* means _____.

# Solar System Match Game

You and a partner may enjoy checking your knowledge of the planets in our solar system by playing the Solar System Match Game found on the following pages.

**Directions:**

1. Study the fact cards (on page 45) for each object.
2. Cut out the cards and place them face down.
3. You and your partner should each have a game card.
4. Take turns with your partner flipping over one card and matching it with the correct object on your game card.
5. The first person to get 3 in a row, up and down, across or diagonally is the winner.

# Solar System Match Game

## Game Card

| | | |
|---|---|---|
| Mercury | Venus | Earth |
| Mars | Jupiter | Saturn |
| Uranus | Neptune | Pluto |

# Solar System Match Game

### Game Card

| | | |
|---|---|---|
| Mercury | Venus | Earth |
| Mars | Jupiter | Saturn |
| Uranus | Neptune | Pluto |

# Solar System Match Game

Mercury | Closest planet to the Sun | This planet orbits the Sun in the fewest number of days—88.

Venus | Known as "Earth's twin" | Earth's nearest planet neighbor

Earth | The only planet with life | Known as the "Blue Planet"

Mars | "The Red Planet" | Orbits the Sun between Earth and Jupiter

Jupiter | Largest planet | Has a "red spot" caused by a huge storm

Saturn | Known for its beautiful rings | Second largest planet

Uranus | This planet was thought to be a comet. | Orbits between Saturn and Neptune

Neptune | Has eight moons and may have rings | Orbits between Uranus and Pluto

Pluto | Dwarf planet | Has the orbit farthest from the Sun

# So Far Apart

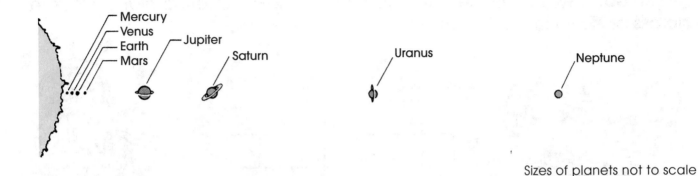

Sizes of planets not to scale

## Planets and Their Average Distances From the Sun

| Mercury | 36 million miles | Mars | 142 million miles | Uranus | 1,781 million miles |
|---|---|---|---|---|---|
| Venus | 67 million miles | Jupiter | 484 million miles | Neptune | 2,788 million miles |
| Earth | 93 million miles | Saturn | 885 million miles | | |

Use the chart and diagram to answer these questions.

1. What is Neptune's average distance from the Sun? _____

2. Which planet has an average distance from the Sun of 142 million miles?

   _____

3. Which planet is closest to the Sun—Saturn, Mars, or Neptune?

   _____

4. How much farther from the Sun is Venus than Mercury?

   _____

5. How much farther is the fourth planet from the Sun than the third planet

   from the Sun? _____

# The Planets' Names

Match each symbol in the puzzle to a clue below. Write the planet's name across or down in capital letters.

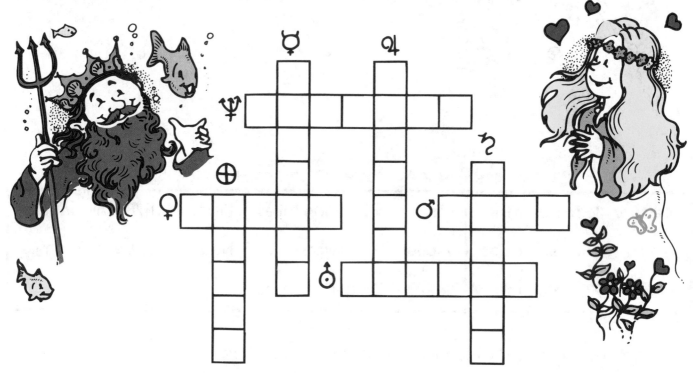

## Across

♆ Neptune was named after the Roman god of the sea.

♀ Venus was named after the Roman goddess of love and beauty.

♂ Mars was named after the Roman god of war.

♅ Uranus was named after the Greek god of the sky.

## Down

☿ Mercury was named after the Roman messenger of the gods.

♃ Jupiter was named after the Roman king of the gods and ruler of the universe.

♄ Saturn was named after the Roman god of farming.

⊕ Earth was named after the Greek Earth goddess.

# Read My Mind

Pretend you have been contacted by NASA to serve as an astronaut on a secret mission. Because of its secrecy, NASA cannot give you your destination. Instead, you must figure it out using the clues below. After each clue, check the possible answers. The planet with the most clues checked will be your destination.

| Destination Clues | Record Answers Here | | | | | | | |
|---|---|---|---|---|---|---|---|---|
| | Mercury | Venus | Earth | Mars | Jupiter | Saturn | Uranus | Neptune |
| It is part of our solar system. | | | | | | | | |
| It is a bright object in the sky. | | | | | | | | |
| It is less than 2,000,000,000 miles from the sun. | | | | | | | | |
| It orbits the sun. | | | | | | | | |
| It has less than 15 known satellites. | | | | | | | | |
| There is weather there. | | | | | | | | |
| It rotates in the opposite direction of Earth. | | | | | | | | |
| It is the hottest planet. | | | | | | | | |
| Its years are longer than its days. | | | | | | | | |
| It is called "Earth's twin." | | | | | | | | |
| It is closest to Earth. | | | | | | | | |
| Secret Mission Destination is _____ I know this because _____ | | | | | | | | |

# Space Trips

Mr. Ward asked his students this question: *What planet would you most like to visit?*

The children made a graph to show their answers.

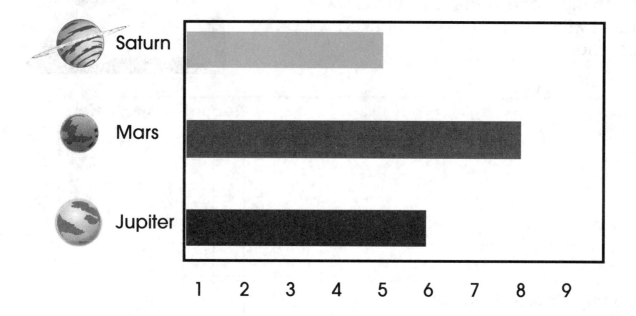

Which planet did the most students choose?

       Saturn          Mars          Jupiter

Which planet did the fewest students choose?

       Saturn          Mars          Jupiter

Which planet would you choose? Why?

_____

_____

_____

_____

_____

# Comparing and Contrasting

Choose two of your favorite planets in the solar system. Now compare and contrast these planets using the Venn diagram below.

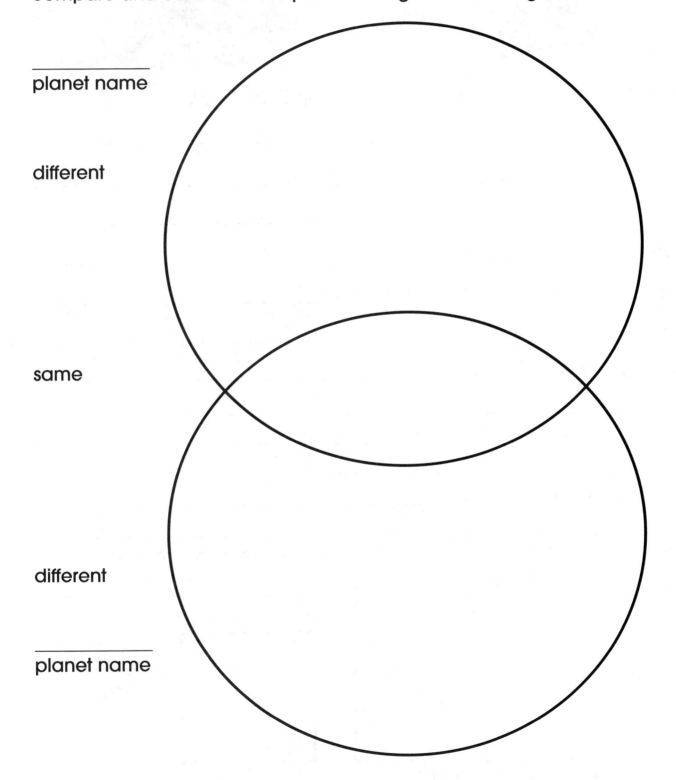

_____
planet name

different

same

different

_____
planet name

The Planets

# My Planet Report

Choose your favorite planet and write a report on it below.

Name of the planet _____

Named after _____

Size of the planet _____

Average distance from the Sun _____

Time needed to revolve around the Sun _____

Time needed to rotate on its axis _____

Facts about the planet's surface _____

_____

Facts about the planet's moon(s) _____

_____

Other interesting facts _____

_____

My information came from

_____

**A picture of my planet**

**My planet's symbol**

# MERCURY

# Fascinating Facts About Mercury

Mercury is the planet nearest to the Sun.

It is the second smallest planet in our solar system.

No planet experiences more radical temperature changes than Mercury. The temperature can rise to 800°F during the day and drop to -275°F at night.

Mercury is a world without an atmosphere. It has no air or life of any kind. It is also covered with thousands of ancient craters.

Because it is so near the Sun, Mercury can actually have two sunrises in a single day!

A solar day on Mercury, from sunrise to sunrise, lasts about six Earth months!

# Mercury

Mercury is one of the smallest of the eight planets in our solar system. It is also the nearest planet to the Sun.

Mercury spins very slowly. The side next to the Sun gets very hot before it turns away from the Sun. The other side freezes while away from the Sun. As the planet slowly spins, the frozen side then becomes burning hot and the hot side becomes freezing cold.

Even though Mercury spins slowly, it moves around the Sun very quickly. That is why it was named Mercury—after the Roman messenger for the gods.

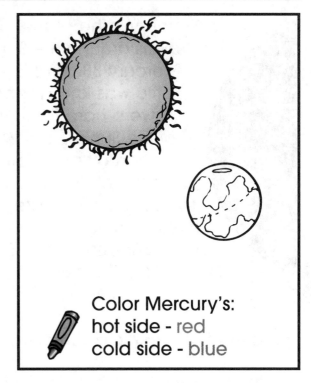

Color Mercury's:
hot side - red
cold side - blue

**Underline:**

Mercury    is the largest planet in our solar system.
           is one of the smallest planets in our solar system.

**Write:**
                    darkest   nearest
Mercury is the_____ planet to the Sun.

**Match:**

How does spinning slowly affect the temperature on Mercury?

The side next to the Sun              is freezing cold.
The side away from the Sun            is burning hot.

**Circle:**

Mercury moves quickly/quietly around the Sun.    Mercury spins very lightly./slowly.

**Check:**

Mercury was named for the    ☐ famous Roman speaker.
                             ☐ Roman messenger for the gods.

# Closest to the Sun

Mercury is the planet closest to the Sun. That is why Mercury travels around the Sun faster than any other planet. It takes Mercury 88 days to revolve once around the Sun.

Little was known about Mercury before 1974. Scientists have a hard time studying Mercury with telescopes because of the Sun's great light. In 1974 and 1975, an unmanned spacecraft named Mariner X flew by Mercury three times and sent scientists new information about the planet. The surface of Mercury is much like the Moon's surface. It has high cliffs and deep craters, or holes. Mercury has almost no atmosphere, or gases, surrounding it. Temperatures on the planet range from over 750°F to -300°F! Mercury does not have a moon.

**Write each answer in a sentence.**

1. Which planet is closest to the Sun? _____

_____

2. How long does it take Mercury to revolve around the Sun? _____

_____

3. Why do scientists have a hard time studying Mercury with telescopes? ___

_____

4. What did Mariner X do? _____

_____

5. Describe Mercury's surface. _____

_____

# A Short Year!

You know that Mercury is the planet located closest to the Sun, right? This little planet, less than half the size of Earth, orbits around the Sun quickly because it is so close to that star.

What is a year? Circle your answer.

A. The time it takes a planet to go around the Sun once.

B  The time it takes for a star to stop shining.

C. The time it takes for a moon to orbit a planet.

*The answer is A!* Mercury's year is the shortest of all the planets—88 Earth days.

A year on Earth is how many days? _____

**Now Try This:**

1. How old would you be on Mercury if you had been there for 440 days?

   _____

2. Write your age: _____

   How many days would you have to be on Mercury to reach your

   present age? _____

   _____

   _____

# The Punching Bag Planet

Mercury is like a punching bag! This little planet is covered with thousands of holes called **craters**. A crater is a hole caused by a **meteorite** hitting the surface of a planet or moon. A meteorite is a piece of rock or metal that flies through space and hits a planet or moon.

Why do you think so many meteorites hit Mercury? There is no air mass or atmosphere to stop them, so they simply bang right into the planet! No wonder Mercury looks like a punching bag!

**Try this experiment and create the surface of Mercury!**

You will need:
    a small flat pan
    dirt or sand to make mud
    small rocks

1. Fill a flat pan with soft mud.
2. Drop small rocks into the soft mud.
3. Push some of the mud up to form mountains.
4. Leave some of the mud flat.
5. When the mud is beginning to dry, remove the rocks. Now you have craters on the surface just like on the planet Mercury!

# Mercury

Mercury is the closest planet to the Sun. It is about 36 million miles from the Sun. Half the size of Earth, Mercury is just a little larger than our Moon. It circles the Sun very fast. It takes Earth 365 days, or one year, to complete one orbit around the Sun. It takes Mercury only 88 Earth days to orbit the Sun. Mercury spins slowly. It takes Earth 24 hours, or one day, to make one complete turn on its axis. Mercury turns once every 59 Earth days.

Because this is close to the length of one Mercury orbit, Mercury has a "day" from one sunrise to the next, of 176 Earth days. Mercury's "day" is twice as long as its year! The surface of Mercury is desertlike, with rocks and giant holes, or craters. Its biggest crater is called *caloris basin*. These craters make Mercury look like our moon. Because of its nearness to the Sun, Mercury is extremely hot — twice as hot as a pizza oven — about 800° F.

**ACROSS**
3. A year on Mercury would last ____-____ Earth days.
4. The closest planet to the Sun
6. Mercury circles the Sun very____.
8. These are found on Mercury.
10. The surface of Mercury is like a____.
11. Mercury is part of our____system.
13. Mercury spins on its____slowly.

**DOWN**
1. A____on Mercury lasts only 88 Earth days.
2. Mercury turns once every__days.
5. Giant holes on Mercury
7. Mercury is very hot because it is so____to the Sun.
9. First word in name of Mercury's largest crater
12. Size of Mercury in comparison with the Earth

# More About Mercury

Do you think you could ever live on Mercury? The side facing the Sun is over 800 degrees! The side away from the Sun is almost -305 degrees!

If you want to know what Mercury looks like, just think of the Moon. Mercury has almost no atmosphere or air mass surrounding it. Without an atmosphere, if you stood on the planet and looked up, the sky would seem black. The Sun looks $2\frac{1}{2}$ times larger from Mercury than Earth.

**Mercury Word Search**
Circle the words you find.

**Word Bank**
meteorite
Mercury
bang
punching
bag
planet
hole
crater
hits
surface
rock
moon
land
air
atmosphere
stop

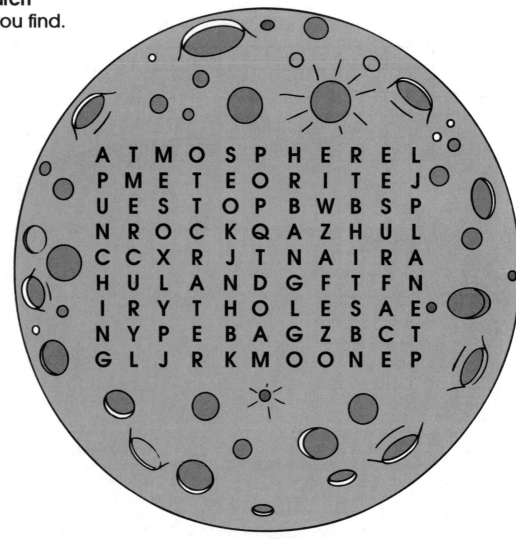

A T M O S P H E R E L
P M E T E O R I T E J
U E S T O P B W B S P
N R O C K Q A Z H U L
C C X R J T N A I R A
H U L A N D G F T F N
I R Y T H O L E S A E
N Y P E B A G Z B C T
G L J R K M O O N E P

# VENUS

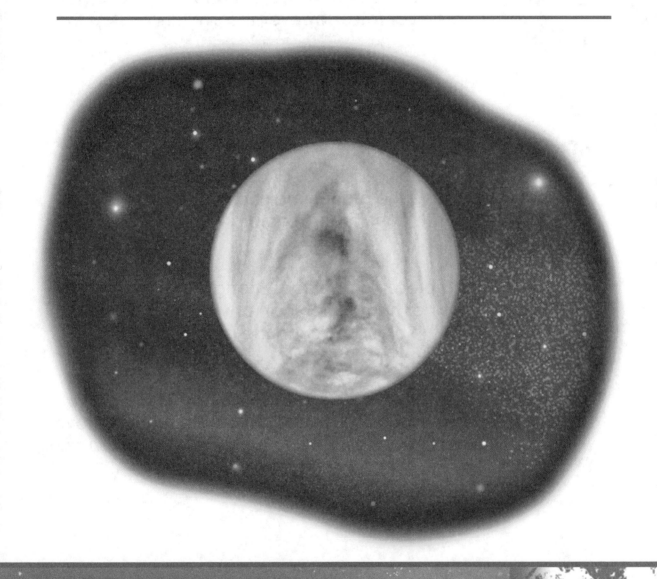

Venus is often called Earth's "sister planet" because it is almost the same size as Earth and orbits the Sun at a similar rate. However, the similarities stop there!

Venus is a hot, hostile place, with an average temperature of 900°F.

Thick, choking clouds of carbon dioxide gas surround the planet, making everything seem a gloomy, dark, orange color.

It is a breezy planet too! Strong winds of up to 220 miles per hour, faster than any hurricane on Earth, whip the clouds around the planet.

Venus's surface is covered with dry, dusty, rocky areas called lava plains. These plains help prove to scientists that Venus was once covered by erupting volcanoes!

# Venus

Venus is the planet nearest to Earth. Because it is the easiest planet to see in the sky, it has been called the Morning Star and Evening Star. The Romans named Venus after their goddess of love and beauty. Venus is sometimes called "Earth's twin."

Venus is covered with thick clouds. The Sun's heat is trapped by the clouds. The temperature on Venus is nearly 900°F!

Space probes have been sent to study Venus. They have reported information to scientists. But they can only last a few hours on Venus because of the high temperature.

Venus turns in the opposite direction from Earth. So, on Venus, the Sun rises in the west and sets in the east!

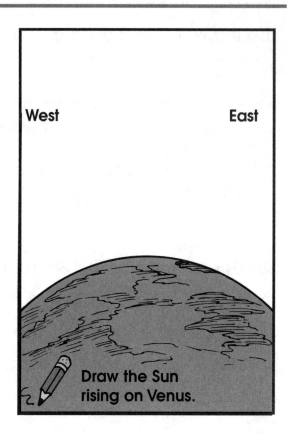

West                    East

Draw the Sun rising on Venus.

**Unscramble and Circle:**

_____ is the friendliest / nearest planet to Earth.

e s V u n
2 5 1 4 3

**Check:**
It is called the
☐ Evening Sun
☐ Morning Star   because it is so easy to see.
☐ Evening Star

**Circle:**
The Romans named Venus for their:

goddess of love and beauty     god of light     goddess of truth

**Circle Yes or No:**

Half of Venus is frozen with ice and snow.                    **Yes    No**
Space probes have reported information from Venus.           **Yes    No**
On Venus, the Sun rises in the east and sets in the west.    **Yes    No**

# Earth's Twin

Use the words in the Word Bank to complete the story.

## Word Bank

| | | | |
|---|---|---|---|
| light | against | lightning | size |
| closest | higher | atmosphere | melt |

Venus has been called Earth's twin because it is about the same _____ as Earth. Venus is the second planet from the Sun and is the planet _____ to Earth. Venus was also the first planet to be studied by spacecraft. Venus has no moon.

Venus has an interesting _____, or blanket of gases around it. It reflects, or bounces off, so much of the Sun's _____ that Venus is easier to see than any other planet. The atmosphere also lets some sunlight in and traps heat _____ the planet's surface. Therefore, temperatures on Venus are high enough to _____ some metals. Clouds move at high speeds in Venus's atmosphere, and bolts of _____ streak across the sky.

Venus has volcanoes on its surface and a mountain _____ than the highest on Earth. There is no liquid water on Venus. Earth's plants and animals could not live on Venus.

# Sparkling Venus

Beautiful Venus is the second planet from the Sun. Why do you think it is brighter than any other planet? Circle the best answer.

A. Its surface is almost as hot as the Sun.

B. Its surface is covered with millions of diamonds.

C. Its thick clouds reflect the Sun's light.

Venus is covered by very thick clouds, so C is correct. Sometimes we can see Venus as a bright, sparkling, starlike object in the morning or the evening sky.

**Something's Wrong!**
There is something wrong with these facts about Venus. Circle the wrong word in each sentence. Write the correct word on the line.

1. Venus is the second planet from the Earth._____

2. Venus looks dull in the sky._____

3. Venus has a thin cloud cover._____

4. At night, Mercury sparkles in the sky._____

# Venus

Venus is the second planet away from the Sun in our solar system. With a diameter of 7,521 miles, it is almost as large as Earth. The diameter of the Earth is 7,927 miles. Venus, the brightest planet seen from Earth, was named after the Roman goddess of love and beauty. It is covered with clouds that reflect the Sun's light. After Earth's moon, Venus is the second brightest light in the night sky. Look for Venus in the western evening sky just after sunset or the eastern morning sky just before sunrise. Some people call Venus the evening star when it is in the evening sky because it looks like a very bright star. Venus is a rocky desert with high mountains and valleys. Maxwell Mountain on Venus is seven miles high. We could not survive on Venus without lots of protection because it is so hot. It takes Venus 225 Earth days to circle the Sun. It turns on its axis slowly. A day on Venus from one sunrise to the next lasts 117 Earth days.

**ACROSS**
1. Position of Venus in the solar system
5. First part of the name of the mountain on Venus
7. Venus is a_____.
8. Venus is a rocky_____.
9. Venus was named after the Roman _____of love.
13. Maxwell is one.

**DOWN**
2. Venus is covered with_____that reflect the Sun's light.
3. Venus is almost as large as_____.
4. Second planet in our solar system
6. Venus is the name of the Roman goddess of_____and beauty.
10. The_____of Venus is 7,625 miles.
11. It is too hot on Venus for_____.
12. There are mountains and_____.

# Hot Stuff!

Venus is not only beautiful, but it is also the hottest planet in our solar system. Space probes like Mariner 2 and the Russian Veneras probes discovered that the thick clouds that surround Venus are not like the clouds we have on Earth. They are made of carbon dioxide gas and hold in the Sun's heat.

Temperatures on Venus reach 900 degrees Fahrenheit. Think how hot you feel when it's only 90 degrees outside!

The sky of Venus seems to be a reddish-orange color. Violent lightening and terrible winds blow across the planet.

Space explorers landing on this planet would have a difficult time. Besides the heat and the poisonous atmosphere, the air pressure on Venus is about 100 times greater than on Earth. That means it would be much harder to move around on Venus. It would be like trying to walk underwater.

The carbon dioxide gas makes the air very dense. The clouds are filled with sulfuric acid droplets. The atmosphere around Venus is thick and deadly.

**Circle the different conditions that space travelers might face on Venus.**

swampy areas
active volcanoes
hail storms
90° temperatures
black ice
thick dense air
dangerous lightening storms
snowstorms
900° temperatures
cool rain showers
muddy roads
terrible winds

### Feel the Heat

1. Get an empty glass jar with a lid. Screw the lid on and set the jar in the sunlight for two hours.
2. Carefully unscrew the jar—it's hot!
3. Put your hand inside the jar. Do you feel the heat?
4. What kept the heat inside?_____
5. The lid kept the heat inside like Venus's clouds hold in the Sun's warmth causing very high temperatures.

# The Cloudy Beauty

Until the early 1960s, we didn't know what was under the thick clouds that color Venus. Then space probes discovered that under the clouds most of Venus is a gently rolling plain. There are two volcanoes and one mountain higher than Earth's Mount Everest. There are craters, but they have been worn down by the winds and the sulfuric acid in the atmosphere.

Like Mercury, Venus has no moon. It rotates in the opposite direction of most of the planets. The Sun rises in the west and sets in the east.

**Make a Venus Mobile!**

1. Use a 3-inch styrofoam ball.
2. Make cotton clouds by pulling cotton balls into long wispy pieces.
3. Glue the clouds on to the planet. Make sure you cover the whole planet with swirling cotton clouds.
4. Push an opened paper clip into your planet and hang with a string.

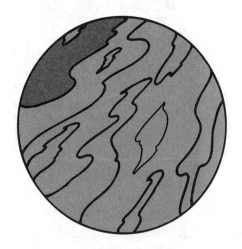

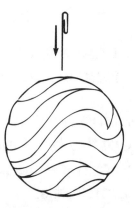

# Our Planet Earth

As far as scientists can tell, Earth is the only planet in the solar system to have water, in liquid form, on its surface.

Earth is also the only planet that is able to support life. This is largely due to its mild, steady temperature and thick, oxygen-rich atmosphere.

The Earth is the largest and densest of the four rocky planets.

Water covers three-fourths of the Earth's surface! Ice covers more than one-tenth!

The surface of the Earth is constantly changing. Great big pieces, or plates, of solid rock are floating on top of molten rock. As they drift, they sometimes bump up against each other. Over thousands of years, a mountain range can form!

Signs of life, such as seasonal changes in plant color, radio signals, and man-made lights, can be observed from space!

# Our Planet Earth

Earth is the planet where we live. Earth has land and water. It gets light and heat from the Sun. Earth has one moon. Earth is the only planet that we know has life. Many people think there is life on other planets. Do you think there is life on other planets?

**Unscramble:**

Earth is the _____ where we live.

l e t p n a

**Check** the sentences about the Earth that are true.

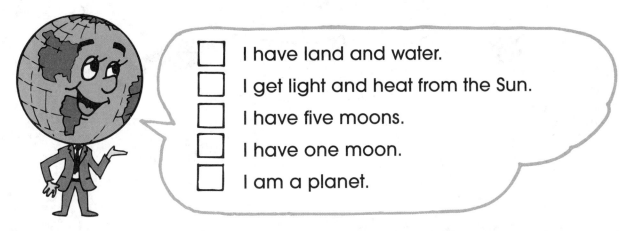

☐ I have land and water.

☐ I get light and heat from the Sun.

☐ I have five moons.

☐ I have one moon.

☐ I am a planet.

**Circle:** Earth is the only planet that we know has

stars.

life.

**Color:** Draw one yellow moon in the picture.

**Draw** and color a picture of the Earth.

# The Earth

Although you can't tell from where you are, the Earth is round, like an orange. You can see this by looking at pictures of Earth taken from space.

We cannot feel it, but the Earth moves around the Sun. There are eight big, round planets that all move around the Sun.

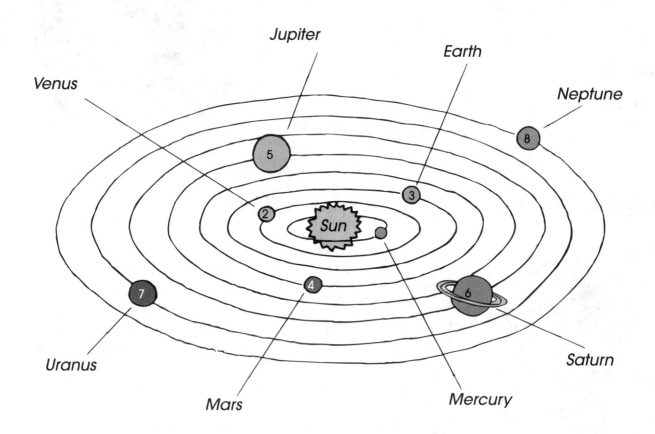

Look at the eight planets in the picture.

Which planet is closest to the Sun? _____

Which planet is farthest from the Sun? _____

# Earth

Earth is about 93 million miles from the Sun. Earth is the only planet in the solar system that has plants, animals, and human beings living on it. Earth is a giant ball of rock and metal about 8,000 miles across. Its crust is made of rock. On top of the Earth's crust are oceans and land. Oceans store heat from the Sun and help keep Earth from becoming too hot or too cold for human life. Earth orbits around the Sun in about 365 days, or one year. As Earth orbits the Sun, it also spins on its axis. One complete spin takes 24 hours, or one day. As it spins on its axis, we experience day and night. When our side of the Earth is turned toward the Sun, the Sun lights up our sky and we experience day. When our side of the Earth is turned away from the Sun, we cannot see its light and we experience night. When our part of the Earth is tipped toward the Sun, the Sun is high in the sky, the days are long and the nights are short, giving us warm summer weather. When our part of the Earth is tipped away from the Sun, the Sun is low in the sky, the days are short and the nights are long, giving us cold winter weather.

**ACROSS**
2. They help keep the Earth cool.
4. It is made up of 24 hours.
6. The planet we live on
9. Earth is a giant ball of rock and_____.
11. They grow on Earth.
12. Opposite of summer

**DOWN**
1. Earth is a giant_____.
2. A colorless, odorless gas found on Earth
3. Earth orbits this star.
5. On top of the Earth's_____are oceans and land.
7. They live on Earth.
8. It is made up of 365 days.
10. Earth is 93_____miles from the Sun.

# Spinning Top

Whir-r-r-ling! Matt's top is spinning very fast. Just like Matt's top, the Earth is also spinning.

The Earth spins about an imaginary line that is drawn from the North **Pole** to the South Pole through the center of the Earth. This line is called Earth's **axis**. Instead of using the word "spin," though, we say that the Earth **rotates** on its axis.

The Earth rotates **one** time every 24 hours. The part of the Earth facing the Sun experiences day. The side that is away from the Sun's light experiences **night**.

Draw a line from each picture of Matt to the correct day or night picture of the Earth.

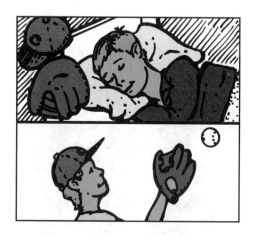

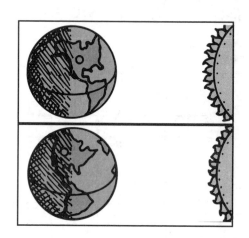

**Directions:**

Use the highlighted words above to solve the puzzle.

1. The part of the Earth not facing the Sun experiences _____.

2. Earth's axis goes from the North to the South _____.

3. The Earth spins, or _____.

4. Number of times the Earth rotates in 24 hours.

5. Imaginary line on which the Earth rotates.

# Our Rotating Planet

Try the experiments below to discover firsthand how our planet rotates and revolves around the Sun.

## Around the Axis

1. Use a large thread spool for the planet.
2. Use a thin round stick for the axis. Sometimes a pencil will work if the hole in the spool is big enough.
3. With a pencil or marker, put a dot on the top of the spool near the edge.
4. Put the stick through the hole in the spool so the spool will spin.
5. Hold the bottom of the stick with one hand so the spool won't fall off.
6. Use your other hand to spin or rotate the spool.
7. Rotate the spool so the dot goes around the stick or axis once. This is called one rotation. It didn't take very long to rotate your planet once, did it?

It takes 24 hours for Earth to rotate once. We call this amount of time a day. Other planets take different amounts of time to rotate on their axis.

While Earth is spinning, it is also revolving or moving around the Sun. We usually say that it takes 365 days for the Earth to orbit the Sun once. Remember, it really takes 365 and $\frac{1}{4}$ days, but to make it easier we say a year is just 365 days.

## Once Around the Sun

1. Put a chair in the middle of the room. Pretend it's the Sun.
2. Start spinning your planet around its axis. At the same time, begin orbiting or walking in a circle around the Sun. Be sure to keep spinning your planet.
3. Stop at the place you started. You have completed one revolution of the Sun.
4. Do this one foot away from the Sun. Then move four feet away from the Sun.

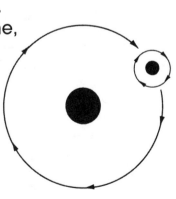

Which orbit took more time to go around the Sun?

_____

Did your planet rotate more times with the longer orbit?

_____

It takes 24 hours, or one full day, for the Earth to rotate completely.

Circle the picture of the Earth that belongs with the last Sun.
Color the suns yellow.

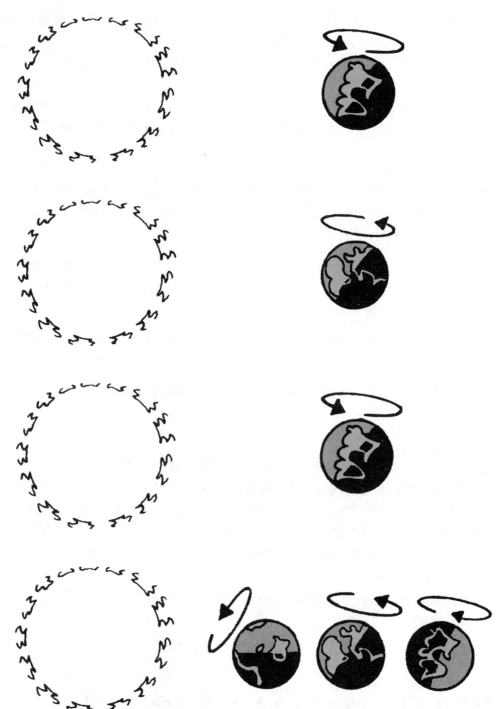

# A Big Ball

Earth is like a big ball.

Most of the Earth is covered by

water . The rest of the Earth is

land .

Color the blue.

Color the green

Why do you think the Earth is called the water planet?

_____

_____

# The Earth's Layers

Now you know that oceans and continents cover the Earth. But what's inside the Earth?

The Earth has three layers — the crust, the mantle, and the core. Unscramble the words below to discover where each layer is located. Write the new words on the lines.

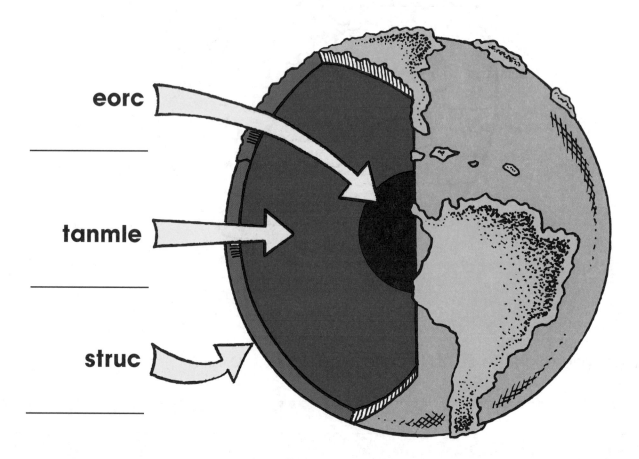

**eorc**

_____

**tanmle**

_____

**struc**

_____

# What's Inside?

The **core** of the Earth is its hardest and hottest part. Around the core lies a thick layer, called the **mantle**, which is hot and rocky. The outside layer of the Earth is the **crust**. This is where the oceans and the continents are. People, plants, and animals live on the Earth's crust.

Find the layer that is hot and hard. Color it black. What is it called?

Color the rocky, hot part of the Earth red. What is it called?

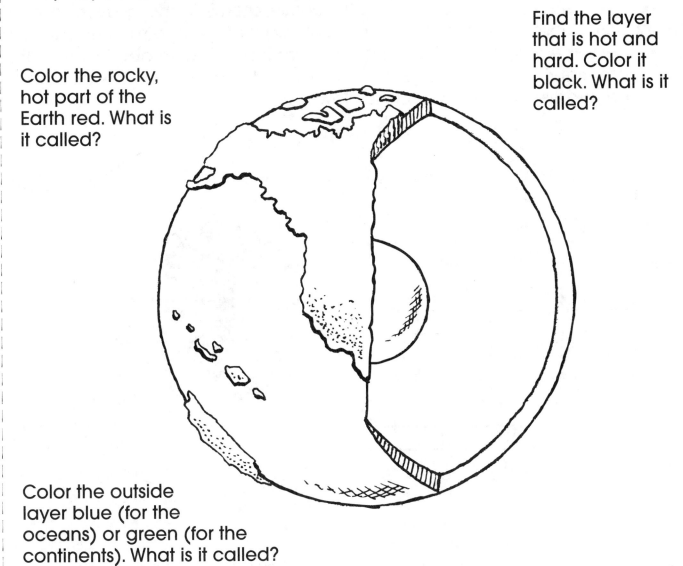

Color the outside layer blue (for the oceans) or green (for the continents). What is it called?

There is nothing alive below the Earth's crust. Why do you think that is?

_____

_____

The air that surrounds the Earth is called Earth's **atmosphere**. The atmosphere is made up of gases that contain tight bundles of atoms called **molecules**. Gravity holds Earth's atmosphere close to the surface of Earth. Near the surface of Earth the atoms are tightly packed together. When the atoms are packed close together, the atmosphere is said to be dense. Feel the air around you. It has high density. On top of a high mountain, the air density is lower because atoms in the gases are not tightly packed. Most airplanes cannot fly more than 20 miles above the Earth because the density of the air is too low.

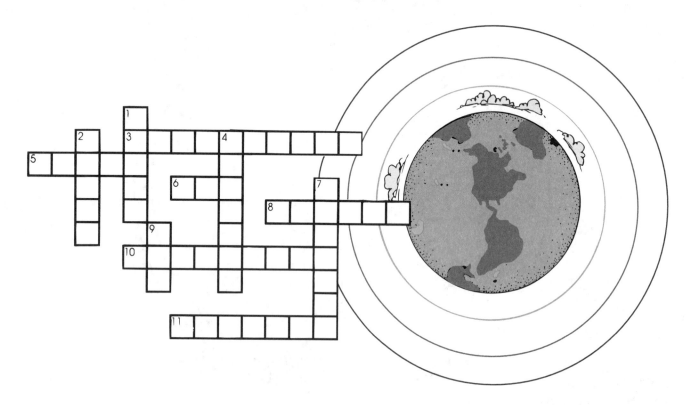

**ACROSS**
3. The air that surrounds Earth
5. The atmosphere is made up of gases that contain tight bundles of_____ called molecules.
6. It is called the atmosphere.
8. Most airplanes can't fly higher than _____miles up in the sky.
10. The gases in the atmosphere are made of bundles of atoms called_____.

11. It holds Earth's atmosphere close to the surface of Earth.

**DOWN**
1. What the atmosphere is made of
2. On the top of a high mountain the air density is_____.
4. Earth's atmosphere is held closely to Earth's_____by gravity.
7. Measurement of the atmosphere
9. Opposite of high

# Leaning Into Summer

Why isn't it summer all year long? The seasons change because the Earth is tilted like the Leaning Tower of Pisa. As the Earth orbits the Sun, it stays tilting in the same direction in space.

Let's look at the seasons in the Northern Hemisphere. When the North Pole is tilting toward the Sun, the days become warmer and longer. It is summer. Six months later, the North Pole tilts away from the Sun. The days become cooler and shorter. It is winter.

**Directions:** Label the Northern Hemisphere's seasons on the chart below. Write a make-believe weather forecast for each season. Each forecast should show what the weather is like in your region for that season.

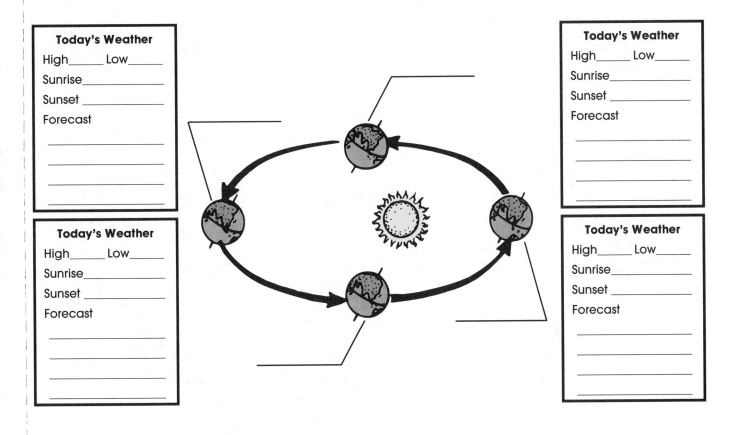

**Today's Weather**

High_____ Low_____

Sunrise_____

Sunset _____

Forecast

_____

_____

_____

_____

**Today's Weather**

High_____ Low_____

Sunrise_____

Sunset _____

Forecast

_____

_____

_____

_____

**Today's Weather**

High_____ Low_____

Sunrise_____

Sunset _____

Forecast

_____

_____

_____

_____

**Today's Weather**

High_____ Low_____

Sunrise_____

Sunset _____

Forecast

_____

_____

_____

_____

# The Earth's Four Seasons

1. Write the season words from the Word Bank under the correct boxes below.
2. Color the clothes for autumn **blue**.
3. Color the clothes for winter **red**.
4. Color the clothes for spring **green**.
5. Color the clothes for summer **yellow**.

**Word Bank**

| | |
|---|---|
| Spring | Summer |
| Autumn | Winter |

# Night and Day Difference

What causes the daily change from daylight to darkness? Day turns into night because the Earth rotates on its axis. The Earth s axis is an imaginary line that cuts through the Earth from the North Pole to the South Pole. The Earth spins in a counter-clockwise direction.

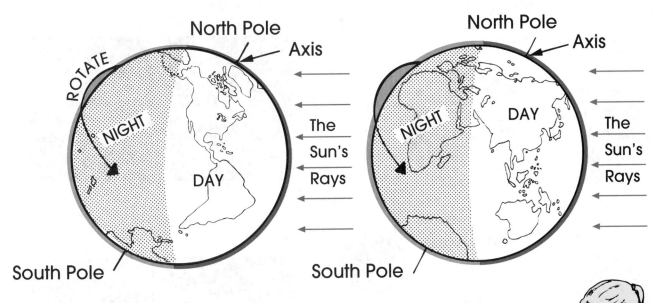

Let's demonstrate the difference between night and day.

**You will need:**

> globe
> flashlight

Directions:

1. In a very dark room, set the globe on a table, as demonstrated in the picture.

2. Standing five to ten feet away, aim the flashlight at the globe.

3. Have a friend slowly rotate the globe on its axis.

4. Discover what parts of the world are sleeping when it is daytime in your community.

Pretend you live on the continent or continents in each picture. Would it be day or night there? Circle the picture to the right that shows what it would be like.

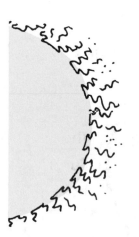

If you live in  then it is

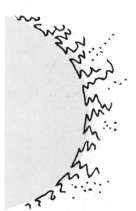

If you live in  then it is

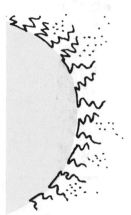

If you live in  then it is

# A Changing Planet

The Earth today is very different from the day it was formed, and it is still changing. There are mountains, deserts, forests, volcanoes, and oceans. They are all changing every day.

Do you know these Earth facts?
- 10% of the land surface is covered with ice.
- The highest point on land is Mount Everest at 29,028 feet.
- The lowest point is the Mariana Trench in the Pacific Ocean at 35,820 feet below sea level.
- Earth is like a giant magnet with north and south magnetic poles.
- Almost 75% or $\frac{3}{4}$ of the land surface is under water!

## Water, Water Everywhere!
1. Use a 3-inch styrofoam ball.
2. Use a blue marker with a wide tip.
3. Draw a line around the middle of the ball.
4. Turn the ball and draw another line as in the picture below.
5. You have just divided the Earth into fourths, or four parts. Color three sections blue and one section green. The blue shows how much land on Earth is covered by water!

# LO-O-O-NG Trip

What is the longest trip you have ever taken? Was it 100 miles? 500 miles? Maybe it was more than 1,000 miles. You probably didn't know it, but last year you traveled 620 million miles.

The Earth travels in a path around the Sun called its **orbit**. Earth's orbit is almost 620 million miles. It takes 1 year, or 365 days, for the Earth to orbit or **revolve** around the Sun.

Earth's orbit is not a perfect circle. It is a special shape called an **ellipse**.

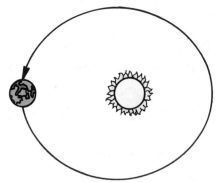

1. How long does it take for the Earth to revolve around the Sun? _____

2. How many times has the Earth revolved around the Sun since you were born? _____

3. How many miles has the Earth traveled in orbit since you were born?

   _____

4. Draw an **X** on Earth's orbit to show where it will be in six months.

**Experiment:**

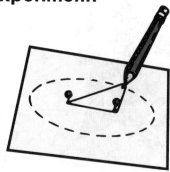

You can draw an ellipse. Place two straight pins about 3 inches apart in a piece of cardboard. Tie the ends of a 10-inch piece of string to the pins. Place your pencil inside the string. Keeping the string tight, draw an ellipse.

Make four different ellipses by changing the length of the string and the distance between the pins. How do the ellipses change?

# Just Imagine

Earth is a very special planet because it is the only planet known to have life. Only Earth has the necessities to support life—water, air, moderate temperatures, and suitable air pressure. Earth is about 92,960,000 miles from the Sun and is 7,926 miles in diameter. Its highest recorded temperature was 136°F in Libya and the lowest was -127°F in Antarctica.

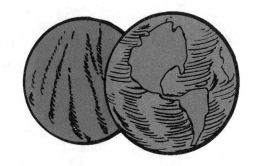

Venus is known as Earth's "twin" because the two planets are so similar in size. At about 67,230,000 miles from the Sun, Venus is 7,521 miles in diameter. Venus is the brightest planet in the sky, as seen from Earth, and is brighter than even the stars. The temperature on the surface of this planet is about 850°F.

Mercury is the planet closest to the Sun. It is about 35,980,000 miles from the Sun and is 3,031 miles in diameter. The temperature on this planet ranges from -300°F to 750°F.

Pretend you were going to Venus or Mercury for spring break. Make a list of the things you would bring (you may have to invent them in order to survive), and draw a picture of the vehicle that would take you there. Write about your experiences on another sheet of paper.

**Things I Need to Take**

**Vehicle**

# Model Earth

Imagine you are flying around in space. You look down and see a big round ball. It is the Earth.

A model of the Earth is called a **globe**. It is a round map that shows land and water. It uses colors to show which is the land and which is the water.

Unscramble the letters below to find out the colors that are used on the globe.

Land is _____. e r g e n

Water is_____. l u e b

**Color** the land on the globe green.

**Color** the water on the globe blue.

# It's a Round World

Use these maps with pages 90 and 91.

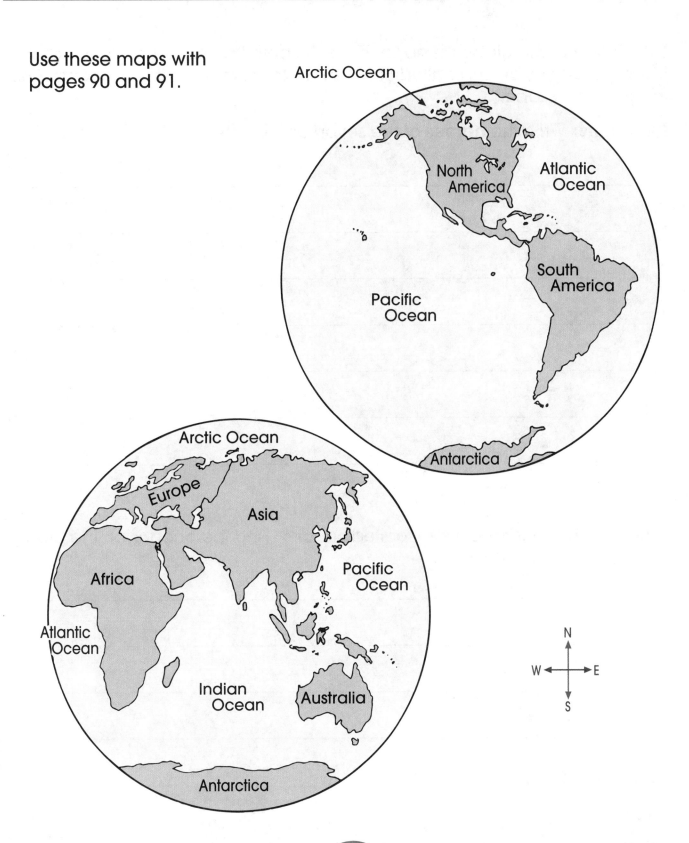

Our Planet Earth

# It's a Round World

The picture of the globe on page 89 shows both halves of the Earth. It shows the large pieces of land called **continents**. There are seven continents. Find them on the globe.

**Directions:** Write the names of the seven continents.

1. _____

2. _____

3. _____

4. _____

5. _____

6. _____

7. _____

There are four bodies of water called **oceans**. Find the oceans on the globe. Write the names below.

1. _____

2. _____

3. _____

4. _____

Use the globe on page 89. Read the clues below. Write the answers on the lines. Then, use the numbered letters to solve the riddle at the bottom of the page.

1. This direction points up.

    ___ ___ ___ ___ ___
    1   2  22  3

2. This direction points down.

    ___ ___ ___ ___ ___
    4      5   6

3. This direction points right.

    ___ ___ ___ ___
    7     8

4. This direction points left.

    ___ ___ ___ ___
    9    10

5. This ocean is west of North America.

    ___ ___ ___ ___ ___ ___ ___
    11  12

    ___ ___ ___ ___ ___
    13     14

6. This ocean is south of Asia.

    ___ ___ ___ ___ ___ ___
    15   16     17

    ___ ___ ___ ___

7. This ocean is east of South America.

    ___ ___ ___ ___ ___ ___ ___
      18  19

    ___ ___ ___ ___ ___
    20      21

Riddle: What does a globe do?

    ___ ___ ___ ___ ___ ___ ___
    15   6    4  11  15  21  8

    ___ ___ " ___ - ___ ___ ___ ___ "
    5  10    12   22  2  5  21  16

    ___ ___ ___ ___ ___ ___ ___ ___ ___ .
    13  5  22   11  19  14  17  7  18

# Our Home Planet

Use the words from the Word Bank to complete the story.

## Word Bank

| | | |
|---|---|---|
| distance | reaches | main |
| planet | liquid | closer |
| soil | Sun | Earth |

The third planet from the _____ is our home planet Earth. Earth has something no other _____ is known to have—living things.

Earth is at the right _____ from the Sun to have the liquid water necessary to support life. Mercury and Venus are too hot because they are _____ to the Sun. The other planets are too far from the Sun to have _____ water. Not much heat or light _____ them, so the water would be in the form of ice.

Earth has a lot of water. Most living things need water. Water helps to control the Earth's weather and climate. Water also breaks rock into _____ which plants need to grow.

Earth is surrounded by a blanket of air called the atmosphere. Oxygen is one of the _____ gases in the atmosphere. Most animals breathe oxygen.

_____ is a special planet!

# Earth's Sister Planet

Venus is often called "Earth's sister planet." Besides the Moon, Venus is Earth's closest neighbor. These two planets are alike in some ways but are quite different in others.

**Earth and Venus: Which Is Which?**

1. Cut out the Earth and Venus planet cards.
2. Fold each card on the dotted line.
3. Glue the two parts together.
4. Turn the cards so all the facts show. Can you divide the facts about Earth from the facts about Venus?
5. Turn the cards over to see if you have put all the Earth cards together and all the Venus cards together.

| Earth | Earth | Venus | Venus |
|---|---|---|---|
| **DIAMETER** 7,927 miles | Solid planet with a core of iron | **TEMPERATURE** 900° Fahrenheit | **DIAMETER** 7,521 miles |
| Earth | Earth | Venus | Venus |
| **MAIN GAS** Oxygen | **TEMPERATURE** Up to 136° Fahrenheit | Sun rises in the west and sets in the east. | **MAIN GAS** Carbon Dioxide |
| Earth | Earth | Venus | Venus |
| **SURFACE** rocky | Sun rises in the east and sets in the west. | Solid planet with a core of iron | **SURFACE** rocky |

# Why Can't We Fall off the Earth?

Everything is held on the Earth by a force called **gravity**. Gravity causes things to fall down toward the center of the Earth. All objects, including planets, stars, and moons, are made up of stuff called matter. The more matter something has in it for its size, the stronger its gravity is. Some objects, like the Sun, have lots of matter. The Sun's gravity is much stronger than the Earth's. The Moon's gravity is weaker than the Earth's. You would weigh a lot less on the Moon than you do on Earth!

1. What brings a rocket ship back down to Earth?

   _____

2. Why is it so difficult to walk up a very steep hill? _____

   _____

3. Why is it so easy to go downhill?

   _____

   _____

4. Why is the Sun's gravity stronger than the Earth's gravity? _____

   _____

   _____

5. Would things weigh more or less on the Sun than on the Earth?

   _____

   _____

   _____

6. Can smaller objects have strong gravity? _____

   _____

   _____

   _____

   _____

95

# Weight and Gravity

## Making a Scale

**Directions:**

1. Use a hole punch or scissors to punch two holes exactly opposite each other at the top of a clear plastic cup.
2. Cut a piece of fishing line 6" long. Tie one end to one hole and the other end to the opposite hole.
3. Tape a ruler to the top of a table so one end hangs over the edge. Then, tape a piece of tagboard to the side of the table.
4. Wrap a rubber band around the fishing line and loop it inside itself. Now hang the rubber band from the ruler. The cup should hang in front of the tagboard.

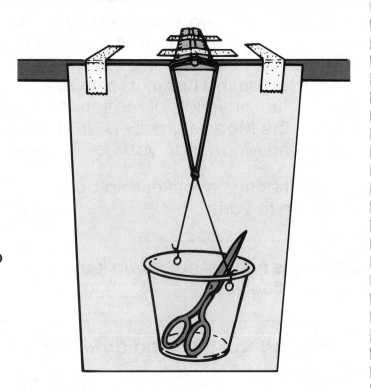

## Comparing Weights

To weigh an object, place it in the cup. The heavier the object, the lower the cup will sag. To record its weight, put a mark on the tagboard even with the bottom of the cup and write the name of the object next to the mark.

Make a prediction. Put all the objects on the table. Line them up in order from the lightest to the heaviest. Now weigh the objects. Number them from lightest to heaviest, with 1 the lightest and 8 the heaviest.

_____scissors      _____small jar of water      _____pencil      _____coin

_____stone        _____crayon box          _____eraser      _____magnifying glass

How accurate was your prediction?

## Extension:

Why is gravity important to human beings? _____

_____

What would happen if there were no gravity?_____

_____

_____

# Gravity

Have you ever wondered why the Earth orbits the Sun and why it doesn't fly off into space? A force called gravity keeps Earth from flying off into space. Everything in the universe has gravity. Every galaxy, every star, every planet and moon, every building, every tree, every person, every bug, every atom has gravity. The gravity of a thing pulls on every other thing in the universe.

Gravity pulls much harder on nearby things than on faraway things, but even the tiniest flower tugs on the farthest galaxy. The more massive the object, the harder it pulls at other things. Since the Sun is the greatest mass in our solar system, it has the strongest pull. The Sun's gravitational pull on Earth and the other planets keeps them from flying off into space.

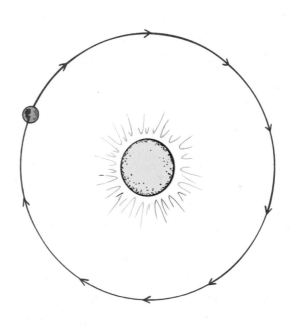

**ACROSS**
4. The planet we live on
5. There are nine_____in our solar system.
8. To move around another planet
9. A force of nature that keeps everything from flying off into space
10. Earth orbits the_____.

**DOWN**
1. The area all around Earth, the planets, galaxies, and stars
2. Gravity is a_____that keeps Earth orbiting the Sun.
3. The more massive the_____the harder it pulls at other things.
6. Earth moves_____the Sun.
7. Everything in the_____system has gravity.

# Fast Fall

Do heavy objects fall faster than light objects?

**Background:**
Gravity is a force, or type of energy, that pulls all objects toward Earth. It holds people on the ground and keeps the Moon from flying off into space. If you pick up an object then let go of it, it falls down because of gravity.

**What You'll Need:**
- book
- rubber ball
- spoon
- pencil
- marble
- ball of crumpled aluminum foil

**What to Do:**
1. Hold the book in one hand and the rubber ball in the other hand.
2. Put your arms straight out in front of you. Make sure the book and the ball are the same distance from the floor.
3. Let go of the book and the ball at exactly the same time. Watch them drop. Do they hit the floor at the same time?
4. Repeat the experiment several times. Use a different pair of objects each time: a ball and a spoon, a pencil and a marble, a book and a ball of crumbled aluminum foil, and so on. Do the objects always hit the floor at the same time?

**What Happened:**
The objects you dropped—the book, ball, spoon, pencil, marble, and ball of crumpled aluminum foil—were pulled down by gravity. The force of gravity on all these objects is equal, no matter how big or heavy they are. Therefore, all the objects fall at the same speed. In each part of this experiment, the pair of items you dropped fell at the same speed and hit the floor together.

## One Step Further:

Try the experiment with a pencil and a flat piece of paper. Now crumble up the paper and try it again. Do the two objects hit the floor at the same time in both cases? Why or why not?

_____

_____

_____

## Questions:

1. Why do objects fall down instead of up?

   _____

   _____

2. If you wanted to travel to Mars, how would you overcome Earth's gravity?

   _____

   _____

3. Gravity is stronger on bigger planets. Pluto is the smallest planet in our solar system. Can you name a planet that has stronger gravity than Pluto?

   _____

4. Earth is larger than the Moon. Could you jump higher on the Moon or on Earth? Explain your answer.

   _____

   _____

   _____

5. The gravity of a black hole is so strong that nothing can escape it, not even light. What do you think happens to things that are pulled into a black hole?

   _____

   _____

   _____

# A Riddle Review

Fill in the blanks below to find out how much you have learned about your home planet, Earth!

1. Three-fourths of the Earth is covered by ___ ___ ___ ___ ___ .

2. Earth is the only planet that can support ___ ___ ___ ___ .

3. The Earth has one ___ ___ ___ ___ .

4. 365 days make up one Earth ___ ___ ___ ___ .

5. It takes 24 hours for the Earth to rotate the ___ ___ ___ .

6. The Earth has four ___ ___ ___ ___ ___ ___ ___ .

7. This keeps us from falling off the Earth ___ ___ ___ ___ ___ ___ ___ .

# Mars

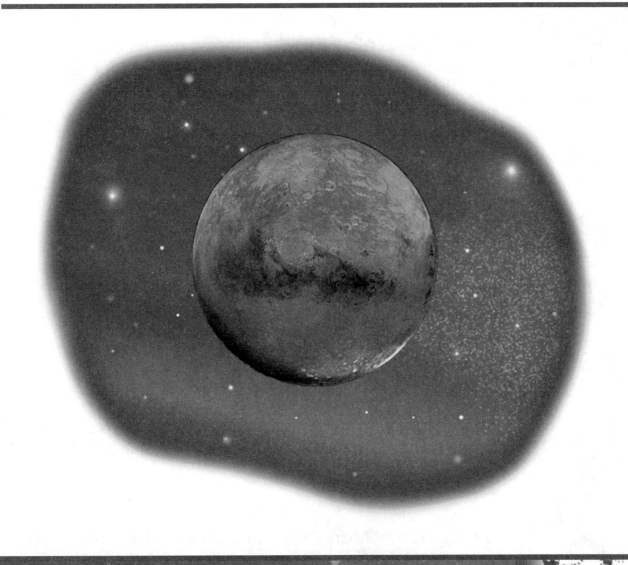

Rusted, or oxidized, iron in the soil on Mars gives the planet a red appearance. That is why Mars' nickname is the *Red Planet*.

Violent winds blow red dust storms across the surface of Mars at hundreds of miles per hour. Even the skies glow reddish pink on Mars, instead of blue!

Mars and Earth are similar in many ways. Both planets have four seasons, polar ice caps, stable temperatures, and magnetic iron cores.

Mars differs from Earth because it has a thinner atmosphere and the only remaining water on Mars is frozen.

Research suggests that at one time Mars was a much warmer and wetter planet. Probes have been sent to Mars to search for traces of life that existed long ago.

The surface of Mars shows clues that volcanoes were once active and erupting there. Its largest volcano is called Olympus Mons and is 15 miles high and 370 miles wide!

# Mars

Mars is the fourth planet from the Sun at 141,600,000 miles. The diameter of Mars is 4,200 miles. Mars is often called the Red Planet because rocks on its surface contain limonite, which is similar to rust. Mars has two moons.

Mars is dustier and drier than any desert on Earth. However, new evidence suggests that Mars may have once been a wetter and warmer planet. According to information gathered at the 1997 landing site of the Mars Pathfinder Mission, there may have been tremendous flooding on Mars about two to three billion years ago. Mars, then, may once have been more like Earth than was earlier thought.

Scientists are now pondering this question—if life was able to develop on Earth two to three billion years ago, why not on Mars too? What do you think about this? Explain your answer on the lines below.

_____

_____

_____

_____

_____

_____

_____

_____

# The Last of the Rocky Planets

Can you name the four planets with rocky surfaces? They are Mercury, Venus, Earth, and Mars. Each planet has a surface you could walk on.

Although Mars is much colder than Earth, it is like Earth in many ways. Mars has polar ice caps just as Earth has the North and South Poles. These caps grow smaller or larger when the Martian seasons get warmer or colder.

Scientists have also seen dark green or blue-grey areas on Mars. These areas grow smaller in the winter season and larger during the Martian summer. Scientists think the areas are covered and uncovered by blowing sand.

Mars also has lines or "canals" running between the dark areas. Scientists know these are not canals that carry water, but they are not sure what they really might be.

**Make a Mars Mobile!**

1. Use a $2\frac{1}{2}$ inch styrofoam ball.
2. Wrap the ball in a single layer of masking tape. The tape will give you ridges and bumps just like the planet.
3. Use a spoon, the flat end of a pen, or anything else you can think of to make craters, volcanoes, canyons, or canals.
4. Use markers to color the planet shades of red. Don't forget the polar ice caps.
5. Push an opened paper clip into your planet and hang it with a string.

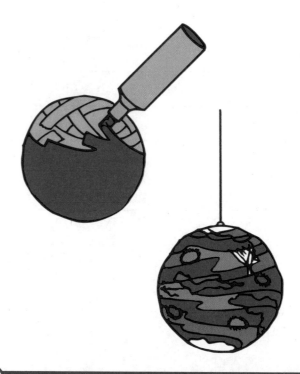

# The Red Planet

Mars, the fourth planet from the Sun, is half the size of Earth. Mars has two moons. It has been called the Red Planet because of its red color. Parts of this planet's surface are covered with sand dunes and dry, reddish deserts. Other areas look like dried up riverbeds. Some scientists believe water may once have flowed on Mars. Mars also has two polar caps made up of frozen water and dry ice. Pink, blue, and white clouds move through the Red Planet's sky.

For a long time, some people thought there might be life on Mars. When two U.S. spacecraft landed on the planet in 1976, they sent back photographs of Mars and did experiments to find out if life exists there. Scientists now believe that Mars does not have plant or animal life like that on Earth.

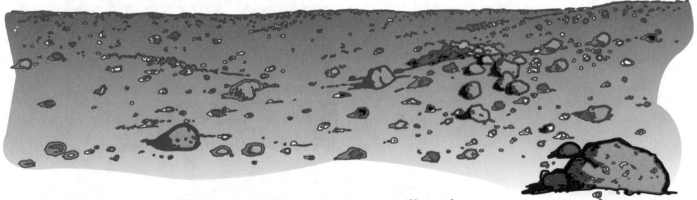

Finish each sentence below with details from the story.

1. Mars is the _____ planet from the Sun, and it has _____ moons.

2. Mars is nicknamed the _____.

3. Two U.S. spacecraft landed on Mars in _____, sent back photographs,

   and did _____.

4. Mars has dry, reddish _____ and what looks like dried up _____.

5. Mars has two _____ made of frozen water and dry ice.

# Climbing Mars' Mountain

Help the astronauts climb to the top of this mountain on Mars!

**Directions:**

You will need the game cards on page 107 and a marker for each player. Each player takes a card and reads the number. The player with the higher number moves his or her marker up one space on the mountain. If the cards are equal, discard them and draw again. The first person to reach the top of Mars' mountain wins!

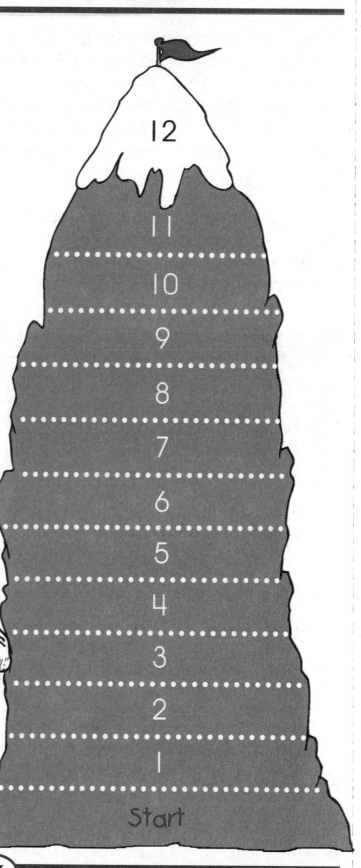

# Climbing Mars' Mountain Game Cards

| | | | | | |
|---|---|---|---|---|---|
| 6 | 12 | 18 | 24 | 30 | 36 |
| 5 | 11 | 17 | 23 | 29 | 35 |
| 4 | 10 | 16 | 22 | 28 | 34 |
| 3 | 9 | 15 | 21 | 27 | 33 |
| 2 | 8 | 14 | 20 | 26 | 32 |
| 1 | 7 | 13 | 19 | 25 | 31 |

# Make a Martian Mini-Book!

*Mini* means very small. Make a mini-book of facts about Mars that is small enough to carry in your pocket.

1. Read the facts about the Red Planet and carefully cut them out.

2. Follow the dashed lines to cut out the pages for your mini-book.

3. Glue one fact to the bottom of each page.

4. Draw and color a mini-picture to go with the fact on each page.

## Mars
### The Red Planet

2. The Sun would look much farther away if you were standing on Mars.

3. Since Martian atmosphere has little oxygen, the sky would probably appear deep blue or violet in color.

4. Mars has mountains three times taller than Mt. Everest, Earth's highest mountain.

| | |
|---|---|
| 1 | 2 |
| 3 | 4 |

# More of Your Martian Mini-Book

Glue all the facts and color pictures on each of your mini-pages. Then do the following:

1. Put all your mini-pages in order, with mini-page one on top.
2. Staple them together.

Does your Martian Mini-Book fit in your pocket? Show it to your friends!

5. Great sand storms of red dust blow across Mars.

6. Mars has a giant volcano, named Olympus Mons, almost 16 miles high.

7. Mars has thousands of craters.

8. Mars has two polar ice caps.

5

6

7

8

# Mars

Mars is a planet half the size of Earth. In some ways, Mars resembles Earth. It has ice caps at its North and South Poles, and some of its surface was shaped long ago by running water and streams. A day on Mars is also very different from Earth. It takes Mars 687 Earth days to circle the Sun. The air on Mars is too thin for human beings to breathe. The rivers that once crossed Mars have dried up, leaving a planet that is covered with deserts and ice caps. During the day, the temperature can be comfortable at 72 degrees Fahrenheit, but at night, it can drop to about 200 degrees below zero! Mars looks red to us because its surface soil is rich in minerals that are like rust. The sky around Mars is pink from the rusty dust that floats in the atmosphere. There are huge wind storms on Mars. Mars has two moons, Phobos and Deimos. It also has huge mountains and deep canyons. Mons Olympus, a giant volcano, is three times higher than Mt. Everest. Robots from the Viking spaceship tested the air and soil of Mars for signs of life. These studies found no trace of life as we know it.

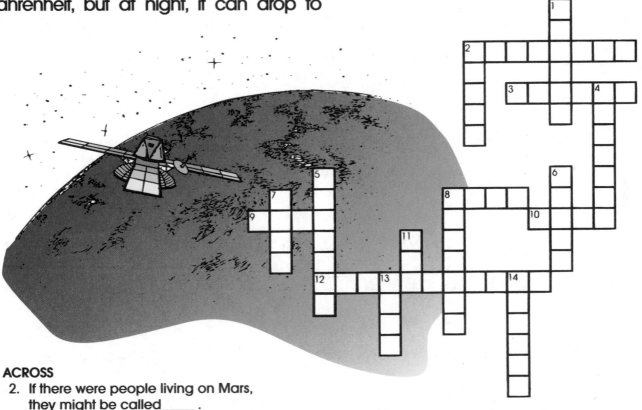

**ACROSS**

2. If there were people living on Mars, they might be called_____ .
3. Name of one of the moons of Mars
8. Mars'____is rich in rust.
9. It is the planet that resembles Earth.
10. First word in the name of the volcano on Mars
12. At night on Mars, the____can drop to –200 degrees.

**DOWN**

1. The name of one of the moons that orbits Mars
2. Phobos and Deimos are_____of Mars.

4. Second part of the name of the volcano on Mars
5. Mars is covered with____and ice caps.
6. A huge wind____is not uncommon on Mars.
7. Size of Mars in comparison with the Earth
8. The_____of Mars was shaped by running water.
11. Type of caps on Mars
13. Color of sky around Mars
14. They tested the air and soil of Mars.

# Marvelous Mars

Can you find the hidden words about Mars in the puzzle below? Use the Word Bank to help you, and circle the words as you find them.

## Word Bank

| | | | |
|---|---|---|---|
| red | dusty | craters | seasons |
| windy | lifeless | volcanoes | stable temperature |
| dry | mountainous | polar ice caps | frozen |

```
S  T  A  B  L  E  T  E  M  P  E  R  A  T  U  R  E
E  A  S  D  I  G  H  E  O  Q  W  E  R  T  Y  E  P
A  Z  X  D  F  V  C  X  U  B  N  M  J  K  W  D  O
S  H  G  J  E  Q  E  E  N  Z  X  C  B  N  N  M  L
O  C  V  E  L  R  R  R  T  M  M  B  V  F  W  E  K
N  Z  D  F  E  E  R  G  A  H  D  S  D  R  S  W  C
S  A  S  G  S  W  R  S  I  T  R  P  O  O  M  N  R
F  D  G  H  S  S  W  I  N  D  Y  S  D  Z  T  R  A
R  T  Y  Q  H  G  B  W  O  Q  W  B  S  E  S  R  T
B  V  S  T  N  N  W  M  U  N  S  S  T  N  T  M  E
W  E  R  T  W  W  D  U  S  T  Y  B  N  M  N  S  R
S  T  U  V  N  V  D  D  L  L  P  B  V  S  T  S  S
P  O  L  A  R  I  C  E  C  A  P  S  S  P  A  C  S
B  V  C  S  D  S  B  S  N  B  S  S  S  F  S  T
S  D  A  V  O  L  C  A  N  O  E  S  G  D  D  B  S
```

# Jupiter

# Fascinating Facts About Jupiter

Jupiter is the biggest planet in our solar system. In fact, it is so big all of the other planets could fit inside it!

Jupiter has a famous "landmark" called the Great Red Spot (GRS). It is thought to be a giant, swirling, storm cloud, three times larger than the Earth!

Jupiter spins faster than any other planet. Jupiter bulges at its equator because it is not solid and it is spinning so fast.

Jupiter's atmosphere is very stormy, with high winds of up to 250 miles per hour and lightening. It is very violent.

One year on Jupiter lasts almost 12 Earth years!

Jupiter has no definite surface, but under the outer cloud layers, the gas thickens as the pressure increases, gradually becoming like a hot liquid.

# Jupiter

Jupiter is the largest planet in our solar system. It has thirty-nine moons. Jupiter is the second-brightest planet—only Venus is brighter.

Jupiter is bigger and heavier than all of the other planets together. It is covered with thick clouds. Many loose rocks and dust particles form a single, thin, flat ring around Jupiter.

One of the most fascinating things about Jupiter is its Great Red Spot. The Great Red Spot of Jupiter is a huge storm in the atmosphere. It looks like a red ball. This giant storm is larger than Earth! Every six days it goes completely around Jupiter.

**Unscramble the words below:**

1. Jupiter is the _____ planet in our solar system.
   e t s l r g a

2. Jupiter has _____ moons.
   h t r i y t - i e n n

3. Jupiter is covered with thick _____.
   d s o c l u

4. Loose rocks and dust form a _____ around Jupiter.
   g i r n

5. The Great Red _____ of Jupiter is a huge storm.
   t S o p

**Circle and Write:**

Jupiter is the second largest brightest planet.

Jupiter is _____ and lighter heavier than all of the planets together.
bigger   redder

# The Great Red Spot

Jupiter has a famous "beauty mark" called the Great Red Spot, or GRS for short. The GRS is a football-shaped globe of gases, first seen in 1664.

What year is it now?_____

How many years ago was the GRS first discovered?_____

The United States spacecraft Pioneer 10 and Pioneer 11 flew past Jupiter in 1973 and 1974. They took pictures of the planet and its moons. They recorded much new information. Scientists learned that the GRS is a huge storm, like a hurricane, big enough to hold two Earth-sized planets. Winds blow at hundreds of miles per hour, causing swirling gases.

Scientists also discovered that Jupiter had a thin, flat ring of particles orbiting it just like Saturn and Uranus.

## Jupiter—The True Story

1. Read the facts about Jupiter. Some are true, others are false.
2. Draw a line to connect the true facts to the planet Jupiter.

The GRS was first seen in 1657.

Two Mars-sized planets could fit inside the GRS.

Jupiter is the largest planet in our solar system.

Jupiter has at least 39 moons.

The Great Red Spot is like a giant, super hurricane.

Winds blow up to 30 miles per hour in the GRS.

Jupiter is a quiet, peaceful planet.

Pioneer 10 and 11 flew by Jupiter in 1973 and 1974.

# The Giant Planet's Moons

Jupiter has many more moons than Mars and Earth! At least 39 moons have been discovered orbiting Jupiter.

How do we decide if something is a moon? Scientists in the United States have a rule: A spacecraft must record the potential moon moving around the planet two separate times before it is counted as a moon. As spacecraft get closer to distant planets, we learn more about them and new moons continue to be discovered.

The surfaces of Jupiter's four largest moons are very different from other moons in our solar system.

**Europa** is bright and smooth like a billiard ball. Scientists think it is covered with a frozen ocean of ice. There are dark streaks and lines all over the surface. It is about the size of our moon.

The moon, **Io**, is the only moon with active volcanoes. Volcanic lava shoots onto its surface. It is a very dry moon with high mountains and cliffs. It is bright orange in color.

**Callisto** is covered with craters. It has more craters than anything else in the solar system—even Mercury. Callisto has been called a ball of frozen slush.

**Ganymede** is the largest of Jupiter's moons. It is bigger than Mercury. It is half ice and half rock. Scientists discovered that the deep grooves in the moon were really mountains, valleys, and craters.

## Jupiter's Moon Facts
Complete the following sentences.

1. Jupiter has at least _____ moons.

2. _____ shoots onto the surface of Io.

3. The largest of Jupiter's moon is _____.

4. Callisto is covered with _____.

5. Ganymede's dark grooves are really _____.

6. _____, the brightest moon, is covered with ice.

# Jumbo Jupiter

Jupiter is the largest of the eight planets. It is more than 11 times larger than Earth. Jupiter is the fifth planet from the Sun, and it travels once around the Sun every 12 years. This jumbo planet rotates in just ten hours—faster than any other planet! Thick clouds surround Jupiter. Most scientists believe that the belts of color in Jupiter's atmosphere are caused by different gases. The planet is a giant ball of liquids and gases with, perhaps, a small rocky core. Its famous Great Red Spot is a huge storm of swirling gases. Lightning streaks across Jupiter's sky. Jupiter has a thin dust ring around its middle and 39 know moons.

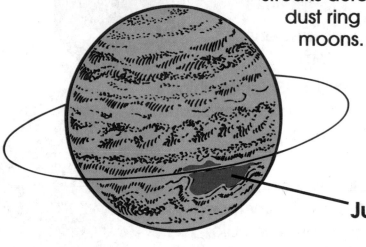

**Jupiter's Great Red Spot**

Write **true** or **false**.

_____ 1. Jupiter is the smallest planet in our solar system.

_____ 2. Earth is larger than Jupiter.

_____ 3. It takes 12 years for Jupiter to travel around the Sun.

_____ 4. Jupiter rotates faster than any other planet.

_____ 5. Jupiter's Great Red Spot is a huge storm of swirling gases.

_____ 6. Jupiter has a thick ice ring around its middle.

_____ 7. Jupiter has more than ten moons.

_____ 8. Jupiter is the sixth planet from the Sun.

# Jupiter

Jupiter is the largest planet and the fifth out from the Sun. Named after the king of the Roman gods, Jupiter is easy to see in the night sky. It shines almost as brightly as Venus does. It is 1,300 times the volume of Earth. Jupiter takes about twelve Earth years to circle the Sun. It spins so rapidly on its axis that its day is only about ten hours long. There is no solid ground on Jupiter. It is a giant ball of liquid and gas. It is made of the same elements as the Sun. Jupiter is called a gas giant because it is a giant planet made mostly of hydrogen and helium rather than rock and metal like the Earth. Storms and swirling clouds continually move through Jupiter's atmosphere that scientists call the Great Red Spot, big enough to hold two Earth's. They have discovered 39 moons orbiting around Jupiter and there are probably lots more. The moon Io has active volcanoes. The moon Ganymede is the largest moon in the solar system, even larger than Pluto and Mercury. There is also a ring around Jupiter made of dust.

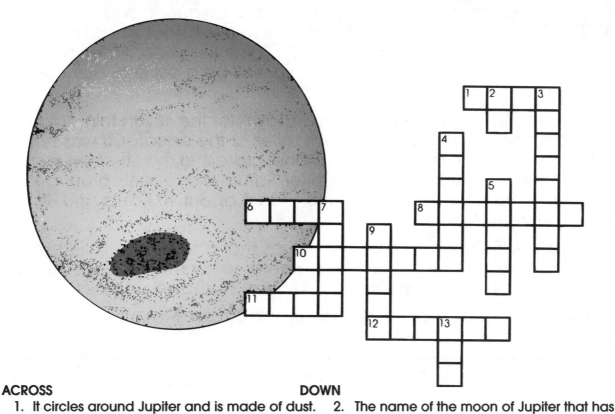

**ACROSS**

1. It circles around Jupiter and is made of dust.
6. Jupiter was named after the_____of the Roman gods.
8. The largest planet and fifth out from the Sun
10. Jupiter is called a "gas giant" because of its _____ surface.
11. What Jupiter's ring is made of
12. Jupiter's atmosphere is very violent and full of _____.

**DOWN**

2. The name of the moon of Jupiter that has an active volcano
3. Name of the largest moon in the solar system
4. Storms and swirling_____move through Jupiter's atmosphere.
5. The_____from Jupiter shines brightly in the night.
7. Jupiter is often called a gas_____.
9. A planet that shines brighter than Jupiter
13. The place on Jupiter that never seems to change is called the Great_____Spot.

# The Large Planets

Jupiter is about 88,733 miles at its equator. Named after the king of the Roman gods, it is the fifth-closest planet to the Sun at about 483,600,000 miles away. Jupiter travels around the Sun in an oval-shaped, elliptical, orbit. Jupiter also spins faster than any other planet and makes a complete rotation in about 9 hours and 55 minutes.

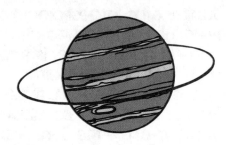

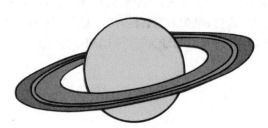

The surface of Jupiter cannot be seen from Earth because of the layers of dense clouds surrounding it. Jupiter has no solid surface but is made of liquid and gases that are held together by gravity.

One characteristic unique to Jupiter is the Great Red Spot that is about 25,000 miles long and about 20,000 miles wide. Astronomers believe the spot to be a swirling, hurricane-like mass of gas.

Saturn, the second-largest planet, is well known for the seven thin, flat rings encircling it. Its diameter is about 74,898 miles at the equator. It was named for the Roman god. Saturn is the sixth planet closest to the Sun and is about 888,200,000 miles away from it. Like Jupiter, Saturn also travels around the Sun in an elliptical orbit, and it takes the planet about 10 hours and 39 minutes to make one rotation.

Scientists believe Saturn is a giant ball of gas that also has no solid surface. They believe it also may have an inner core of rocky material, like Jupiter. Whereas Saturn claims 30 satellites, Jupiter has 39 known satellites.

Fill in the chart below to compare Jupiter and Saturn. Make two of your own categories.

| Categories | Jupiter | Saturn |
|---|---|---|
| 1. diameter | | |
| 2. origin of name | | |
| 3. distance from Sun | | |
| 4. rotation | | |
| 5. surface | | |
| 6. unique characteristics | | |
| 7. | | |
| 8. | | |

Jupiter

# Saturn

# Fascinating Facts About Saturn

Saturn is a very cold planet.  Its average temperature is around -274°F!

Saturn is most famous for its rings.  Saturn is the only gas planet whose rings are visible through a telescope or even with a pair of binoculars!

Saturn's rings stretch out into space for a distance of nearly 50,000 miles.  They are made up of a mixture of ice, rock, and dust.

Saturn has a density lower than water. That means that if there were a tub of water big enough, Saturn would float in it!

One of Saturn's moons is named Titan.  Titan is one of only three terrestrial worlds in the solar system supporting a thick atmosphere.  Astronomers are uncertain whether Titan is covered by oceans, land, or ice.

# Saturn

Saturn is probably most famous for its rings. These rings are made of billions of tiny pieces of ice and dust. Although these rings are very wide, they are very thin. If you look at the rings from the side, they are almost too thin to be seen.

Saturn is the second-largest planet in our solar system. It is so big that 758 Earths could fit inside it!

Saturn is covered by clouds. Strong, fast winds move the clouds quickly across the planet.

Saturn has 30 moons! Its largest moon is called Titan.

Draw 30 moons around Saturn!

**Circle:**
Saturn is most famous for its        spots.        rings.

**Write:**
Saturn's rings are made of _____ and _____.
                            mud   ice              dust   moons

**Check:**
Saturn's rings are ☐ red, yellow, and purple.
                   ☐ wide, but thin.

**Underline:**

Saturn...

is the second-largest planet in our solar system.
is big enough to hold 758 Earths inside it.
is farther from the Sun than any other planet.
is covered by fast, strong winds.
has 30 moons.

**Unscramble:**
Saturn's largest moon is called _____.
                                i T a n t

# Stunning Saturn

Saturn is the sixth planet from the Sun and is best known for the beautiful rings around its middle. The rings are thin and flat and made of pieces of rock and ice. They stretch more than 100,000 miles across!

Some scientists believe the rings are made of particles left over from the time when Saturn first became a planet. Others believe the rings are made of pieces of a moon that was torn apart when it came too close to Saturn.

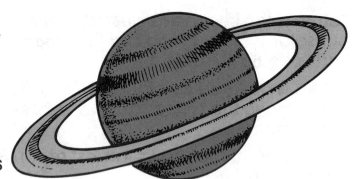

Saturn is the second largest planet. Since Saturn is more than nine times farther than Earth is from the Sun, it is much colder than Earth. The planet is a giant ball of spinning gases. Saturn has at least 30 moons.

**Write each answer in a sentence.**

1. For what is Saturn best known? _____

_____

2. What is one idea scientists have about how Saturn's rings were made?

_____

3. How does Saturn compare in size with the other planets? _____

_____

4. Why is Saturn colder than Earth? _____

_____

5. How many moons does Saturn have? _____

_____

# The Light, Cold Planet

Like Jupiter, Saturn is a planet made mostly of gases. Saturn is the lightest of all the planets. If placed in a gigantic ocean, Saturn would float!

Saturn is a cold planet. It takes 30 Earth years to complete one orbit around the Sun. Winds blow as high as 900 miles per hour in its atmosphere. Temperatures at the top of Saturn's clouds are colder than 240 degrees below zero! Why do you think Saturn is so cold? Write your answer below.

_____

_____

## A Visit to Saturn
1. Below are ten items you want to take for your spaceship journey to Saturn.
2. You can only take five! Select the five most important items.
3. Color your five items, cut them out, and glue them to the spaceship.

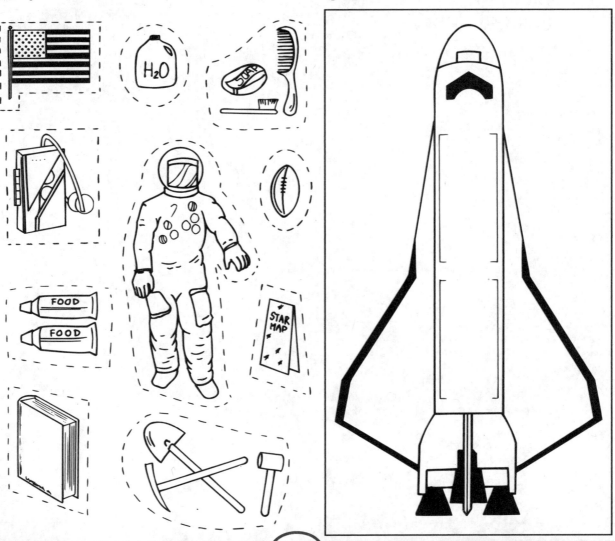

Saturn

# Moons, Moons, And More Moons!

Saturn has many, many, many moons! Scientists know that more than 30 moons orbit Saturn. They do not know the exact number. They are still studying information sent back to Earth from the Pioneer and Voyager spacecraft. Remember the scientists' rule: A moon must be seen two different times orbiting a planet before it can be called a moon. Perhaps even more moons will be found orbiting Saturn!

One moon is named Titan. The word *titan* means "very big," and that's the perfect name for Saturn's biggest moon. Titan is larger than the planet Mercury, but smaller than Ganymede, Jupiter's moon. Scientists believe that Titan is the only moon in the solar system with an atmosphere. The surface may have oceans and lakes of methane gas. Other areas are filled with methane ice. The nitrogen in the atmosphere gives the sky a red-orange color.

**Watch Out—Moons Ahead!**

You are in a spacecraft visiting all of Saturn's moons.

Use a pencil or a crayon to draw a path through the moon maze.

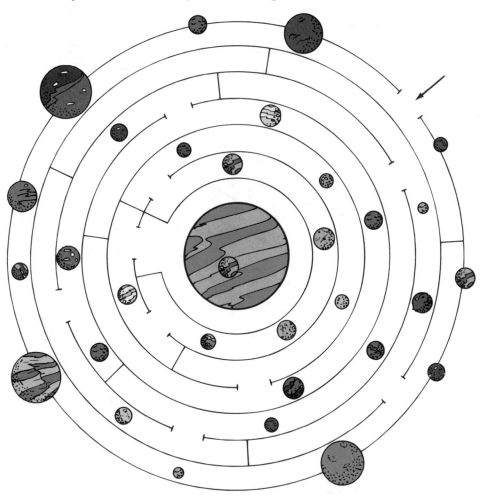

# Saturn's Rings

Use the code to color Saturn's rings.

If the number has:

7 ten thousands, color it red.

1 thousand, color it blue.

4 hundred thousands, color it green.

6 tens, color it brown.

8 ones, color it yellow.

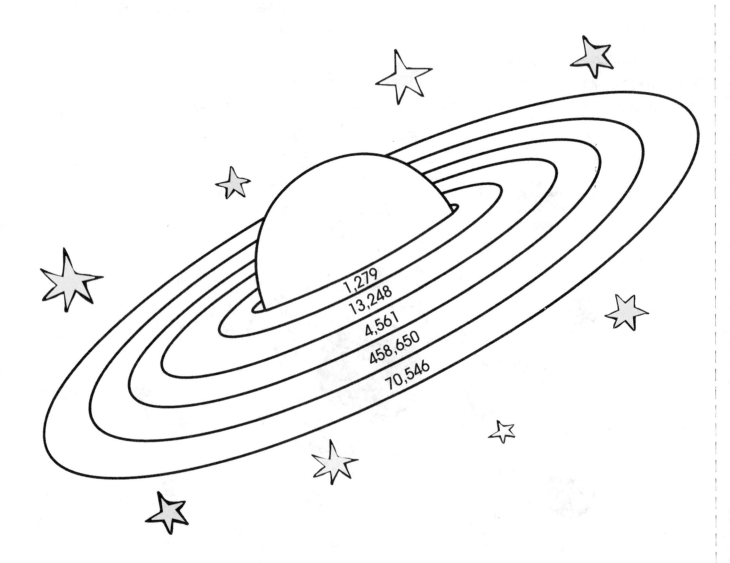

1,279
13,248
4,561
458,650
70,546

# Saturn

Saturn, the sixth planet out from the Sun, is often called the "ringed planet" because it has bright rings around it. Saturn is a gas giant planet like Jupiter. It's 758 times the volume of Earth. It takes Saturn nearly 30 Earth years to circle the Sun, but only ten hours and fourteen minutes to turn once on its axis. The center of Saturn is very hot, and the tops of the clouds are very cold. The rings around Saturn look solid, but they actually are not. They are made of billions and billions of pieces of ice and rock. The ring particles orbit Saturn like tiny moons. Saturn also has 30 moons. Its largest moon is called Titan. Titan has an atmosphere, but it is poisonous to human beings.

**ACROSS**
3. Saturn is a gaseous ball like_____.
6. The air on Titan is_____to human beings.
8. Sixth planet in the solar system
10. Saturn is the _____planet in our solar system.
11. Saturn is called the "_____planet."
13. Saturn's rings are made of pieces of _____and ice. (plural)

**DOWN**
1. Saturn has 30_____.
2. The rings of Saturn look_____, but they are not.
4. Saturn is one.
5. Number of Earth years it takes for Saturn to circle the Sun
7. It is found in the rings of Saturn.
9. Not hundreds but_____
12. Saturn is_____hundred times larger than the Earth.

# What Is Missing?

As you know, Saturn is most famous for its beautiful rings. Saturn is the only gas planet whose rings are visible through a telescope and can even be seen with some binoculars!

This picture of Saturn is missing something. Use crayons or markers to draw what is missing from the picture below.

# URANUS

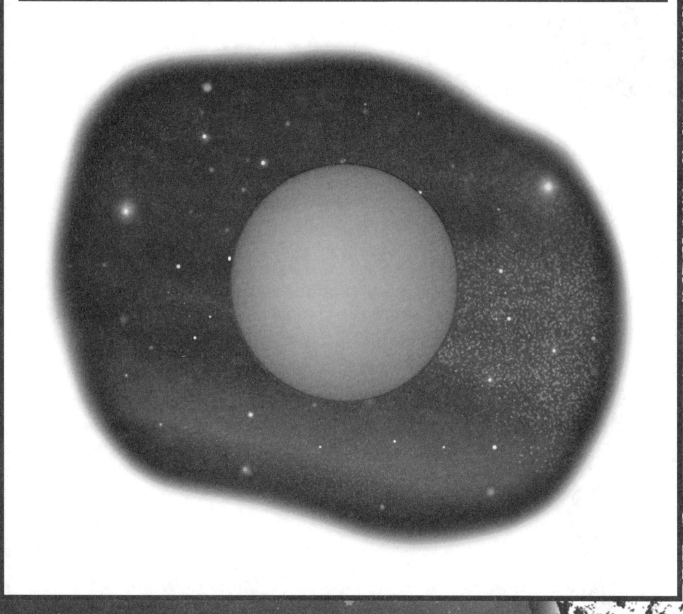

# Fascinating Facts About Uranus

Uranus is unusual because it orbits the Sun along its side — all of the other planets orbit in an upright position.

Some scientists think Uranus was struck by a large meteor at some point long ago and knocked sideways into its current position.

Uranus is so big that sixty planets the size of Earth could fit inside it!

Uranus is a "new" planet. It was discovered in 1781! This might seem like a long time ago, but compared to the other planets, it is recent.

Uranus was the first planet to be discovered with the help of a telescope. All of the other planets were bright enough to be seen from Earth without one.

# Uranus

Did you know that Uranus was first thought to be a comet? Many scientists studied the mystery comet. It was soon decided that Uranus was a planet. It was the first planet to be discovered through a telescope.

Scientists believe that Uranus is made of rock and metal with gas and ice surrounding it.

Even through a telescope, Uranus is not easy to see. That is because it is almost two billion miles from the Sun that lights it. It takes Uranus 84 Earth years to orbit the Sun!

Scientists know that Uranus has twenty moons and is circled by ten thin rings. But there are still many mysteries about this faraway planet.

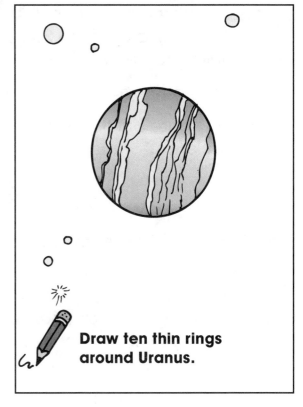

**Draw ten thin rings around Uranus.**

**Circle:**
Uranus was first thought to be a   moon.
                                        comet.

**Write:**
Uranus was the first planet to be discovered through a _____.
                                      telescope    TV

**Check:**
Scientists believe that Uranus is made of:

☐ rock    ☐ oil    ☐ metal    ☐ oceans    ☐ gas    ☐ ice

**Match:**

two billion miles         . . . the number of Uranus's moons
84 Earth years           . . . the distance of Uranus from the Sun
twenty                     . . . the number of Uranus's rings
ten                       . . . the time it takes Uranus to orbit the Sun

# The Green Planet

Uranus, a frozen dim world, is the seventh planet from the Sun.  Uranus takes 84 Earth years to orbit the Sun one time!  If you were 42 Earth years old, how old would you be on Uranus?

_____

Can you figure out the nickname for Uranus?  Unscramble each of the two words below.

NEGRE          LPNAET

Write Uranus's nickname: _____

**Add the Rings!**
Remembering its nickname, color the picture of Uranus below.  Then add Uranus's rings with a pencil or crayon.

# A Spin or a Roll

Planets spin as they orbit the Sun on an imaginary line called an axis. This line runs from the top to bottom through the planet. The top end of the planet is called the North Pole and the bottom end is called the South Pole.

Uranus does not spin like the other eight planets. Its axis is tipped over, so Uranus appears to be lying down. Uranus looks like a big, round watermelon rolling in space!

One complete spin on an axis is one day.

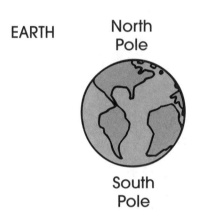

EARTH

North Pole

South Pole

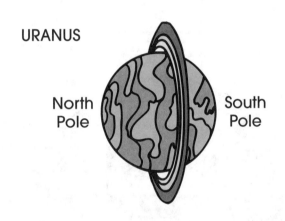

URANUS

North Pole

South Pole

## Move Like a Planet!

1. Standing up, spin around slowly five times.

2. Turn five somersaults in a row.

3. Circle which movement you would prefer if you were a planet.

　　　　to spin　　　to roll

4. Explain your answer.

_____

_____

# Uranus

Uranus, the seventh planet out from the Sun, is also a gas giant. It is the furthest planet that can be seen without a telescope and was discovered in 1781 in England. It is 60 times the volume of Earth. It is a blue-green color. It is probably very hot at the center, but the tops of its clouds are cold. It has ten rings that are very dark and thin compared to those of Saturn. Scientists believe that the rings are made of dark dust. It also has 20 known moons. Most of them were discovered in photographs of Uranus sent back by the Voyager spacecraft that flew by in 1986. Uranus orbits the Sun once every 84 Earth years. It takes Uranus 17 hours to complete one turn on its axis.

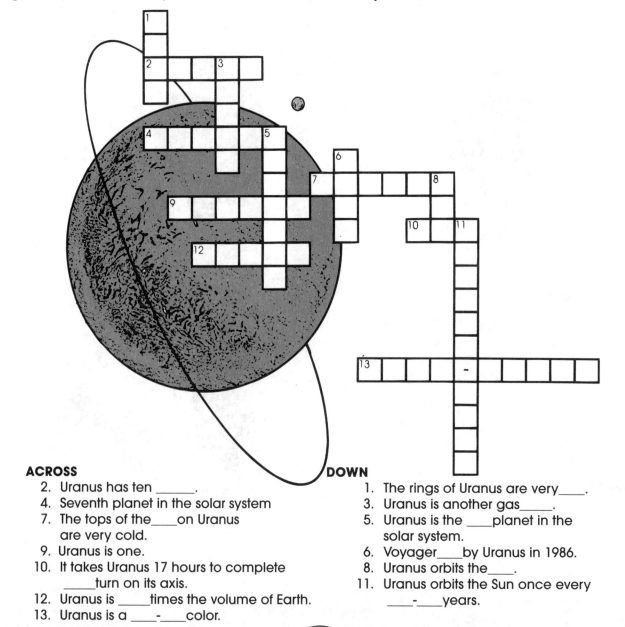

**ACROSS**
2. Uranus has ten _____.
4. Seventh planet in the solar system
7. The tops of the____on Uranus are very cold.
9. Uranus is one.
10. It takes Uranus 17 hours to complete _____turn on its axis.
12. Uranus is _____times the volume of Earth.
13. Uranus is a ____-____color.

**DOWN**
1. The rings of Uranus are very____.
3. Uranus is another gas_____.
5. Uranus is the ___planet in the solar system.
6. Voyager____by Uranus in 1986.
8. Uranus orbits the____.
11. Uranus orbits the Sun once every ____-____years.

# Strange Rings

In 1986, the Voyager spacecraft passed by Uranus. It photographed small rings encircling the Green Planet. The rings are made of rocks, gases, and dust.

These rings go around the middle of the planet like the rings around Jupiter and Saturn. But, since its axis tips Uranus on its side, the rings appear to go around the top and bottom!

**Make a Uranus Mobile!**

1. Use a 4–inch styrofoam ball.

2. Wrap the ball in a single layer of masking tape.

3. Color the ball using green markers or paint.

4. Then use pipe cleaners to make Uranus's rings. Twist the ends of two pipe cleaners together to make a ring. Ask an adult for help and attach the rings to Uranus using straight pins.

5. Use a paper clip and string to hang your Uranus mobile from the ceiling!

Remember, Uranus's rings go around from top to bottom!

# Unusual Uranus

Uranus is almost four times larger than Earth. Scientists think it has a thick, cloudy atmosphere made of hydrogen and helium gases. Deep inside is probably a solid core.

How many Earth years does Uranus take to orbit the Sun once?_____

While orbiting the Sun, Uranus turns on its axis very quickly, one turn every 17 hours.

How many hours are there in one Earth day?_____

Uranus has two days for every day on Earth. Scientists know the Green Planet is very cold. Temperatures probably drop lower than 240 degrees below zero.

## A Crossword Puzzle About Uranus

### Across
2. The atmosphere is made of hydrogen and
_____ .
4. Nicknamed the "_____ planet."
5. A day on Uranus is almost 17 _____ long.
7. The atmosphere is _____ and thick.
8. Uranus doesn't spin on its axis. It _____ .

### Down
1. An axis is an imaginary _____ .
3. Uranus is four times larger than this planet.
6. The seventh planet from the Sun.
7. Temperatures on Uranus are very
_____ .

# Close Encounter of a Mysterious Kind?

Do you know why the planet Uranus and its system of moons and rings tipped over?

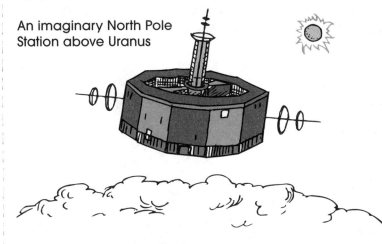

An imaginary North Pole Station above Uranus

*Pretend the year is 2020. You are living at Uranus North Pole Station. This is no ordinary, land-based station—this station floats just above the blue-green clouds, for Uranus has no "surface" as we know it. Down beneath the station the liquids are so thick and dense that any Earthly spaceship would be crushed.*

*At midsummer, the tiny Sun hovers near the top of the sky. It moves through a small circle every 17 hours. But as Earth years go by, the circle becomes bigger and bigger, until 21 years later the Sun moves in a giant circle that hugs the horizon. Finally, the Sun sets. For 42 years the Sun is not seen—it is winter. Luckily, because you are so far from the Sun, winter isn't much colder than any other season. Unluckily, it is always a lot colder than any place on Earth. After 42 years of winter, the Sun slowly, slowly rises in a giant circle near the horizon. Finally, for 21 more years, the Sun slowly spirals up to the center of the sky, and once again it is midsummer.*

The particular view of the Sun and sky that Uranus has is totally different from anyplace else in our solar system. Why? Imagine that all the planets orbit our Sun within a giant, flat "pancake." All the planets spin like a top. But all the planets, except Uranus, spin with their north poles pointing out of the top of the pancake. Uranus's north pole points toward the thin edge of the pancake. And this is not the only strange thing about Uranus!

Uranus has at least 20 moons. These moons orbit over the planet's equator. But because its north and south poles are tipped over, Uranus's equator must also be. So the entire Uranian system is tipped over. This includes Uranus's system of rings, too!

# The Twin Planets

1. Uranus and Neptune are similar in size, rotation time, and temperature. Sometimes they are called twin planets. Uranus is about 1,786,400,000 miles from the Sun. Neptune is about 2,798,800,000 miles from the Sun. What is the difference between these two distances?_____

2. Neptune can complete a rotation in 18 to 20 hours. Uranus can make one in 16 to 18 hours. What is the average time it takes Neptune to complete a rotation? _____ Uranus?_____

3. Can you believe that it is about -353°F on Neptune and about -357°F on Uranus? Brrr! That's cold! What is the temperature outside today in your town?_____
How much warmer is it in your town than on Neptune?_____Uranus?_____

4. Uranus has at least five small satellites moving around it. Their names are Miranda, Ariel, Umbriel, Tatania, and Oberon. They are 292, 721, 727, 982, and 945 miles in diameter, respectively. What is the average diameter of Uranus's satellites?_____

5. Neptune was first seen in 1846 by Johanna G. Galle. Uranus was first discovered by Sir William Herschel in 1781. How many years ago was Neptune discovered?_____Uranus?_____
About how many years later was Uranus discovered than Neptune? _____

6. Both Uranus and Neptune have names taken from Greek and Roman mythology. Use an encyclopedia to find their names and their origins.

_____

_____

_____

# NEPTUNE

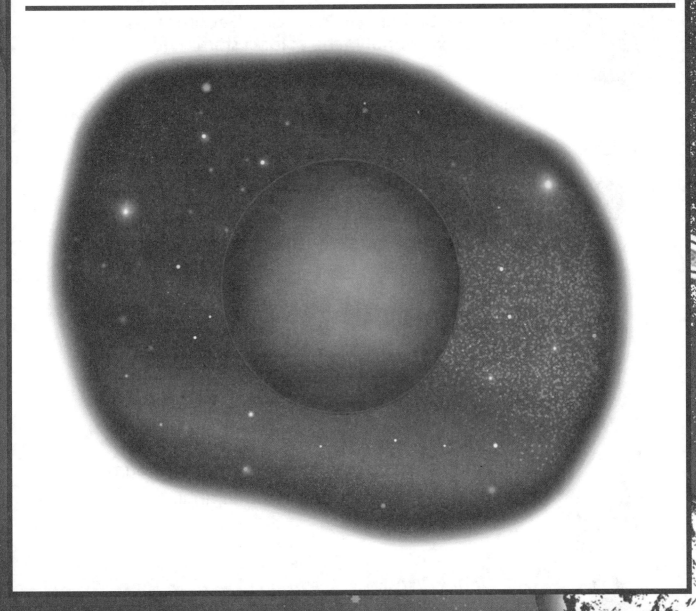

# Fascinating Facts About Neptune

Neptune is the eighth planet from the Sun—but not always! For 20 out of every 250 years, Neptune switches places with Pluto and becomes the outermost planet in the solar system.

Neptune is a very cold planet and a very windy one. Winds whip around Neptune at an awesome 1,400 miles per hour!

Neptune is a brilliant blue color, but on a closer look, it is colored by bands of different shades of blue. This coloring is due to a gas called methane in the atmosphere.

One of Neptune's moons is called Triton. Triton is thought to be one of the coldest worlds in our solar system. It has an average temperature of -455°F!

Neptune is 30 times farther away from the Sun than the Earth and is $3\frac{1}{2}$ times larger than Earth!

# The Blue-Green Giants

Uranus and Neptune are giant planets more than a billion miles from the Sun and Earth. They are about the same size. Each is more than $3\frac{1}{2}$ times larger than Earth. They look blue-green in photos because both have a gas called methane in their atmospheres. Uranus and Neptune are very cold planets where life probably doesn't exist.

Uranus is the seventh planet from the Sun. It is known to have at least 20 moons and 11 thin rings. Uranus rotates in the direction opposite of Earth. It can be seen from Earth without a telescope.

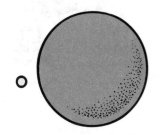

Neptune is farther from the Sun than Uranus. It has eight known moons and also has rings. Neptune cannot be seen without a telescope.

Decide which planet or planets each fact describes. If it describes Uranus, write *Uranus*. If it describes Neptune, write *Neptune*. If it describes both Uranus and Neptune, write *both*.

1. rotates in the opposite direction _____

2. called a blue-green giant _____

3. cannot be seen without a telescope _____

4. is more than a billion miles from Earth _____

5. has methane in its atmosphere _____

6. has at least 11 rings _____

7. can be seen without a telescope _____

8. has eight known moons _____

# Neptune

Neptune is the eighth planet from the Sun. It is difficult to see Neptune—even through a telescope. It is almost three billion miles from Earth.

Scientists believe that Neptune is much like Uranus—made of rock, iron, ice, and gases. Neptune has eight moons. Scientists believe that it may also have several rings.

Neptune is so faraway from the Sun that it takes 164 Earth years for it to orbit the Sun just once!

Scientists still know very little about this cold and distant planet.

Draw 8 moons around Neptune.

**Write, Circle, or Unscramble:**

**N** eptune is the   sixth / eighth   planet from the Sun.

**E** arth is almost three _____ miles from Neptune.
million   billion

**P** eople know   very little / very much   about Neptune.

**T** elescopes are used to see Neptune.   **Yes**   **No**

**U** ranus and Neptune are made of:   rock   soap   gases   ice

**N** eptune is a _____ and _____ planet.
warm   cold         distant   near

**E** very orbit around the _____ takes Neptune 164 Earth years.

# How Many Moons?

Neptune's moons are a mystery!  Scientists know at least eight moons move around the planet. One, Triton, is large and rocky and almost as big as Earth's Moon. It is almost as close to Neptune as our Moon is to Earth. Triton circles Neptune one time every six Earth days. Triton is the only moon in our solar system which revolves around a planet in the opposite direction that the planet rotates.

One of Neptune's other moons is called Nereid. It is very small and is $3\frac{1}{2}$ million miles from Neptune!  Tiny Nereid takes 360 Earth days to go around Neptune once. That is almost one year on Earth.

**Know the Moons**

1. Read the facts about Neptune's moons below.
2. Draw a line from the fact to the moon it describes.

I am much bigger than Neptune's other moon.

I am the smaller moon.

I am $3\frac{1}{2}$ million miles from Neptune.

It takes me 360 days to go around Neptune once.

I am almost as big as Earth's moon.

**TRITON**

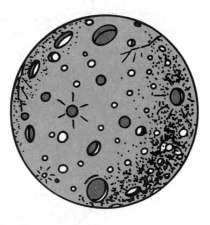

**NEREID**

I am as close to Neptune as Earth's moon is close to Earth.

It takes me almost one Earth year to orbit Neptune.

I revolve in the opposite direction of Neptune's rotation.

I circle Neptune once in six days.

147

# Neptune

Neptune, the eighth planet out from the Sun, is another gas giant. It is about the same size as Uranus. It is blue in color. Scientists know that Neptune gives off more heat than it gets from the Sun. It takes 165 Earth years for Neptune to orbit the Sun. It completes one turn on its axis every 16 to 18 hours. Neptune can only be seen in the night sky with a telescope. Scientists do not yet know if Neptune has any rings, but they know it has eight moons including Triton and Nereid.

**ACROSS**
3. The eighth planet in the solar system
5. This planet is the farthest from the Sun.
7. Neptune is a giant ball of _____.
9. Neptune completes one turn on its axis once every 16 to _____ hours.
10. Neptune is about the same size as this planet.
11. Biggest moon orbiting Neptune

**DOWN**
1. Color of Neptune
2. Name for a small moon orbiting Neptune
4. Neptune is called the _____ planet.
6. You can see Neptune only with a _____.
8. Neptune gives off more _____ than it gets from the Sun.

# PLUTO

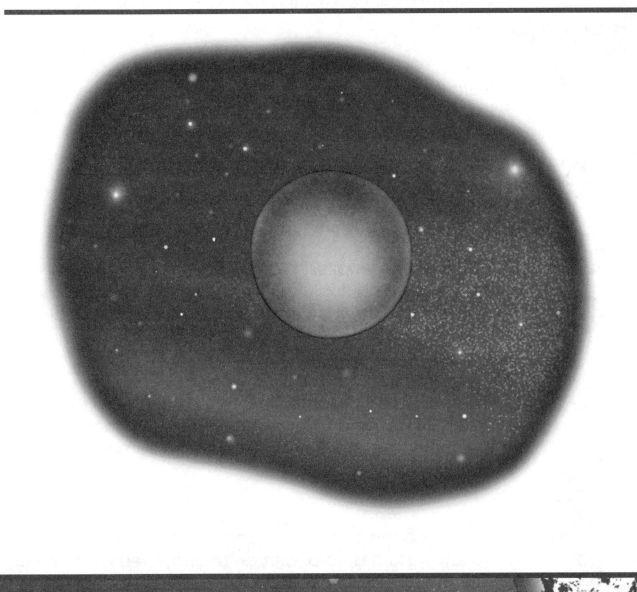

# Fascinating Facts About Pluto

Although astronomers predicted Pluto's existence in the early twentieth century, it was not officially discovered until 1930! It became a dwarf planet in 2006.

Pluto is so faraway that it appears as only a tiny speck in the largest telescopes and has not been visited by any space probes.

One year on Pluto equals 248 years on Earth!

Pluto was the smallest planet in our solar system. Its diameter is only 1,430 miles, which is smaller than our own Moon! Now it is considered a dwarf planet, along with Ceres and Eris.

Charon, Pluto's moon, is the largest satellite in the solar system. Pluto and Charon orbit so closely together that they have locked in rotation—the same sides always facing each other.

Little has been discovered about faraway Pluto, but we do know Pluto is cold, with an average temperature of -380°F.

# Pluto

Pluto used to be considered the ninth planet. Now, along with Ceres and Eris, it is considered a dwarf planet.

If you stood on Pluto, the sun would look just like a bright star in the sky. Pluto is so far away that it gets little of the sun's heat. That is why it is freezing cold on Pluto.

Some scientists think that Pluto was once one of Neptune's moons that escaped from orbit and drifted into space.

Pluto is so far away from the sun that it takes 248 Earth years just to orbit the sun once!

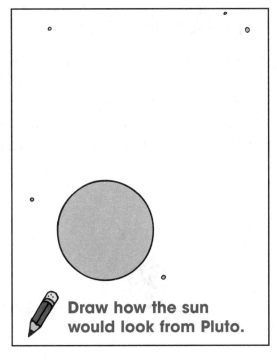

Draw how the sun would look from Pluto.

## Unscramble and Circle:

_____ is  farther  to the sun than Earth.
    l t P o u        closer
    2 4 1 5 3

Pluto, Ceres, and Eris are  large  _____ .
                             dwarf
                                    l a e n p t s
                                    2 3 5 4 1 6 7

## Check:

### Pluto Facts

☐ On Pluto, the sun looks like a bright star.

☐ Pluto gets very little of the sun's heat.

☐ Pluto has very hot weather.

☐ Pluto takes 248 Earth years to orbit the sun.

## Circle:

Some scientists believe that Pluto was once Neptune's  sun.
                                                        moon.

151

# Faraway Pluto

At Pluto's farthest point, it is more than four billion miles from Earth!

Pluto is smaller than Earth's moon.

Scientists know very little about Pluto because it is so faraway.
It is believed to be like a rocky snowball in space. Charon is Pluto's only moon. Scientists don't think any life exists on faraway Pluto.

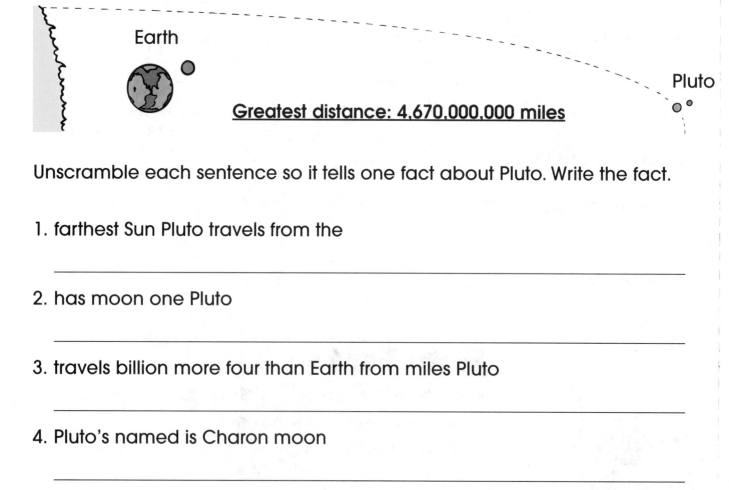

Earth

Pluto

**Greatest distance: 4,670,000,000 miles**

Unscramble each sentence so it tells one fact about Pluto. Write the fact.

1. farthest Sun Pluto travels from the

   _____

2. has moon one Pluto

   _____

3. travels billion more four than Earth from miles Pluto

   _____

4. Pluto's named is Charon moon

   _____

# Measure the Distance!

Pluto is even smaller than Earth's Moon!

What is Pluto like? This ball of frozen ice appears white. It may be partly covered by frozen methane gas. It has little or no atmosphere.

Pluto is 39 times farther away from the Sun than the Earth is. Scientists do not have much information about distant Pluto.

**Measure the Distance!**
1. Cut out the three name cards below.
2. Place one marble on the floor next to the "Sun" label.
3. Measure one inch from the Sun and place another marble and the "Earth" label.
4. Measure 38 inches and place a third marble and the "Pluto" label on the floor. Stand back and look at the distances between the three marbles. Now can you understand why Pluto takes 248 Earth years to travel once around the Sun?

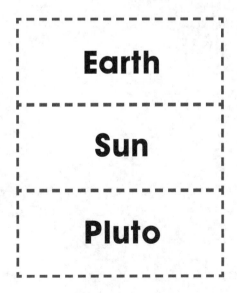

**Earth**

**Sun**

**Pluto**

# Pluto and Planet X

Pluto's orbit forms a long, thin oval shape that crosses the path of Neptune's orbit every 248 years. So, for about 200 Earth years, Pluto is actually closer to the sun than Neptune! Try this art project:

**You will need:**
crayons or chalk
glue
yarn (various colors)
pencil

## Directions:

1. Use a crayon to draw the sun in the center of page 156.
2. Use your pencil to draw each orbit, being careful to cross Pluto's with Neptune's.*
3. Color the planets along the orbits.
4. Trace the orbits in glue, then lay yarn on top.

*Only Pluto's and Neptune's orbits should cross.

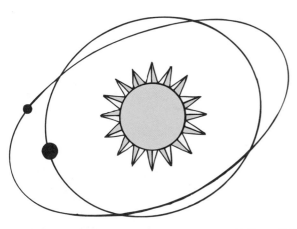

Imagine there is another planet called Planet X. Write a name for it below and use information about the other planets to estimate and create answers in the chart.

| Planet Name | Diameter | Distance from Sun | Revolution | Rotation | Satellites |
|---|---|---|---|---|---|
|  |  |  |  |  |  |

# A Discovery!

An exciting discovery was made in 1978! An astronomer in Washington, D.C. discovered a moon orbiting tiny Pluto. Until 1978, scientists did not think Pluto had any moons.

This moon is called Charon. Even with a telescope this moon is difficult to see because it is so close to Pluto. Charon is only 840 miles in diameter.

Charon does not weigh very much. Like planet Jupiter, this moon may not have a lot of heavy matter inside. Scientists think it may be as light as a comet!

It takes Charon 6 days, 9 hours, and 17 minutes to go around Pluto one time. This is exactly the same amount of time it takes Pluto to spin once on its axis. So, during one day on Pluto, Charon orbits the planet once.

Charon orbits close to Pluto. The pull of gravity from Charon is very strong. The pull causes **geysers**, jet sprays of water, to burst up from inside Pluto. The moment the water hits the surface, it freezes. This occurs all the time, causing Pluto to be continuously covered by new coats of frozen ice.

## Pluto Quiz

1. What would you have named Pluto's moon?

   _____

2. How long is one day on Pluto?

   _____

3. What is an astronomer?

   _____

   Would you like to be an astronomer? Tell why or why not.

   _____

4. How big is Charon?

   _____

5. Do you remember what "diameter" means? Draw where the diameter would be on this planet.

6. Why do you think no one had found Charon before 1978?

   _____

7. What is a jet spray of water called?

   _____

157

# Planet Fact Cards

Cut apart the cards on the pages that follow to create your own set of planet fact cards! Use them to learn fascinating information about the planets in our solar system. Practice on your own with the cards or grab a friend and test both of your knowledge about the planets!

**Mercury**

Mercury is the planet nearest to the Sun.

It is the second smallest planet in our solar system.

Mercury experiences radical temperature changes.

The temperature can rise to 800°F during the day and drop to -275°F at night!

Mercury has no atmosphere. It also has no air or life of any kind.

It is covered with thousands of ancient craters.

# Planet Fact Cards

# Planet Fact Cards

# Planet Fact Cards

# Planet Fact Cards

Earth

Mars

Venus

Neptune

Mercury

Jupiter

Saturn

Uranus

IN9660479A

**Venus**

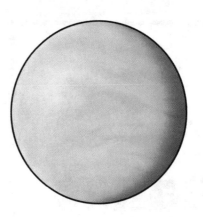

Venus is Earth's "sister planet."

Venus and Earth are almost the same size and orbit the Sun at the same rate.

Venus is a hot, hostile planet.

It has an average temperature of 900°F.

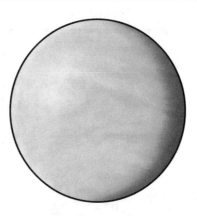

Venus is the planet nearest to the Earth. This makes it the easiest planet in the sky to see.

# Planet
# Fact
# Cards

# Planet
# Fact
# Cards

# Planet
# Fact
# Cards

# Planet
# Fact
# Cards

**Earth**

$E$arth is the third planet from the Sun.

It takes the Earth about 365 days to orbit the Sun.

$E$arth is the only planet in the solar system that is able to support life.

This is largely due to its mild, steady temperature and thick, oxygen-rich atmosphere. Earth is also the only planet that has water in flowing form.

$E$arth is the largest and densest of the four rocky planets. It has a diameter of approximately 8,000 miles.

Almost 75% or three-fourths of the Earth is covered by water.

# Planet Fact Cards

# Planet Fact Cards

# Planet Fact Cards

# Planet Fact Cards

**Mars**

Mars is the fourth planet from the Sun.

It has a thin atmosphere and the only remaining water on the planet is frozen.

Mars is nicknamed the "Red Planet." Rusted iron in the soil on Mars gives the planet a red appearance.

Mars and Earth are similar in many ways. Both planets have four seasons, polar ice caps, stable temperatures, and magnetic iron cores.

# Planet Fact Cards

# Planet Fact Cards

# Planet Fact Cards

# Planet Fact Cards

**Jupiter**

Jupiter is the biggest planet in the solar system. It is so big all of the other planets could fit inside of it!

Jupiter has a famous landmark called the Great Red Spot (GRS). It is thought to be a giant, swirling storm cloud.

Jupiter's atmosphere is very stormy and violent.

Winds circle Jupiter at 250 miles per hour.

# Planet
# Fact
# Cards

# Planet
# Fact
# Cards

# Planet
# Fact
# Cards

# Planet
# Fact
# Cards

**Saturn**

Saturn is a very cold planet. Its average temperature is around -274°F.

Saturn is most famous for its rings.

It is the only gas planet whose rings are visible through a telescope or even a pair of binoculars!

Saturn has a density lower than water. That means if there was a tub of water big enough, Saturn would float in it!

# Planet Fact Cards

# Planet Fact Cards

# Planet Fact Cards

# Planet Fact Cards

**Uranus**

Uranus is the seventh planet from the Sun.

It is almost two billion miles away from the Sun.

Uranus is unusual! It orbits the Sun along its side. All of the other planets orbit in an upright position.

Uranus is a very large planet. It is so big that 60 planets the size of Earth could fit inside it!

# Planet Fact Cards

# Planet Fact Cards

# Planet Fact Cards

# Planet Fact Cards

**Neptune**

Neptune is usually the eighth planet from the Sun but not always!

For 20 out of every 250 years, Neptune switches places with Pluto to become the outermost planet.

Neptune is a very cold and windy planet.

Winds whip around Neptune at an unbelievable 1,400 miles per hour!

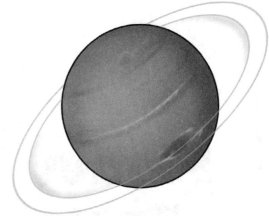

Neptune is a brilliant blue color. On a closer look, it is colored by bands of different shades of blue. This coloring is due to a gas called methane in the atmosphere.

# Planet Fact Cards

# Planet Fact Cards

# Planet Fact Cards

# Planet Fact Cards

# Planet
# Fact
# Cards

# Planet
# Fact
# Cards

# Planet
# Fact
# Cards

# Planet
# Fact
# Cards

# Planet Fact Cards

# Planet Fact Cards

# Planet Fact Cards

# Planet Fact Cards

# Planet
# Fact
# Cards

# Planet
# Fact
# Cards

# Planet
# Fact
# Cards

# Planet
# Fact
# Cards

# THE SUN

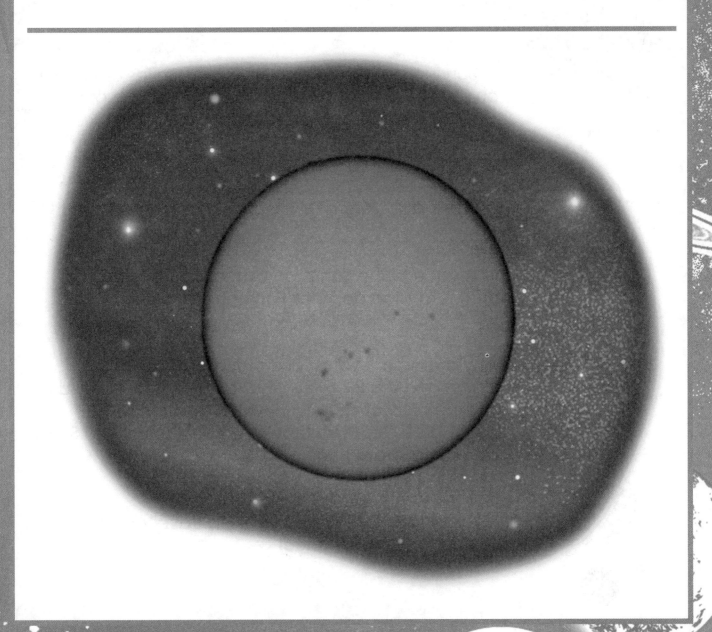

# Fascinating Facts About the Sun

The Sun is a star! It is a huge ball of burning, condensed gases.

The Sun is really big — almost 900,000 miles around! It would take 1.3 million Earths to equal the size of the Sun. However, compared to other stars, the Sun is just average size.

The Sun is also very old. It is over 5 billion years old!

The surface of the Sun is an extremely hot one. It is about 27 million degrees Fahrenheit at its core!

Many dramatic events take place on the Sun's surface, and this is called **solar activity**. **Sun flares** are one type of solar activity in which streams of superheated gas leap thousands of miles off the Sun's surface into space!

It takes the Sun 220 million years to travel around the center of the galaxy once!

# The Spectacular Sun

The Sun is the center of our solar system. The Earth and all the other planets travel around the Sun.

The Sun is made up of gases. Hydrogen makes up most of the Sun, but it also contains a lot of helium. There are small amounts of many other gases.

Use the information on this page and on the page that follows to help you complete the crossword puzzle below.

## Across

3. The Sun is the center of the _____system.

4. The Sun is mostly made of _____.

6. The Sun also contains lots of _____.

## Down

1. The _____travels around the Sun.

2. The Sun is a _____.

3. This puzzle is about the  S U N .

4. The Sun gives off _____.

5. The Sun is the nearest star to _____.

7. The Sun makes its own _____.

Every day, as the Earth spins, the Sun comes up in the east and goes down in the west.

The Sun is very, very bright. It gives off its own light. The sunlight makes our days bright, and it makes plants grow.

On some days, we cannot see the Sun because the sky is cloudy. But the Sun is always there.

The Sun is also very, very hot. It sends us lots of heat that keeps us warm. Without the Sun, we could not live.

What would happen to these flowers if the Sun didn't shine?

_____

_____

What else do plants need to live?

_____

_____

# Our Sun

When you see the Sun shining during
the day, you are seeing a star.
A star is a huge glowing ball of gases.
The Sun is the only star in our solar system.
It looks much larger than the stars we see at
night because it is closer to us than the others.
Even so, the Sun is 93 million miles from Earth.

Our Sun is really only a medium-sized star.  Some
other stars in the universe are much bigger, and
many stars are much smaller.  The Sun is a yellow star.
Hotter stars are blue, and cooler stars are red.

Copy the sentence from the story that answers each question.

1. What is a star? _____

_____

2. Which star is in our solar system?_____

_____

3. How far is the Sun from Earth? _____

_____

4. What color is the Sun?_____

5. Why does the Sun look larger to us than other stars?_____

_____

_____

_____

# Sunny News

The Sun is the closest star to Earth. How close? The Sun is 93,000,000 miles away. This great distance is fairly close when you think of the vast distances in outer space.

How long does light from the Sun take to travel 93 million miles to Earth?
Circle your answer.

$8\frac{1}{2}$ days          8 years          8 minutes, 20 seconds

In just 8 minutes and 20 seconds, light from the Sun travels all that distance and lands on you!

Why is sunlight so important? Place your hand on a window where sunlight is shining in. You will feel the Sun's heat. The Sun's heat keeps the ground and air warm.

Plants need sunlight to make food that keeps them growing. When plants make food they give off oxygen, a gas people and animals breathe. We also eat plants to live.

The Sun helps you when you are lost! If you face the Sun in the morning, your direction is east. In the afternoon, you face the Sun to the west. How can this help if you are lost?

### Sun Talk
People talk about the Sun all the time! Look at the words and pictures below. Draw a line connecting the picture with the "sun" word that matches it. Then color the pictures in a way that makes sense.

sunfish

sunflower

sunset

sunbonnet

sunglasses

sundial

Can you think of three more "sun" words? Write them here.

_____     _____     _____

# Sizing up the Sun

Our star, the Sun, is very important to our solar system. This huge ball of fiery gases provides heat and light, making life, as we know it, possible on Earth.

center
diameter

How large is the Sun? The diameter, or distance across the middle, is 860,000 miles. That's 109 times longer than the Earth's diameter. The Sun is about the size of one million Earths all piled together.

Our Sun is only a medium-sized star. Imagine how big other stars might be!

**The Comparison Test**

1. Cut out a one-inch piece of yarn and place it on the floor.
2. Cut out the "Earth's Diameter" card and place it by the small piece of yarn.
3. Unroll a very long, straight piece of yarn across the floor. Place a 12-inch ruler at the end of the yarn and measure 12 inches.
4. Measure 12 inches of yarn 8 more times to get 108 inches. Then, measure one more inch and cut the yarn. Your one straight piece of yarn is 109 inches long.
5. Cut out the "Sun's Diameter" card and place it next to the long piece of yarn.
6. Compare the length of Earth's diameter to the Sun's. The Sun's diameter is 109 times longer than Earth's.

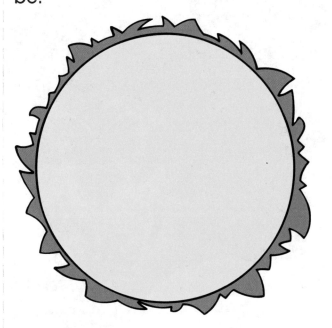

Earth

**Earth's Diameter**

**Sun's Diameter**

# Sun-sational Puzzle

If we could travel from the Sun's core, or center, to the surface we would be at the **photosphere**, which is the surface part of the Sun seen from Earth. Flashes of light seen by scientists on the surface of the Sun are called **flares**, and dark patches are called **sunspots**. Sometimes eruptions of gas, called **prominences**, can also be seen during a solar eclipse. Just above the Sun's surface is a layer of bright gases called the **chromosphere**. The **corona**, the region beyond the chromosphere, consists of white concentric circles of light that radiate from the Sun.

Use words from the Word Bank to complete the crossword puzzle.

**Word Bank**
Sun
flares
sunspots
chromosphere
core
corona
photosphere
prominences

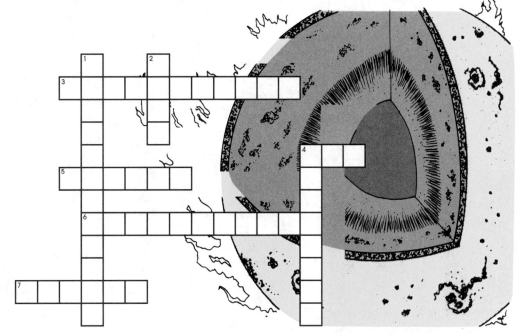

**Across:**
3. The part of the Sun you can see
4. Huge glowing ball of gases at the center of our solar system
5. The region of the Sun's atmosphere above the chromosphere
6. Big, bright eruptions of gas
7. Flashes of light on the Sun's surface

**Down:**
1. The middle part of the Sun's atmosphere
2. The center of the Sun
4. Dark patches that sometimes appear on the Sun

# Follow the Sunbeams

The Sun's rays provide the energy source for every living thing on Earth. Begin at the center of the Sun and find a path that allows the energy to beam toward Earth.

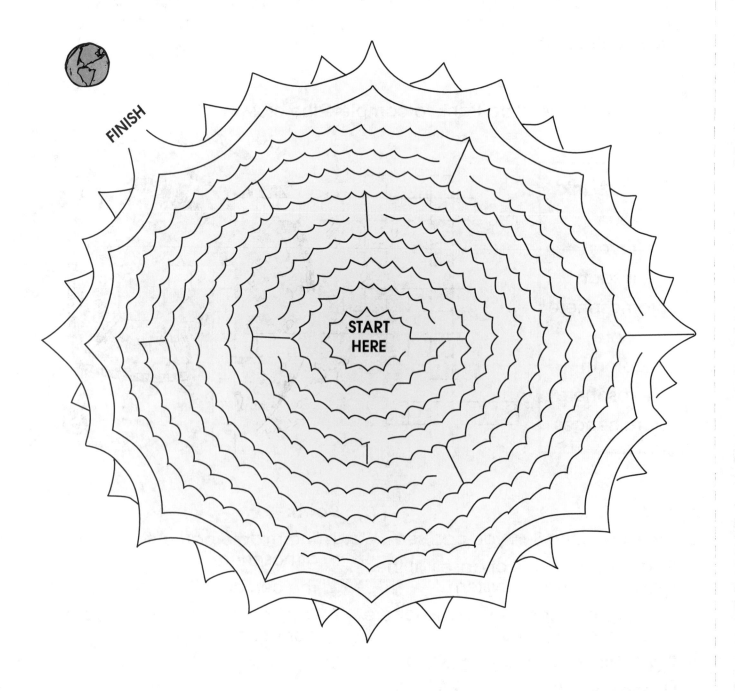

FINISH

START HERE

# Sun

The Sun is a star. It is the only star in our solar system. Our Sun is just one of many billions of stars in the Milky Way galaxy. The Sun is a medium-sized star. It looks bigger than the other stars in the sky because it is closer to Earth than the stars we see at night. The Sun is a huge ball of hot, glowing gases that move and boil. The light from the hot gases of the Sun is so bright that you cannot look straight at it without hurting your eyes. The Sun is 93 million miles from Earth. If a spaceship could fly to the Moon in two days, it would take the same ship more than two years to fly to the Sun. The hottest part of the Sun is the center, or core. Nuclear energy from the core heats the outer parts of the Sun so they are hot enough to glow with light. It takes about eight minutes and twenty seconds for the Sun's light to travel across space and reach Earth.

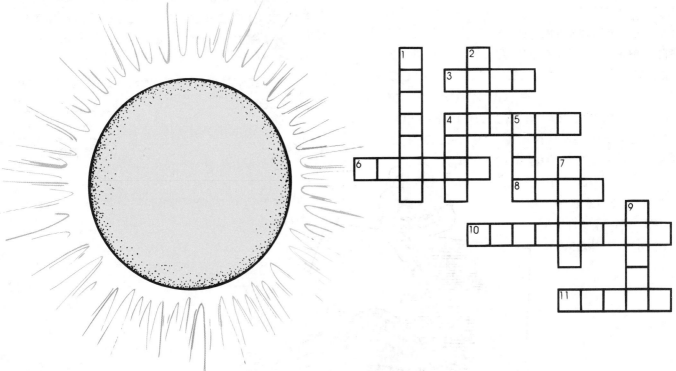

**ACROSS**
3. Center of the Sun
4. Nuclear____heats the outer parts of the Sun.
6. Core of the Sun
8. The Sun is one.
10. If a_____could fly to the Sun, the trip would take a long time.
11. The planet we live on

**DOWN**
1. The gases of the Sun are always moving, _____, and spinning.
2. A satellite of the Earth
4. Looking straight at the Sun can hurt your_____.
5. The Sun's_____give us light; rhymes with days.
7. The Sun is made of hot, glowing_____.
9. Waves of the Sun's_____reach Earth in eight minutes and twenty seconds.

# Amazing Shadow

Place this page flat on a table. Hold your hand over the paper. A shadow will appear. Your hand blocks light creating a dark shadow.

Outside, when objects block sunlight, shadows appear. When you sit under the shade of a tree on a hot day, you sit in a shadow.

A shadow can turn day into night before your very eyes! To make this happen, something must block all sunlight from falling on Earth. The Earth's Moon can do just that! Twice a year the Moon blocks sunlight from an area of Earth. As the Moon blocks the sunlight, the Sun looks smaller and smaller. When the Moon hides all of the Sun, the sky goes dark. The Sun's red fringe surrounds the dark moon for a short while until the Moon moves and slowly the Sun reappears. Day returns. When the Moon passes in front of the Sun and blocks the sunlight, we have a solar eclipse.

## Me and My Shadow

1. Use a piece of white paper larger than yourself. Get a friend to help you.
2. Take the paper outside on a sunny day. Lay the paper on a flat surface.
3. Position yourself so your shadow falls on the paper.
4. Have your friend trace your shadow with a color marker.
5. Try this at three different times of the day—in the morning, around noon, and in the afternoon. Use the same piece of paper but a different color marker each time. Put the paper back in the same place each time.
6. Label each shadow with the time of day.
7. Look at your shadows. How are they different?_____
_____

8. Did you have to move to a new position each time to find the shadow?_____
Why?_____
_____
_____

# The Sun: What a Gas!

The Sun is not solid! This burning star is made of the gases helium and hydrogen. The Sun's energy comes from the Sun's hot core. Hot gases explode inside the Sun, making the surface temperature about 10,000 degrees Fahrenheit.

Not all of the Sun's surface is this hot. Areas of gas that are a "cool" 1500 degrees Fahrenheit are called **sunspots**. They look darker because their temperature is so much lower than the rest of the Sun.

**Prominences** are huge clouds of fiery gases that shoot into space as far as 20,000 miles above the Sun. Some disappear after a few hours. Others can last for days or weeks.

## Make a Sun Mobile
1. Use an 8-inch styrofoam ball.
2. Use yellow and orange crayons or markers to color the fiery surface of the Sun.
3. Cut out the small black ovals for sunspots. Glue them onto the surface of your Sun.
4. Color the prominence patterns orange or red. Cut out the prominences. Attach them to your Sun.
5. Open one end of a paper clip, and push it into the ball. Hang the Sun with a string.

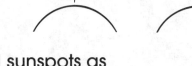

You can also use these prominences and sunspots as patterns to make as many as you want to add to your Sun.

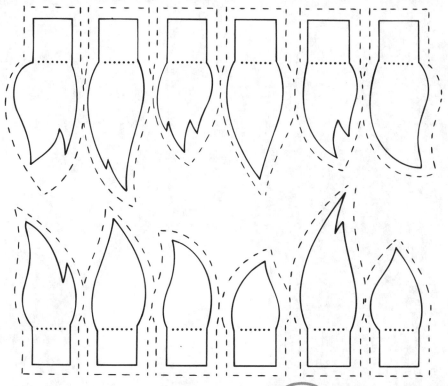

# A Matter of Time

The Sun can help you tell time with shadows. A **sundial**, or shadow clock, has something that sticks up from a flat surface, casting a shadow in the sunlight. During the day, the shadow moves. By watching the shadows, you can mark off hours and keep track of the time.

Why can't you tell time with a sundial at night?

_____

_____

## Make a Sundial
1. Take a notebook-sized piece of cardboard.
2. Stick a 4-inch pencil into a small ball of clay.
3. Press the clay near one end of the cardboard as shown in the picture.
4. Take your cardboard outside early on a sunny morning. Lay it on a flat surface away from any possible shade.
5. Use a **compass**, an instrument for finding directions, to make sure the side of cardboard with the pencil is to the north.
6. Every hour trace the pencil's shadow on the cardboard. Write the time next to the point.
7. At day's end, connect the points of the shadows into a curve.
8. What time was the line the shortest?_____
   Why?_____

## From an Hour to a Year
The shadows moved on your sundial. When we look in the sky, the Sun seems to move. We say that the Sun rises in the east and the Sun sets, or goes down, in the west. Sometimes this can be confusing. It seems the Sun moves, and we stand still. Actually, the Sun stays in one place and Earth rotates like a top. It takes 24 hours for Earth to rotate one time. We call this amount of time one day.

The Sun also helps us to tell time in another way. The time it takes for a planet like our Earth to travel around the Sun is called a year. It takes 365 and $\frac{1}{4}$ days for Earth to travel around the Sun once. The extra $\frac{1}{4}$ days add up to one full day every four years. That year is called a **leap year**.

How many days are in a leap year?_____

# What Is a Light-Year?

A light-year is the distance that light travels in one year. Light travels at 186,282 miles per second. That's equal to about seven and a half times around the Earth in one second! In one year, light travels almost 6 trillion miles—or 6,000,000,000,000 miles!

Astronomers measure distances in space by light-years because most things in space are so faraway. **Proxima Centauri**, the nearest star to Earth after the Sun, is more than four light-years away.

1. Which is bigger, a billion or a trillion? _____
_____

2. What is an astronomer? _____
_____

3. What instruments do astronomers use to study space? _____
_____

4. Why is it important for scientists to continue investigating space? _____
_____

5. Why is the Sun important to life on Earth? _____
_____
_____

6. What does the expression "Today's computers are light-years ahead of the first computers" mean? _____
_____

# Solar and Lunar Eclipses

A solar eclipse happens when the Moon passes directly between the Earth and the Sun. It blocks the sunlight to Earth and total darkness can happen in the middle of the day!

A lunar eclipse occurs when the Earth is lined up between the Sun and the Moon. The Moon shines by reflecting the Sun's light, but during a lunar eclipse, Earth is in the way. There is no moonlight during a lunar eclipse!

**Solar or Lunar?**

Read the facts below. Mark an **S** if the fact is describing a solar eclipse or an **L** if it is describing a lunar eclipse.

1. ____ The Earth lines up between the Sun and Moon, blocking the sunlight from the Moon.

2. ____ The Moon blocks the Sun's light from reaching Earth.

3. ____ Complete darkness occurs in the middle of the day.

4. ____ There is no moonlight at all.

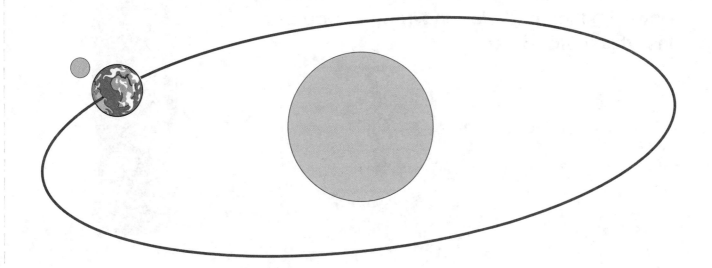

# Solar Eclipse Viewing Tube

**Materials Needed:**
Aluminum foil
Pin (to make a pinhole)
White cardboard
Long cardboard tube (an old paper towel roll will work great)

**Directions:**
1. Cover one end of the cardboard tube with aluminum foil and make a pinhole in the foil at the top.
2. Carefully cut a square viewing port, or hole, on the side of the tube near the opposite end.
3. Cover that end, but not the viewing port, with white cardboard.

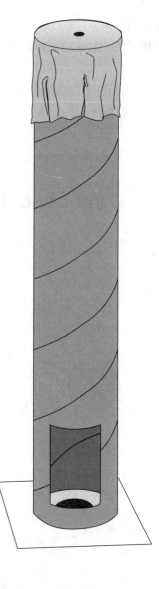

**To Use:**
1. Stand with your back towards the Sun. Do not look at the Sun.
2. Hold the viewing port end in one hand and rest the foil end on your shoulder.
3. Move your hand until the sunlight shines directly down the tube and the Sun's image appears on the white cardboard!

The Sun

# The Moon

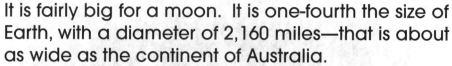

# Fascinating Facts About the Moon

The Moon is Earth's only satellite!

It is fairly big for a moon. It is one-fourth the size of Earth, with a diameter of 2,160 miles—that is about as wide as the continent of Australia.

The Moon is a dry, rocky place. It has no air, atmosphere, water, or live organisms at all! It is basically a giant ball of stone!

The gravitational pull of the Moon causes the tides in the Earth's oceans and seas.

At nighttime, the Moon shines brightly because it is reflecting the light of the Sun. It does not produce light of its own.

The Moon is the only satellite or planet to which men have traveled. On July 20, 1969, Neil Armstrong was the first man to walk on the Moon. Because there is no weather on the Moon, his historical first footsteps will last for centuries!

# We See Our Moon

Earth has one moon. It is the Moon that we see in the sky. The Moon is Earth's partner in space. It **orbits** the Earth. It also orbits the Sun along with the Earth.

The Moon looks large because it is closer to Earth than the Sun or planets. Four moons would stretch across the **diameter** of the Earth.

In 1969, **astronaut** Neil Armstrong took the first steps on the Moon. Scientists have studied rocks brought back from the Moon.

The surface of the Moon has many deep holes called **craters**. It has flat areas called **maria**. The Moon also has rocky mountain areas called **highlands**. There is no air, wind, or water on the Moon. No life exists there.

Write the boldfaced word from the story that matches each definition.

1. deep holes in the Moon's surface _____

2. to make a path around _____

3. flat land on the Moon _____

4. the widest part of the Earth _____

5. areas with rocky mountains _____

6. a person who travels in space _____

Write two sentences about the Moon using two of the boldfaced words.

1. _____

   _____

2. _____

   _____

# Earth's Nearest Neighbor

Although the Moon looks round, it is slightly egg-shaped and is much smaller than Earth. It is a little more than one-fourth the size of Earth. The Moon does not have an atmosphere to protect it, so it can get as cold as -200°F at night or as hot as the boiling point of water during the day!

While planets in the solar system orbit the Sun, moons travel around the planets. Our Moon orbits Earth 27.3 days, nearly a month.

   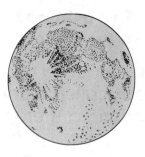

Look at the chart below to find out how many moons each of the planets in our solar system have.

## The Planets and Their Moons

| The Planets | Number of Moons |
| --- | --- |
| Mercury | 0 |
| Venus | 0 |
| Earth | 1 |
| Mars | 2 |
| Jupiter | 39 |
| Saturn | 30 |
| Uranus | 20 |
| Neptune | 8 |

# That's a Fact!

Study the chart below.
Then answer the questions.

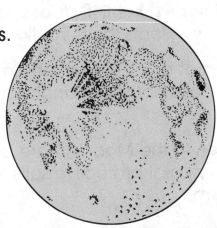

| The Moon at a Glance! | |
|---|---|
| **Age:** | about 4.6 billion years |
| **Distance from Earth:** | average of 237,083 miles |
| **Diameter:** | about 2,160 miles |
| **Circumference:** | about 6,790 miles |
| **Surface Area:** | about 14,670,000 square miles |
| **Rotation Period:** | about 27 days |
| **Average Speed Around Earth:** | 2,300 miles per hour |
| **Length of One Day and Night:** | about 15 Earth days |
| **Temperature at Equator:** | 260°F |

1. Write the number for 4.6 billion years._____

2. What is the distance of the Moon from the Earth?_____

3. About how many miles is the diameter of the Moon?_____

4. How many days are in 5 rotation periods of the Moon?_____

5. How much hotter is the temperature at the Moon's equator than the

   temperature outside your house today?_____

6. How many Moon days equal 45 days on Earth?_____

# The Moon

The Moon does not give off its own light.  It does not give us heat.  We can see the Moon only because it reflects the Sun's light like a mirror.

Sometimes we see the Moon at night, sometimes in the day.  When we see the Moon in the daytime, it does not seem bright at all.  But at night the Moon lights up the land.

Several astronauts have been to the Moon.  There is no air there to breathe.  The astronauts had to wear special protective suits with helmets so that they could breathe and stay warm.

Would you like to go to the Moon?_____

What would you bring with you?_____

_____

Think of something you could leave on the Moon that would tell future astronauts you had been there. _____

_____

# Moon's "Faces"

As the Moon orbits the Earth, we often see different amounts of the Moon's lighted part. Sometimes it looks like a circle, half-circle, or thin curved sliver. These different shapes are the Moon's **phases**.

**Directions:**

Cut out the Moon's phases (as seen from Earth) at the bottom of this page. Glue them next to the Moon phase as seen from space. Label the pictures using the words in the Word Bank. Use a science book to help you.

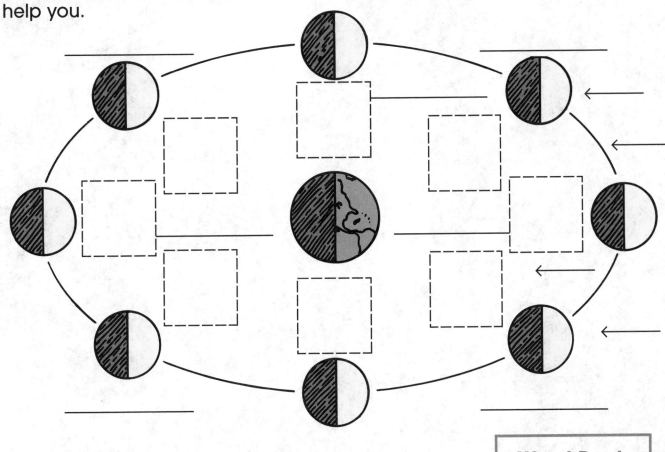

## Word Bank

Full Moon
New Moon
Crescent Moon
Half Moon
Gibbous Moon

# Earth's Moon

Earth's closest neighbor is its moon. The Moon is about 240,000 miles from Earth. The Moon orbits Earth just as Earth orbits the Sun. Just as the Sun's gravity keeps Earth from spinning off into space, Earth's gravity keeps the Moon in place. The Moon is roughly a quarter the diameter of Earth. It would take about 81 moons to make up the same weight as Earth. The Moon's gravity is very weak, one-sixth as great as the Earth's gravity. The Moon's gravity is too weak to hold an atmosphere. The Moon is a stark, arid place, hot in the day and very cold at night. The surface of the Moon is a desert of rock and dust. The light that we see from the Moon is reflected sunlight. As the Moon orbits Earth, we see varying parts of the Moon lit up by sunlight. The changing appearance of the Moon is called its cycle of phases. The Moon spins on an axis, but it always keeps the same face to Earth because it rotates and spins at the same rate. Astronauts learned from their trip to the Moon that people could live there if they brought their own water, air, and food.

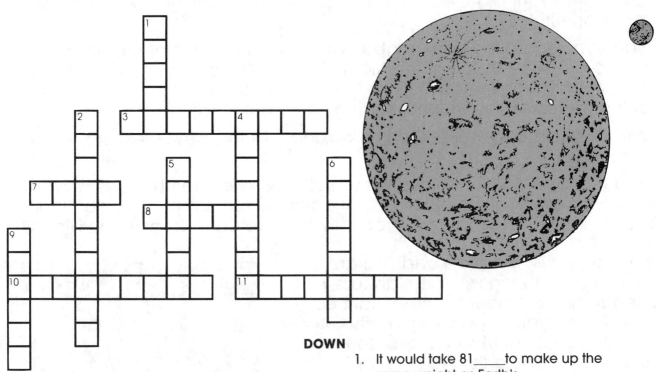

**ACROSS**
3. A person who walked on the Moon
7. It orbits Earth.
8. Planet that humans live on
10. The Moon is a _____ of Earth.
11. The Moon shines from _____ sunlight.

**DOWN**
1. It would take 81 _____ to make up the same weight as Earth's.
2. The Moon's gravity is too weak to hold an _____.
4. The Moon is Earth's closest _____.
5. Earth is a _____ .
6. The Moon keeps its same face to Earth because it _____ and spins at the same speed.
9. The surface of the Moon is like a _____.

# Moon Logs

Keep a log of the Moon's phases.

**You will need:**

four sheets (8"x 12") of black construction paper
a stapler
a white crayon
a large calendar

**Directions:**

Create a Moon log by folding four sheets of black construction paper in half and stapling them together. Using a white crayon, create a title, and decorate the cover.

It is best to begin the Moon observations with the "new moon." Observe the Moon twice a week, or every three days, weather permitting. If clouds interfere with your planned dates to observe the Moon, you may be forced to postpone it.

In your log, record the date of observation, and use half of a page on which to draw the shape of the Moon. Pay careful attention to which side of the Moon is illuminated. Be sure to draw it exactly as you see it. As the month progresses, record your findings on a calendar.

Look up vocabulary words such as waxing, waning, new, crescent, full, and first quarter.

Find out: Why the Moon shines? Why its shape seems to change? Why we see only one side of the Moon? What does the surface of the Moon look like from Earth? What has NASA recently discovered regarding the Moon?

When the log is complete and you are observing another new Moon, discuss with your parent the amount of time that has passed since you began logging the Moon. Relate the cycle of Moon phases to the calendar. Make predictions regarding specific phases of the upcoming month (i.e., How much time will pass between the new moon and the full moon? Predict the date we will see the next full moon). You can add the final touch to your log by writing a poem about the Moon and writing the final draft on the inside cover of your Moon log.

The Moon

# Moon Phases

## You will need:

a ping-pong ball
heavy thread
brass fasteners
scissors
a flashlight
index cards
needles
a shoe box

### Response Card

| Position | 1 | 2 | 3 | 4 |
|----------|---|---|---|---|
| Phase    |   |   |   |   |

Explain what conditions would be like when the Moon is full. _____
_____
_____

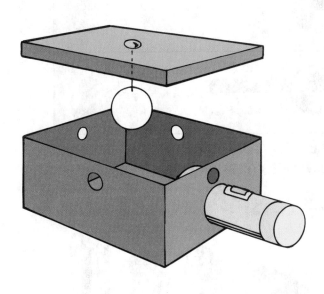

## Directions:

Have an adult help you cut an opening at one end of a shoe box large enough for a flashlight to fit through from the inside of the box. Cut a 1 inch viewing hole on all four sides of the box. Thread a needle with heavy thread and tie a knot. Put the needle through the top of the ping-pong ball, through its opposite side and through the bottom of the box lid up through the top. Cut the thread off close to the needle. Put a fastener into the lid near where the needle entered. Tie the thread around the fastener so that the ball hangs into the box about an inch and a half.

Put the lid on the box. Turn on the flashlight. Number each side of the box 1, 2, 3, 4. Look through the viewing holes. Write which phase of the Moon you see from each position on the card. Think of yourself as an observer on Earth, the flashlight as the Sun, and the ball as the Moon. Tell what conditions would actually be when you see each phase.

# Space Shadows

Have you ever held your hand up in front of a bright light to make shadow pictures on the wall? The Sun and Moon can cast shadows on the Earth just like the light and your hand cast shadow pictures on the wall.

Sometimes the Moon passes between the Earth and the Sun in just the right place to cast a shadow on the Earth. The sky darkens. The air becomes cooler. It seems like the middle of the night. This is called a **solar eclipse**.

**Directions:**

Write "solar eclipse" on the picture which best shows one.

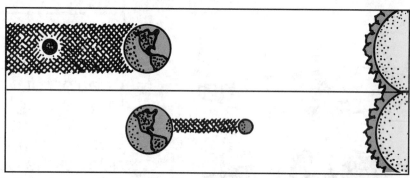

The Moon casts an eerie shadow on the Earth during a solar eclipse. Ordinary objects can also cast eerie shadows when the light hits them at different angles.

Circle the object that formed the shadow.

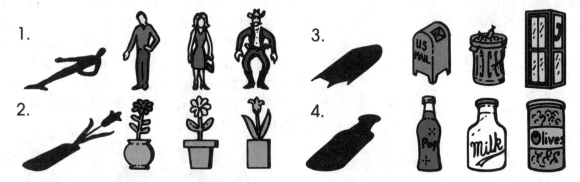

Draw a shadow for the objects below.

# A Time Capsule on the Moon

Scientists have studied the rocky surface of the Moon, our closest neighbor in space. By studying samples the astronauts have brought back to Earth, we know the Moon is probably $4\frac{1}{2}$ billion years old! They also know the Moon is very different from the Earth. Large holes on the surface of the Moon are called craters. Scientists have discovered the Moon has no air, gravity, wind, or water. Because of this, everything stays the same on its surface. The U.S. flag placed on the Moon by our astronauts should stay for millions of years. That means future visitors on the Moon will see it long after we're gone.

What do you think would be important to show millions of years from now? Design a space time capsule to be sealed and left on the Moon. What will you put in it? Why?

Use some of these items and make a time capsule. Seal it until the end of the year.

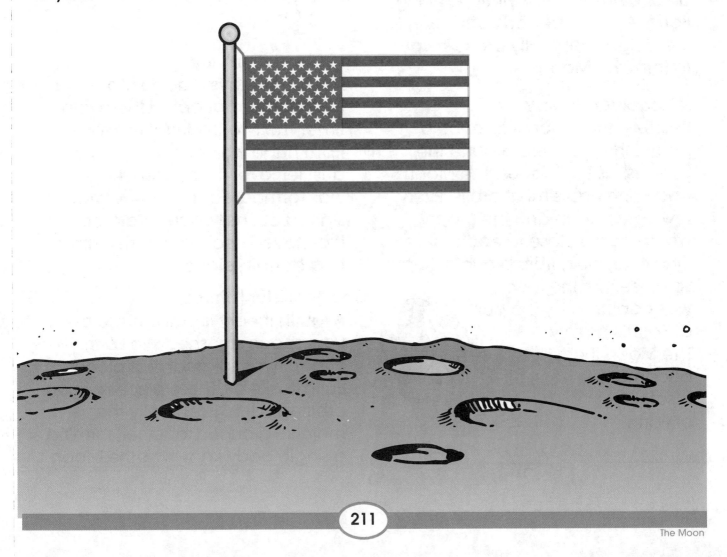

# Origin of the Moon

**Directions:** Look for facts and details as you read these paragraphs.

The Moon is over four billion years old. How the Moon formed remains a mystery. Here are four theories that scientists use to explain the Moon's origin.

### The "escape" theory

Some scientists believe that Earth and the Moon were once a single body. Earth was spinning much faster than it does today. The Sun's gravitational pull caused a bulge on one side of the rapidly spinning Earth. As the lopsided Earth spun, the bulge eventually broke away to form the Moon.

### The "capture" theory

Possibly, the Moon was once a planet that traveled around the Sun, just as Earth does. The Moon and Earth had similar orbits. Every few years, Earth and the Moon would come close to each other. One time, their orbits brought them so close that the Moon was captured by the pull of Earth's gravity. The Moon then became a satellite of Earth.

### The "formation" theory

This theory says that the Moon and Earth formed at about the same time. The two bodies were formed from huge whirlpools of gas and dust left over from when the Sun was formed. Earth and the Moon started out as two separate bodies that stayed near each other, similar to a double planet.

### The "collision" theory

A fourth theory is that a huge body from space smashed into Earth. The impact was so great that pieces of Earth broke off. These pieces began orbiting Earth. Eventually the material grouped together, forming a single body known as the Moon.

# Moon Facts

Write a word from "Origin of the Moon" on the previous page that matches each given detail.

1. _____  A theory that says the Moon originally had an orbit that was much like Earth's orbit.

2. _____  A theory that says Earth and the Moon were formed from gas and dust left by the Sun.

3. _____  A theory that says the Moon was pulled out of Earth by the pull from the Sun's gravity.

4. _____  A theory that says a piece of Earth broke off when a body from space smashed into it.

5. _____  The escape theory explains that the Sun's gravity created this on one side of Earth.

6. _____  This word for a collision may have caused pieces of Earth to break off.

7. _____  Earth and the Moon were double planets in this theory.

8. _____  This word describes what the Moon became after it was captured by Earth.

# Why Don't People Live on the Moon?

There is no air and no water on the Moon. It would be almost impossible to live there unless special places were built in which people could live. Since there is no air around it to protect it from the heat of the Sun, the Moon is boiling hot during the day, but at night it is freezing cold! You would need special gravity boots to help you walk on the Moon, because the Moon's gravity is not as strong as the Earth's.

1. How could you breathe on the Moon? _____
   _____

2. Could plants grow on the Moon?  Why or why not? _____
   _____
   _____

3. Where could you jump higher, on the Earth or on the Moon? _____
   _____

4. Does the American flag that astronauts left on the Moon wave in the
   wind?_____

5. Does the Moon always look the same to someone on the Earth?_____
   _____

6. If you could build a city on the Moon, what would it look like?  How would
   you get water and food? _____
   _____
   _____
   _____
   _____

# Measuring the Moon

Sometimes, when it's close to the horizon, the Moon appears larger than when it is high in the sky. Is it really larger, or is it just an optical illusion? Try this experiment and find out!

**You will need:**

flat piece of glass (like from a picture frame)
pair of work gloves
crayon or marker
help from an adult!

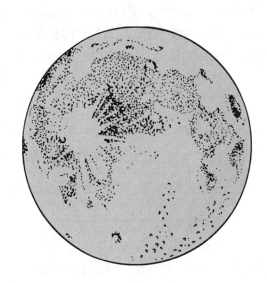

**Here's what to do:**

1. Ask an adult to help you and wear work gloves when handling the glass. As the Moon appears over the horizon, look at it through the square of glass held out at arm's length and trace its shape onto the glass with a crayon.

2. After the Moon is high in the sky, look at it again through the glass. Does it still fill the circle you drew earlier? What conclusions can you draw from this observation?

_____

_____

_____

_____

_____

_____

# What Is the Temperature on the Moon?

The temperature on the Moon gets hotter or colder than any place on Earth. Temperatures as cold as –280 degrees Fahrenheit have been recorded during the Moon's lunar nights, the two-week period when the Moon is in darkness. The temperature is always near –400 degrees in some deep craters at the Moon's poles. But the Moon can also be very hot. At the Moon's equator, which is halfway between the poles, the temperature can go as high as 260 degrees.

1. If you wanted to warm up food on the Moon's surface, where would you put it?

   _____

   _____

   _____

2. How do spacesuits help to protect astronauts on the Moon? _____

   _____

   _____

3. Why do you think it's so cold during the Moon's lunar nights? _____

   _____

4. Would you like to explore the Moon? Why or why not? _____

   _____

   _____

5. Do you think there really is a "man in the Moon"? _____

   _____

6. How would you design a space station that would allow you to live on the Moon? Sketch a diagram and label all its parts on a separate piece of paper.

# Moonbeams

A **statement of fact** can be proven true or false. An **opinion** is what you believe or think.

**Examples:** **Fact:** An Apollo Mission landed a man on the Moon.
**Opinion:** My favorite astronaut is Neil Armstrong.

Write **F** if the sentence is a statement of fact. Write **O** if the sentence is an opinion.

1. _____ The most beautiful object in the sky is the Moon.

2. _____ The Moon is about 240,000 miles from our planet.

3. _____ Plants would make the Moon a prettier place.

4. _____ The surface of the Moon has mountains and craters.

5. _____ Apollo 13 was the most exciting mission ever.

6. _____ Astronauts first walked on the Moon in 1969.

7. _____ The Moon is a satellite of Earth.

8. _____ The Moon reflects light from the Sun.

9. _____ People on Earth can only see one side of the Moon.

10. _____ Neil Armstrong was the bravest of all the astronauts.

11. _____ The force of gravity on the Moon's surface is weaker than that on Earth's surface.

12. _____ Everyone should make a trip to the Moon someday.

# Interesting Moons

Use the code to discover the names of some of the moons in our solar system.

| A | B | C | D | E | F | G | H | I | J | K | L | M |
|---|---|---|---|---|---|---|---|---|---|---|---|---|
| 1 | 2 | 3 | 4 | 5 | 6 | 7 | 8 | 9 | 10 | 11 | 12 | 13 |

| N | O | P | Q | R | S | T | U | V | W | X | Y | Z |
|---|---|---|---|---|---|---|---|---|---|---|---|---|
| 14 | 15 | 16 | 17 | 18 | 19 | 20 | 21 | 22 | 23 | 24 | 25 | 26 |

1. Jupiter's moon named __ __ has at least eight active volcanoes.
   9  15

2. __ __ __ __ __ __ travels around Mars in $7\frac{1}{2}$ hours.  No other moon
   16  8  15  2  15  19
   travels so fast.

3. Jupiter also has the largest moon in the solar system.  It is named

   __ __ __ __ __ __ __ __.
   7  1  14  25  13  5  4  5

4. __ __ __ __ __ is known to have a thick atmosphere.  It is one of
   20  9  20  1  14
   Saturn's moons.

5. Neptune's moon __ __ __ __ __ __ orbits the planet
   20  18  9  20  15  14
   backwards.

6. __ __ __ __ __ __ is the smallest Martian moon.
   4  5  9  13  15  19

7. __ __ __ __ __ __ is one of Jupiter's 39 moons.
   5  21  18  15  16  1

8. The first footsteps on another surface in

   space were taken on Earth's __ __ __ __.
   13  15  15  14

# Moon Dust

Scientists have been able to better understand the Moon's surface by studying the rocks and soil brought back by the astronauts. Soil from the Moon collected by the first astronauts consisted of tiny pieces of ground-up rock, bits of glass, and scattered chunks of rock. Nothing grows or lives in moon soil. It also contains no animal or plant fossils. However, it is interesting to note that some plants on Earth grow better when the soil has been sprinkled with dust from the Moon!

Pretend you have just discovered why moon dust helps plants on Earth grow better. Write your findings below!

_____

_____

_____

_____

_____

_____

_____

_____

_____

_____

_____

# Moon Sums

Add to find the sum on the moons. If the sum is 5, color the moon yellow.
How many yellow moons are there? _____

1
+ 1
____

0
+ 3
____

2
+ 2
____

1
+ 2
____

4
+ 0
____

2
+ 1
____

1
+ 4
____

0
+ 0
____

2
+ 3
____

3
+ 0
____

0
+ 5
____

0
+ 4
____

4
+ 1
____

0
+ 2
____

3
+ 2
____

1
+ 0
____

1
+ 3
____

5
+ 0
____

3
+ 1
____

# The Stars and Beyond

It would take a car traveling 100 miles per hour more than 29 million years to reach our nearest star!

Stars vary in size, surface temperature, and color.

Our solar system has only one star!  That star is the Sun.

A galaxy is a collection of stars bound together by gravity and orbiting around a core.  Galaxies can contain millions or billions of individual stars!

A black hole is what is left after a small, dense, fast-burning star explodes.  Its gravitational pull is so strong that nothing can escape, not even light!

A constellation is a collection of stars that has a name and a recognizable shape.  There are a total of 88 constellations in the sky!

# Star Light, Star Bright

Lie on your back. Gaze up into the night sky. Which star is the brightest? On a clear night, you can see hundreds of stars—some are bright and others are dim.

Why are some stars brighter than others? Let's try to find out by looking at the picture on this page.

1. Look at the two streetlights in the picture. Which streetlight appears the brightest?_____

   Why?_____

   _____

2. Look at the bicycle and the truck.

   Which headlights appear the brightest? _____

   _____

   Why? _____

3. Some stars appear brighter than other stars for the same reasons as the lights in the picture. What are the two reasons?

   a. _____

   b. _____

## Color Me Hot

Stars differ not only in brightness, but also in color. As the star gets hotter, the color changes.

Color these stars. Use the chart to find the correct color.

| Star Color | |
|---|---|
| **Temperature** | **Color** |
| 36,000°F | Blue |
| 18,000°F | White |
| 9,000°F | Yellow |
| 5,400°F | Red |

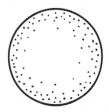

Spica
36,000°F

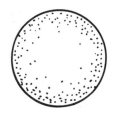

Sirius
18,000°F

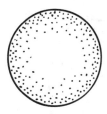

Sun
9,000°F

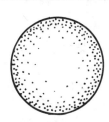

Betelgeuse
5,400°F

The Stars and Beyond

The skies overhead are filled with stars, some near and bright, some far away and very dim. The universe has many different types of stars. They range in surface temperature from 3,000 to 100,000 degrees Fahrenheit. The color of a star reveals how hot it is. Hot stars are blue, and cool stars are red.

Use the guide below to learn more about the different types of stars in our solar system. Color each star in a way that makes sense.

1. **Black Dwarf:** A white dwarf that has become black after burning up all its fuel.

2. **Blue Giant:** A very large, hot, bright star.

3. **Brown Dwarf:** A failed star larger than a planet but unable to produce thermonuclear reactions and shine.

4. **Dwarf Star:** A small star that glows very dimly.

5. **Orange Giant:** A large star with medium-cool surface temperature.

6. **Pulsating Star:** A star that varies in brightness.

7. **Red Dwarf:** A small, dim star with low temperature.

8. **Red Giant:** A large star with low surface temperature.

9. **White Dwarf:** A small, cold star at the end of its life cycle.

10. **White Supergiant**: A very large, medium-hot, bright star.

11. **Yellow Star:** An ordinary star of medium temperature, such as our Sun. Yellow stars emit white light but can appear yellow when viewed from a planet's surface.

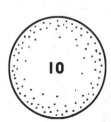

# Stars

Stars are suns in the distant sky. Our Sun is a star of our solar system. Beyond the planet Pluto, beyond our solar system, are millions of other stars. Our Sun is a medium-sized star, but stars come in many sizes. Stars also range in color. There are red, blue, yellow, and white stars. Some stars circle each other like Earth and the Moon. Sometimes a rare giant star will explode, sending its energy into space and creating a giant cloud of gas.

Clouds of gas and dust in space are called **nebulae**. The Orion nebula is a huge glowing cloud where new stars are forming. A galaxy is a gigantic system of billions of stars held together by gravity. Our solar system is a tiny part of the spiral galaxy called the Milky Way. Scientists think that many other stars may have planets circling them, but the stars are too far away for scientists to know for certain.

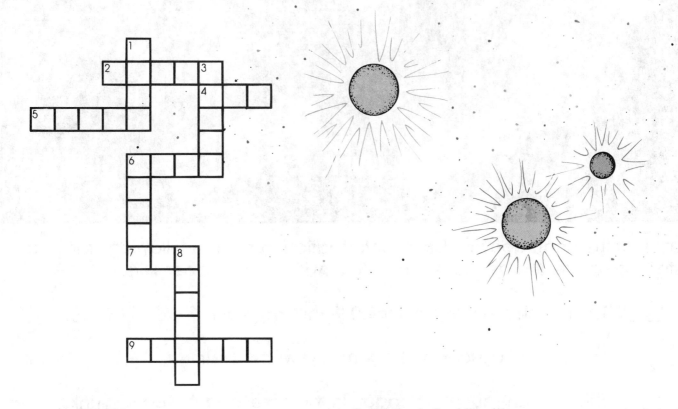

**ACROSS**
2. A dwarf planet
4. A color of a star
5. Another color of a star
6. Orion is not the only nebula in space. The name for another rhymes with "fawn" and is the name of a bird.
7. A star in our solar system

9. We live in the Milky Way_____.

**DOWN**
1. A color of a star
3. The_____nebula is a huge glowing cloud where new stars are forming.
6. They are fiery suns in the distant sky.
8. Star cloud

225

# A Star Is Born!

1. Formed in the clouds of gas and dust in space.

2. Shines steadily as a main-sequence star for 1,000 million years, turning hydrogen into helium in its central core.

3. Starts to run out of hydrogen in the core. The core shrinks and the outer layers expand to make the star a red giant, a hundred times larger than the present size of the Sun.

4. Star's outer layers thrown off to form a shell of glowing gas, known as a **planetary nebula**.

5. The collapsed central part of the star, a **white dwarf**, is all that remains. About the size of the Earth, it contains almost the mass of the Sun, so that a teaspoonful would weigh over a ton. The white dwarf gradually cools and fades.

Look at the chart above. Use the information to put the following stages of a star's life cycle in order from 1 to 5. Start with what happens first.

_____ The star shines steadily for 1,000 million years.

_____ The star collapses and becomes a white dwarf.

_____ The star runs out of hydrogen in the core, and the core shrinks.

_____ The star is formed out of dust and clouds of gas.

_____ The star's outer layers form a shell of glowing gas, known as a planetary nebula.

# Light-Years

Distance to the stars is measured in light-years. A light-year is the distance light travels in a year. Light travels at 186,282 miles per second. In one year, light will travel almost six trillion miles. The distance to our neighboring galaxy, Andromeda, is about two and a half million light years. This means that it would take a spaceship traveling at light-speed almost two and a half million years to get to the Andromeda galaxy.

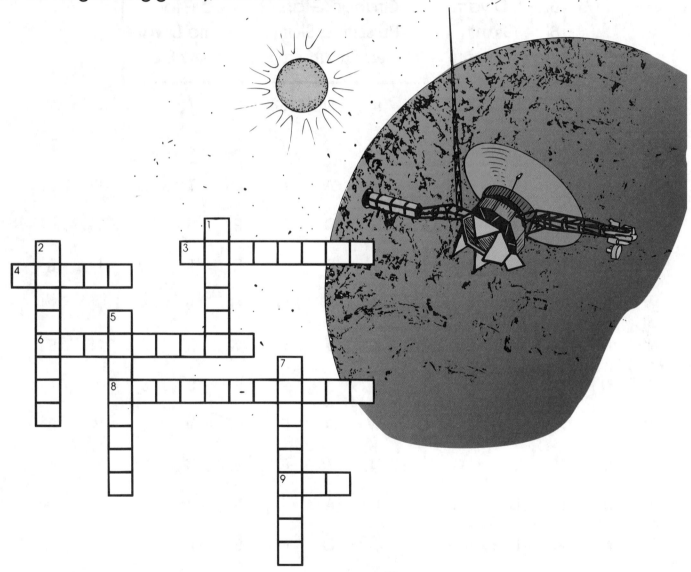

**ACROSS**
3. Distance to the stars is____in light-years.
4. It travels at 186,282 miles per second.
6. Our neighboring galaxy
8. The speed of light can be called__-__.
9. One more than five

**DOWN**
1. Not first, the next one
2. A light-year is the____light travels in a year.
5. Light travels almost six____miles in a year.
7. A vehicle that travels through space

# Seeing Stars!

Stars are divided into different categories according to their color, size, and temperature. Can you find the names of the different types of stars in the puzzle below? Use the Word Bank to help you, and circle the words as you find them.

## Word Bank

| | | |
|---|---|---|
| Black Dwarf | Orange Giant | Red Giant |
| Blue Giant | Pulsating Star | White Dwarf |
| Brown Dwarf | Red Dwarf | Yellow Star |

```
P  U  L  S  A  T  I  N  G  S  T  A  R  R
R  S  D  T  G  H  J  D  K  L  A  E  E  T
B  L  A  C  K  D  W  A  R  F  T  D  D  D
R  G  K  K  R  R  H  D  E  E  S  E  G  M
O  W  E  R  T  T  S  P  D  R  T  R  I  B
W  B  V  X  B  W  W  E  D  N  V  S  A  T
N  M  D  W  L  W  K  L  W  W  R  S  N  S
D  N  D  S  U  T  S  T  A  E  S  S  T  T
W  H  I  T  E  D  W  A  R  F  V  U  W  B
A  R  S  T  G  S  N  W  F  B  X  W  S  N
R  B  D  D  I  S  T  A  A  R  K  J  P  W
F  N  Q  U  A  E  S  O  M  S  T  U  N  N
T  O  R  A  N  G  E  G  I  A  N  T  P  W
S  N  B  Y  T  T  R  G  T  A  N  T  T  B
U  Y  E  L  L  O  W  S  T  A  R  S  O  R
```

On a clear night, you can see about two thousand stars in the sky. Scientists can use giant telescopes to see billions of stars.

Stars in groups form pictures called **constellations**. These constellations have been recognized for years. Ancient people named many constellations for animals, heroes, and mythical creatures. Many of these names are still used.

Some constellations can be seen every night of the year. Others change with the seasons.

Since all stars are constantly moving, these same constellations that we now see will be changed thousands of years from now.

Connect the stars to form the constellation called the Little Dipper.

**Write:**

Stars in groups form pictures called _____.

telescopes    constellations

**Check**:
Ancient people named many constellations for:

☐ animals   ☐ heroes   ☐ oceans   ☐ mythical creatures

**Match:**

Billions of stars can be seen.
About two thousand stars can be seen.

**Circle Yes or No**:

| | Yes | No |
|---|---|---|
| Some constellations can be seen every night. | **Yes** | **No** |
| Some constellations change with the seasons. | **Yes** | **No** |
| In thousands of years, all constellations will be the same. | **Yes** | **No** |

The best way to learn about the stars is to have a hands-on approach—so go stargazing! It is best to go stargazing right after the Sun goes down on a clear night. Ask an adult to go with you and be prepared to sit patiently while you look up at the stars.

First, find the Big Dipper, a group of seven stars that seem to form a saucepan with a long handle. From there, you should be able to find the North Star, the Little Dipper, Draco, Cassiopeia, and Perseus. Once you find the Big Dipper, look at the map below to find the other constellations. It may be hard to pick them out at first, because there are so many other stars around the main ones you are looking for.

Here are some helpful hints:
- Once you find the Big Dipper, follow the two end stars in its bowl in a straight line to locate the North Star.
- The North Star is very bright and is the end star of the Little Dipper's handle.
- Draco's tail loops around the cup of the Little Dipper.
- If you have found the North Star, the Big Dipper is on one side, and Cassiopeia is on the opposite side.

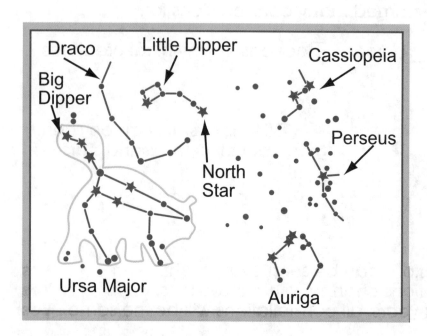

Cut out the names of the constellations below. Then match them to their correct place in the sky.

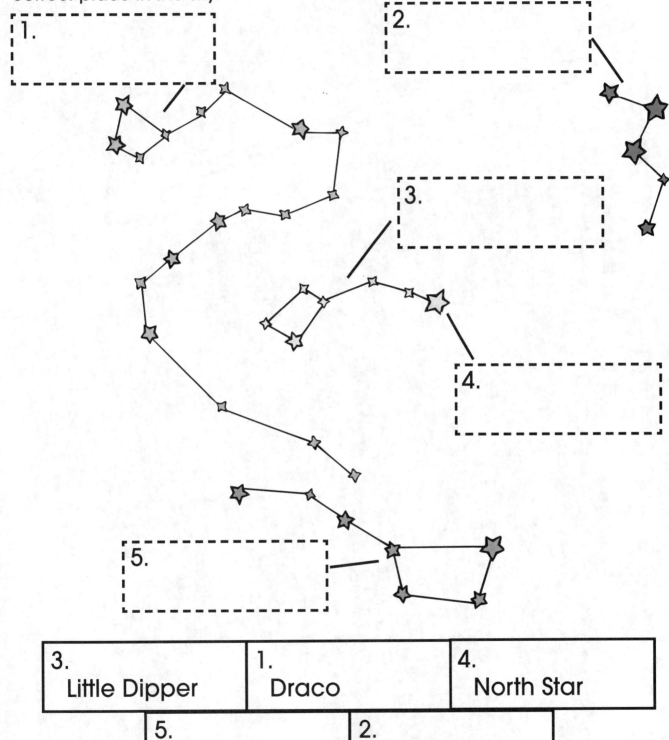

| 3. Little Dipper | 1. Draco | 4. North Star |
| --- | --- | --- |

| 5. Big Dipper | 2. Cassiopeia |
| --- | --- |

# Pictures in the Sky

Color and cut out the constellations on this page. Make a mobile as pictured. Use a science book or other books to make pictures of other constellations for your mobile.

Cover a hanger with black paper and punch in holes to show some of your favorite constellations.

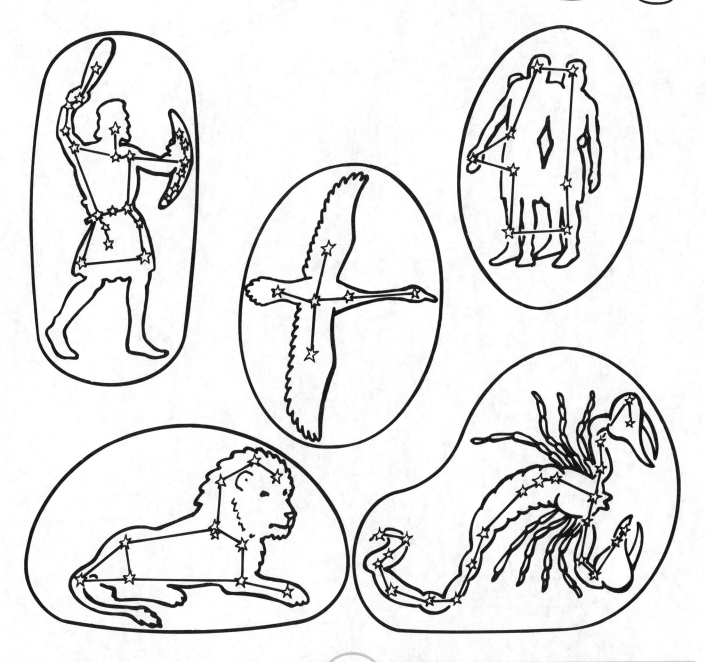

The Stars and Beyond

# Create a Constellation

Thousands of years ago, people believed that there were many gods in the heavens above. They believed that the gods made the Sun rise, the weather change, the oceans move, and even made people fall in love! The people made up stories, or myths, about the gods and their great powers. Many of the characters in these myths can be found in the shapes of the stars. These "star pictures" are called constellations. There are 88 constellations in the sky, but not all of them can be seen from one location. Some are only visible in the Southern Hemisphere while others can only be seen in the Northern Hemisphere. Some are also best observed only in certain seasons. Look at some of the constellations on the previous pages. Pick one or create your own and write a myth about it. Follow the directions below.

1. On a lined sheet of $8\frac{1}{2}$" x 11" paper, write your name, the title of your myth, and the myth.
2. Glue the paper on the right side of a 12" x 18" piece of black construction paper.
3. In the box below, design your constellation using star stickers.
4. Connect the stars to show your constellation and add details.
5. Cut out and glue your constellation on the left side of the construction paper.

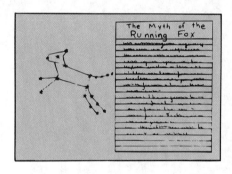

# Constellations

On a clear night, you can see constellations. A constellation is a group of stars named after a mythological character, inanimate object, or animal. There are 88 named constellations that astronomers use to divide the sky. The Big Dipper, in the constellation of Ursa Major, is an easy star pattern to spot. The Pleiades is a compact cluster of stars in the constellation Taurus. The Pleiades is also called the Seven Sisters because it is named after seven beautiful sisters in ancient Greek mythology. American Indians once used the Pleiades as a way of testing the keenness of a warrior's eyesight. There are about 400 stars in the Pleiades. In comparison with the Sun, the stars of the Pleiades are young. They are only a few tens of millions years old.

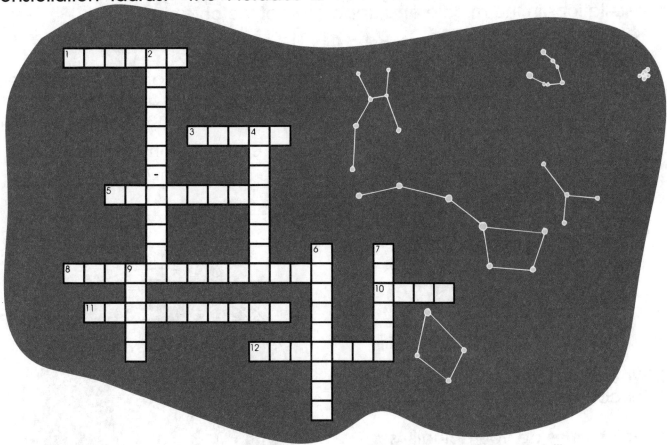

**ACROSS**
1. The Big_____is easy to spot.
3. Number of sisters represented by the Pleiades
5. A group of stars in the Taurus constellation
8. They are a group of stars that resemble a character, animal, or object.
10. The Big Dipper is located in____Major.
11. Some constellations resemble mythological____.

12. Some constellations look like___.
**DOWN**
2. Number of constellations in the night sky
4. Indians used the Pleiades to test__.
6. Some constellations resemble___ objects.
7. The Pleiades is in the____ constellation.
9. A constellation is a group of____.

# Star Search

On a clear dark night, you can look up in the sky and see about 2,000 stars without the help of a telescope. But unless you know which stars form constellations, all you will be seeing are stars.

Carefully poke holes in the Constellation Patterns sheet on page 239, using a sharp pencil. Then, tonight, when it is dark, hold a flashlight behind the paper to make the constellations appear.

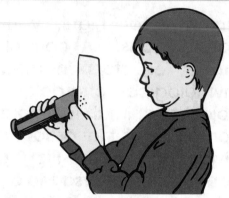

Below are star charts to further help you recognize the constellations. To use the charts, turn them until the present month is at the bottom. Depending on your position and the time of night, you should be able to see most of the constellations in the middle and upper part of the chart.

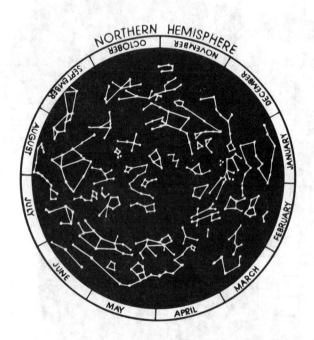

**Directions:**

1. Using the Constellation Patterns sheet to help you, label as many of the constellations in the chart as you can.

2. Which constellations should you be able to see tonight?_____

   _____

   _____

3. When it is dark, go outside to look for constellations.

4. Which ones do you actually see?

   _____

   _____

5. On paper, draw the night sky you see. Draw a small **X** in the center. This should be the point in the sky directly above you.

The Stars and Beyond

# Constellation Patterns

See Star Search, page 238, for directions.

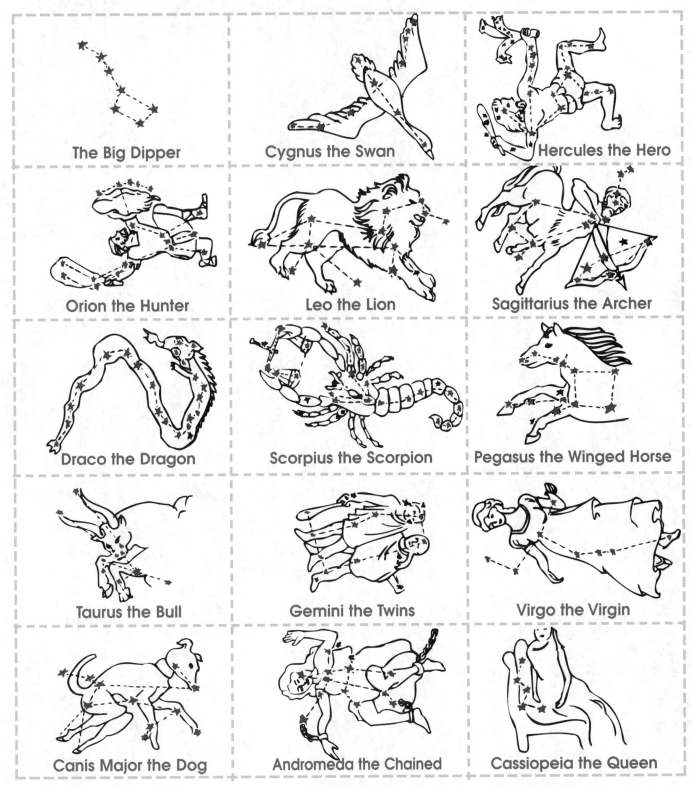

The Big Dipper

Cygnus the Swan

Hercules the Hero

Orion the Hunter

Leo the Lion

Sagittarius the Archer

Draco the Dragon

Scorpius the Scorpion

Pegasus the Winged Horse

Taurus the Bull

Gemini the Twins

Virgo the Virgin

Canis Major the Dog

Andromeda the Chained

Cassiopeia the Queen

The Stars and Beyond

**You will need:**

a cylindrical oatmeal box with a lid
a pencil
flashlight
a thin nail
black tape
a black pen and scissors

Select a constellation visible in the Northern Hemisphere. Use a pencil to mark each star in the constellation on the box lid. Then, poke a hole for each star using a nail. Write the constellation's name on the side of the box using a pen. Next, cut a hole in the bottom of the box just large enough for a flashlight to fit through from the inside. Put the black tape around any air holes. Put the lid on. Darken the room and project your constellation on the ceiling.

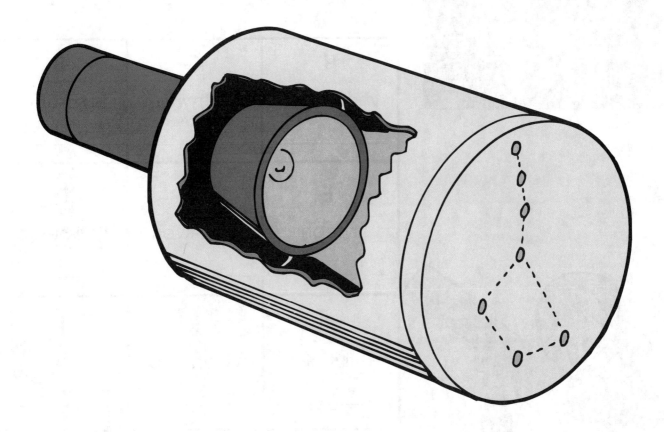

Use the Word Bank to unscramble the number words. Write them correctly on the lines in the box below. Answer the question by writing the letters from the boxes on the lines.

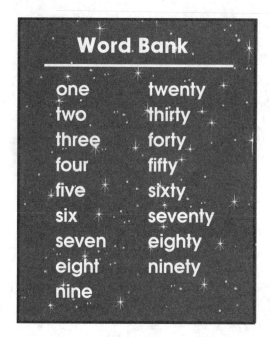

**Word Bank**

| | |
|---|---|
| one | twenty |
| two | thirty |
| three | forty |
| four | fifty |
| five | sixty |
| six | seventy |
| seven | eighty |
| eight | ninety |
| nine | |

**QUESTION:** What was Molly looking at through her telescope?

| ___ | ___ | ___ | ___ | ___ | ___ |
|---|---|---|---|---|---|
| 97 | 38 | 80 | 64 | 60 | 52 |

| ___ | ___ | ___ | ___ | ___ | ___ |
|---|---|---|---|---|---|
| 58 | 60 | 35 | 35 | 80 | 24 |

| **H** yhrtti-ihget <br> _____ | **G** fiyft-wto <br> _____ | **B** siyxt-ofur <br> _____ |
|---|---|---|
| **E** iytegh <br> _____ | **T** ytnnie-svene <br> _____ | **D** fftyi-hietg <br> _____ |
| **P** htriyt-eifv <br> _____ | **R** wytent-ruof <br> _____ | **I** tixsy <br> _____ |

The zodiac is a band of constellations that the Sun travels through in its annual trip around the sky. As the Earth travels around the Sun once a year, it looks like the Sun travels around the sky. The Sun travels through the 13 constellations, not just the 12 most people think of, and these are the constellations of the zodiac. The Moon and planets also stay within this band most of the time. The constellations of the zodiac are well known because the Sun, Moon, and planets travel through them, but many of them are minor constellations that contain no bright stars.

Have you ever heard the song "The Age of Aquarius"? Well, the true Age of Aquarius will begin in about 600 years, when, for the first time, the Sun will be in Aquarius on the first day of spring. Read more about the constellations that make up the zodiac on pages 244–252.

# Aries the Ram

**Aries** (AIR-eez) is a large constellation with only three medium-bright stars in its northern part. These three stars form a simple pattern that is easy to recognize, but—despite its fame as a member of the zodiac—the constellation is not very interesting to observe. Aries is in the east in the autumn and high overhead in late December and January.

In Sumerian times, these stars were a "day laborer" who plowed a field to plant grain. It has been called a ram since at least the time of the ancient Greeks.

Four thousand years ago, the Earth was oriented so that the Sun was in Aries on the first day of spring, March 22, a day that then was considered the first day of the year. At that time, the Sun's position was called the "first point of Aries." The Sun is now in Pisces on the first day of spring, but Aries is still called the first constellation of the zodiac in memory of this ancient alignment. When any planet is "visiting" Aries, the planet is brighter than any of the constellation's stars.

# Cancer the Crab

**Cancer** (KAN-sir) is one of the faintest constellations of the zodiac. If it weren't for its membership in the zodiac, few people would have heard of it. It has no bright stars.

Cancer is midway between the major constellations Leo and Gemini. It is in the early evening sky from February through May. In Greek mythology, Cancer was a crab that was sent to bite Hercules. Hercules squashed it easily. Ancient Egyptians saw it as a scarab beetle, the Babylonians may have seen it as a turtle, and on some old star maps it was a lobster!

# Libra the Balance Scales

**Libra** (LEE-bruh) is a box of four medium-bright stars to the right of Scorpius. The box is standing on one end, resembling a diamond. It is at its best spot for viewing in the early summer, when it is in the southern sky.

Libra is a set of balance scales that work by balancing two pans hanging from a lever, like the scales of justice seen on court buildings. The Sumerians may have originally called these stars scales because the Sun was in front of these stars on the first day of autumn, when day and night are balanced in length.

Libra is the only constellation in the zodiac that isn't an animal. The stars of Libra were once seen as claws that belonged to Scorpius to the east. If you look at the Scorpion carefully, it is missing its claws. While it may make more sense for Libra's stars to be Scorpion's claws, ancient astronomers who wanted to divide the zodiac into 12 equal parts borrowed these stars to form a separate constellation.

# Taurus the Bull

**Taurus** (TORE-us) is one of the major constellations of the winter sky. It contains three bright stars and—even more importantly—two very bright star clusters. The Bull is above and to the right of Orion the Hunter, who is fighting the Bull and driving it westward across the sky.

Taurus looks like the front end of a giant bull.

245

# Leo the Lion

**Leo** (LEE-oh) is a major constellation that is best seen in the springtime. The first appearance of Leo in the evening sky in March announces that spring is coming, and the Lion remains in the evening sky through June. It is one of the few constellations that can be made to look like what it is named after. *Leo* is Latin for "lion" and is one of the zodiacal constellations. *Regulus*, Leo's brightest star, is Latin for "Little King."

Few of us see lions today except at the zoo, but to ancient Sumerians 5,000 years ago, lions were familiar predators who ventured down to the river valleys during hot summer days and hunted sheep and goats. These stars have been seen as a lion since those prehistoric days.

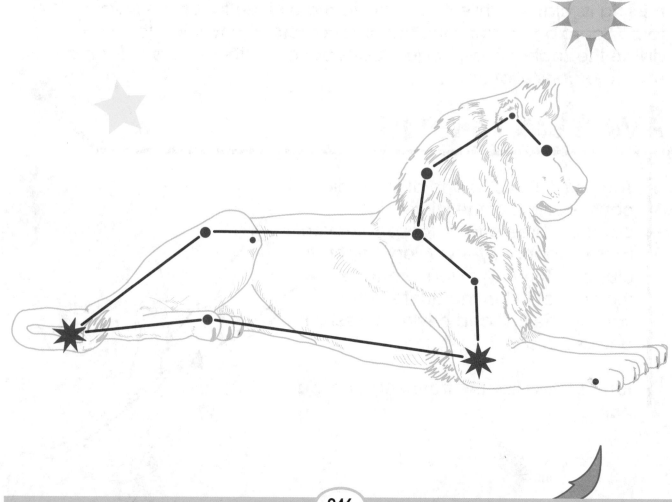

# Scorpius the Scorpion

The Scorpion, a member of the zodiac, is a major constellation in the summer sky. From the United States, it is low on the southern horizon, where we lose much of its splendor. Far south of the equator, where it passes overhead, it is a magnificent group of bright stars.

**Scorpius** (SKOR-pee-us) truly looks like a scorpion, and people have been calling it the Scorpion since prehistoric times— at least 6,000 years.

Scorpius now has only three stars for stubby claws, but long ago the claws included the stars of Libra, to the right.

In Greek mythology, Scorpius was the enemy of Orion. Orion died from the scorpion's bite. Both he and the scorpion were placed in the sky, but on opposite sides, so one sets while the other rises.

The Milky Way runs through Scorpius. Like Sagittarius, it is filled with star clusters that are visible through binoculars or a small telescope. Two star clusters, M6 and M7, are bright enough to see without binoculars. They lie between the Scorpion's stinger and the western end of Sagittarius.

# Capricornus the Sea-Goat

The Sun, Moon, and planets pass through **Capricornus** (kap-rih-KORN-us) as they travel around the sky, making it a constellation of the zodiac. Capricornus is best visible in the early autumn.

A sea-goat, also called a goat-fish, is an odd creature you will not find at the zoo. It is a goat with a fish's tail. In Sumerian times about 5,000 years ago, the Sumerians created imaginary new animals by combining familiar animals in strange ways. Sagittarius, half-man and half-horse, and Pegasus, a horse with wings, are two other examples. Capricornus has no bright stars.

# Pisces the Fishes

**Pisces** (PIE-seez) is a large zodiacal constellation of mostly faint stars in the autumn and winter sky. It is two fish swimming in different directions with their tails tied together.

While there are ancient myths about the fish and their adventures, little information exists that tells us why these stars were originally named fish. In one Greek myth, the fishes' tails were tied together so they would not be separated. We still see them this way today.

# Aquarius the Water Carrier

Before indoor plumbing, water was delivered door to door by water carriers like **Aquarius** (uh-KWARE-ee-us). On antique star charts, Aquarius is shown as a man on his knees pouring from a jug of water. In the sky, Aquarius, is a large but shapeless group of faint stars that lies south and west of Pegasus.

Aquarius seems to be associated with the "great flood" that we are told once inundated the entire world—a story that had its origin in Sumeria and that later appeared in the Old Testament of the Bible, among other places.

You can see Aquarius in the southern sky from August through October.

# Virgo the Virgin or Young Maiden

**Virgo** (VER-go) is the second largest constellation. This member of the zodiac is in the evening sky in late spring and early summer.

Virgo is a young maiden who is associated with agriculture and especially with planting and with ploughing the first furrow of spring, when a barren field is seeded and becomes fertile.

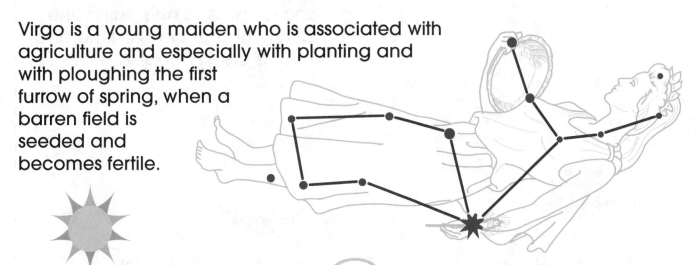

249

# Sagittarius the Archer

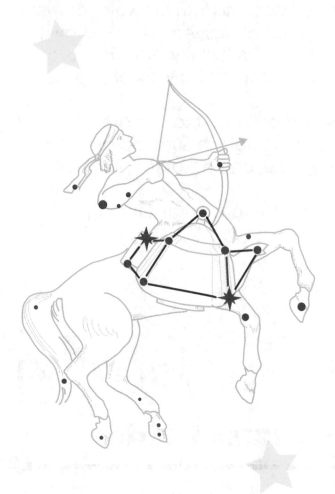

The Archer is a prominent and ancient constellation that has many bright stars. You can see **Sagittarius** (sa-juh-TAIR-ee-us) in summer and early fall evenings, when it is low in the south.

A constellation of the zodiac, Sagittarius is a centaur. However, some people see Sagittarius as a teapot. When Sagittarius is in the southwest, the pot is tipped and is pouring tea on the tail of Scorpius.

Many ancient imaginary creatures are made of two or more animals combined into one. One of the strangest was a centaur, half-man and half-horse. A centaur was the ultimate hunter-warrior, combining the skill of men with the speed of horses. Generally armed and dangerous, centaurs were a wild bunch that were best avoided. Sagittarius carries a bow and arrow, and he's called the Archer. An unarmed centaur named Centaurus is also in the sky.

# Gemini the Twins

The winter sky is full of bright stars. Two that are equal in brightness and close together have been known as the "twin stars" for thousands of years. They are the heads of **Gemini** (JEM-uh-neye), twin brothers Castor (KASS-tor) and Pollux (POL-uks) in Greek mythology. Gemini is a constellation of the zodiac.

Gemini is overhead in winter and early spring. In the middle of May, the Twins stand upright on the northwest horizon around 8:00 p.m.

Gemini looks like two boys standing or lying side by side. It is two strings of stars stretching westward from the bright stars Castor and Pollux. To remember which is which, Castor is nearest to Capella, the brightest star in Auriga, and Pollux is next to Procyon, the brightest star in Canis Minor.

In Greek mythology, these heroic twins were best known for their travels with Jason. Castor was an expert horseman, his twin, Pollux, an expert boxer, and together they had lots of fun battling bad guys. Because they rose before the Sun as winter storms ended and as the sailing season resumed, they were popular with Greek sailors, who also looked to them for protection from pirates.

# Ophiuchus the Serpent Bearer

This outline of a man occupies a large area of the summer sky north of Scorpius. **Ophiuchus** (OH-fee-YOO-kuss) is holding a snake, or serpent, which is the constellation Serpens, in his bare hands. The serpent's head is to the right of Ophiuchus, his tail to the left, and his body seems to cross in front of Ophiuchus. One constellation cannot be in front of another, so Ophiuchus divides the snake into two parts— the head and the tail. No constellations are more closely connected than the snake handler and his serpent.

Ophiuchus is high in the south in early evening through July and August. With a bit of imagination, it is not hard to see the outline of a giant man, even though he has no especially bright stars.

According to modern constellation boundaries, the Sun passes through the southern edge of Ophiuchus, making it a constellation of the zodiac. Ophiuchus is not part of the traditional astrological zodiac of 12 equally spaced signs, but it is the 13th constellation of the astronomical zodiac.

Ophiuchus is a doctor. The Greeks knew him by the name of Aesculapius, and he was a super-physician who possessed the ultimate medical skill—reviving the dead. This alarmed Pluto, god of the underworld, who was afraid he'd received no new visitors. Pluto protested to the god Zeus, who banished Aesculapius to the sky. When physicians take the Hippocratic oath today, they begin by swearing to Aesculapius, or Ophiuchus, to do their duty.

# Zodiac Puzzlers

Now test your knowledge of the zodiac! Fill in the blanks with the name of the constellation that matches the description. The first one has been done for you. Then, design a symbol for the last zodiac puzzler in the space below.

♈ the Ram  A R I E S

♒ the Water Carrier  __ __ __ __ __ __ __ __

♋ the Crab  __ __ __ __ __ __

♊ the Twins  __ __ __ __ __ __

♌ the Lion  __ __ __

♏ the Scorpion  __ __ __ __ __ __ __ __

♑ the Sea-Goat  __ __ __ __ __ __ __ __ __ __ __

♍ the Young Maiden  __ __ __ __ __

♐ the Archer  __ __ __ __ __ __ __ __ __ __ __

♎ the Balance Scales  __ __ __ __ __

♉ the Bull  __ __ __ __ __ __

♓ the Fishes  __ __ __ __ __ __

the Serpent Bearer  __ __ __ __ __ __ __ __ __ __ __

Look at the pictures of constellations below. Draw a line from each constellation to the picture on the next page that you think it represents.

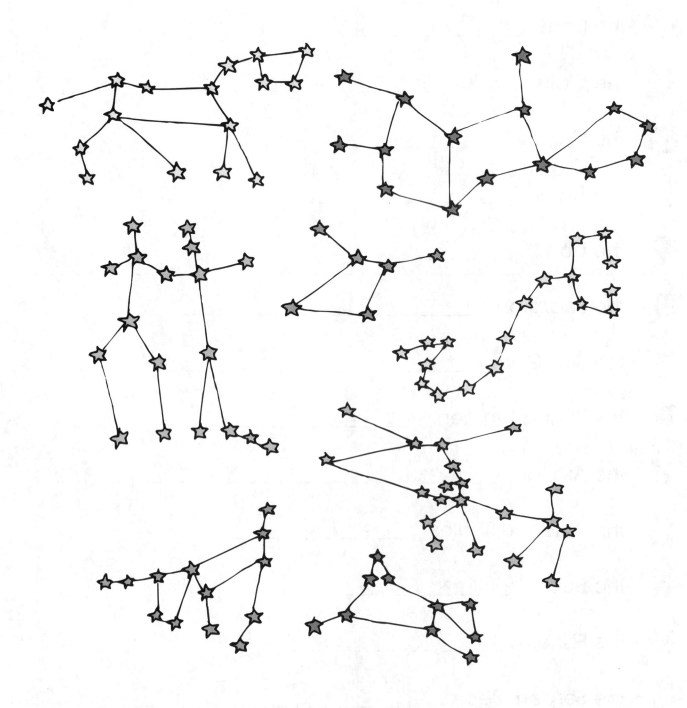

# Constellation Matchup

Look at the pictures of constellations below. Draw a line from each constellation to the picture on the next page that you think it represents.

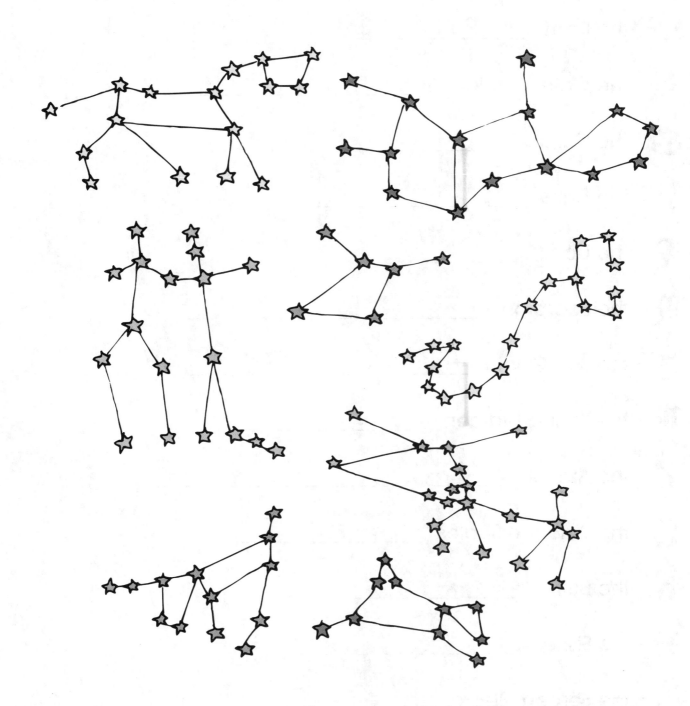

# Zodiac Puzzlers

Now test your knowledge of the zodiac! Fill in the blanks with the name of the constellation that matches the description. The first one has been done for you. Then, design a symbol for the last zodiac puzzler in the space below.

the Ram   <u>A</u> <u>R</u> <u>I</u> <u>E</u> <u>S</u>

the Water Carrier   __ __ __ __ __ __ __ __

the Crab   __ __ __ __ __ __

the Twins   __ __ __ __ __ __

the Lion   __ __ __

the Scorpion   __ __ __ __ __ __ __ __

the Sea-Goat   __ __ __ __ __ __ __ __ __ __

the Young Maiden   __ __ __ __ __

the Archer   __ __ __ __ __ __ __ __ __ __ __

the Balance Scales   __ __ __ __ __

the Bull   __ __ __ __ __ __

the Fishes   __ __ __ __ __ __

the Serpent Bearer   __ __ __ __ __ __ __ __ __

# Alpha Centauri

Alpha Centauri is the star system nearest to our solar system. Alpha Centauri is much farther away than the farthest planet in our solar system. How far is far? Let's pretend that you had a spaceship that could travel 100 thousand miles an hour. With that spaceship, you could reach the Moon in two and one-half hours. It would take you almost five years to reach Pluto. To reach Alpha Centauri would take about 30 thousand years! You can see that there is a lot of space between the stars.

**ACROSS**

2. Earth is one.
6. First part of the name for the star system nearest to our solar system
7. The Sun is one.
9. Planet we live on
10. Number of years it would take a spaceship to reach Pluto

**DOWN**

1. Second part of the name of the star system nearest to ours
3. System pertaining to the Sun
4. Alpha Centauri is a star_____.
5. A vehicle for traveling in space
8. From Pluto it would take you another___ thousand years to reach Alpha Centauri.

# I See Stars!

We use the words **see** or **sees** to tell about something happening now. We use **saw** to tell about something that already happened. Write **see**, **sees**, or **saw** in the sentences about stars below.

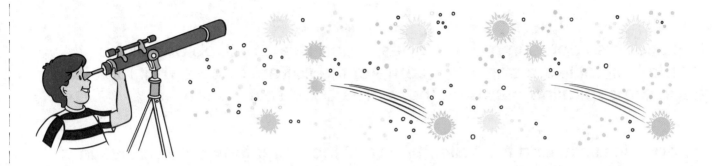

1. Last night, we _____ the stars.

2. John can _____ the stars from his window.

3. He _____ them every night.

4. Last week, he _____ the Big Dipper.

5. Can you _____ it in the night sky, too?

6. If you _____ it, you would remember it!

7. John _____ it often now.

8. How often do you _____ it?

# What Is a Galaxy?

A **galaxy** is a very large collection of stars, planets, moons, gas, and whatever other kinds of matter lurk in space. Galaxies come in many sizes. Small ones contain several billion stars, while the largest ones contain more than a trillion stars!

Galaxies also come in many shapes: round like a ball, oblong like a football, or flat like a pancake. Some of the flat ones have what look like huge arms spiraling outward. These are called spiral galaxies.

All galaxies spin, and the faster they spin, the flatter they are. We live in a pancake-shaped, spiral galaxy. Do you know its name?

Unscramble the letters below to discover the name of the galaxy in which we live.

___ ___ ___   ___ ___ ___ ___ ___   ___ ___ ___!

  E   H   T     L   M   K   Y   I     A   W   Y

# Our Galaxy

Look up at the sky. During the daytime, treetops, birds, airplanes, clouds, and a blue sky seem to stretch forever. A ball of light shines too brightly to look at.

At night, you see something different—a dark sky with a moon and stars. Billions of stars shine in the far distance. Each star is a fiery ball of hot gas. All the stars you see travel together as a large group through space in one galaxy called the Milky Way. The Milky Way is one of many galaxies in space.

One star is closer to you than any other. This star shines daylight on you, provides heat, and helps plants grow. This star is called the Sun.

## Two Different Skies
1. Take two pieces of construction paper, one black and one blue.
2. Glue these papers back to back.
3. Look at the sky on a clear day and on a clear night.
4. Decorate the papers using cotton balls, cut-out construction paper, glitter, or any items that you have

to make the daytime and nighttime skies you see.
5. Use string on two corners to hang your two skies from a hanger.

## Day and Night
Can you name five things that make day different from night?

1._____
2._____
3._____
4._____
5._____

259

# The Milky Way Galaxy

The Milky Way galaxy is made up of the Earth, its solar system, and all the stars you can see at night. There are over 100 billion stars in the Milky Way!

The Milky Way is shaped much like a c.d. It has a center which the outer part goes around.

The Milky Way is always spinning slowly through space. It is so large that it would take 200 million years for the galaxy to make one complete turn.

Many stars in the Milky Way are in clusters. Some star clusters contain up to one million stars!

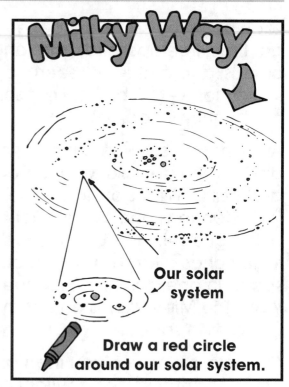

**Our solar system**

**Draw a red circle around our solar system.**

**Check:**

The Milky Way galaxy is made up of
- ☐ Earth.
- ☐ no sun.
- ☐ our solar system.
- ☐ 100 billion stars.

**Circle Yes or No:**

| | | |
|---|---|---|
| The Milky Way is shaped like a pencil. | Yes | No |
| The Milky Way is always slowly moving in space. | Yes | No |
| Many stars in the Milky Way are in clusters. | Yes | No |
| Some star clusters have one million stars. | Yes | No |

**Circle:**

It would take
200
90   million years for the galaxy to spin once.
600

**Underline:**

Which object is the Milky Way shaped like?

   **c.d.**         **ruler**

# Milky Way Galaxy

Our solar system is only a tiny part of the Milky Way galaxy. A galaxy is a giant collection of billions of stars. Our Milky Way galaxy contains over 100 billion stars including our Sun. On a clear night, we can see part of the Milky Way from Earth. It looks like a long, white cloud stretched across the sky. Beyond our galaxy, there are billions of other galaxies.

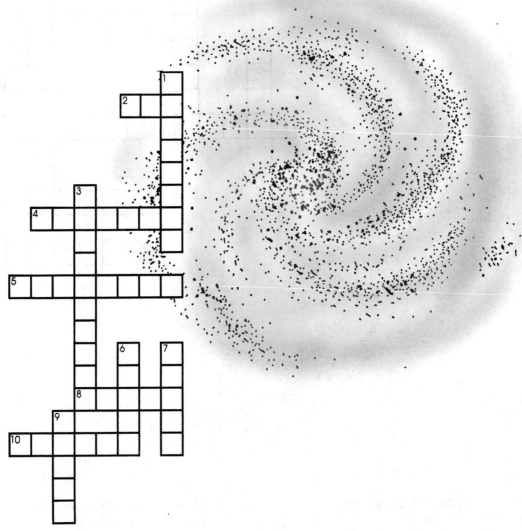

**ACROSS**

2. This star is the center of our solar system.
4. Earth is one of nine____that make up the Milky Way galaxy.
5. Number of galaxies in the universe
8. Earth is part of this system.
10. A giant collection of billions of stars

**DOWN**

1. All of the galaxies and the space between make up the____.
3. Moons are____of planets.
6. First word in the name of our galaxy
7. ____is part of the Milky Way galaxy.
9. From Earth, the Milky Way looks like a long, white____.

# The Andromeda Galaxy

The Andromeda galaxy is the closest big galaxy outside our own Milky Way. It is the most distant object in the sky that you can see without a telescope. It looks like a faint smudge of light in the northern sky. In 1923, Edwin Hubble proved that it was at least two million light-years from Earth. It is shaped like the Milky Way galaxy. It has "arms" made of billions of stars, which orbit around its galactic center.

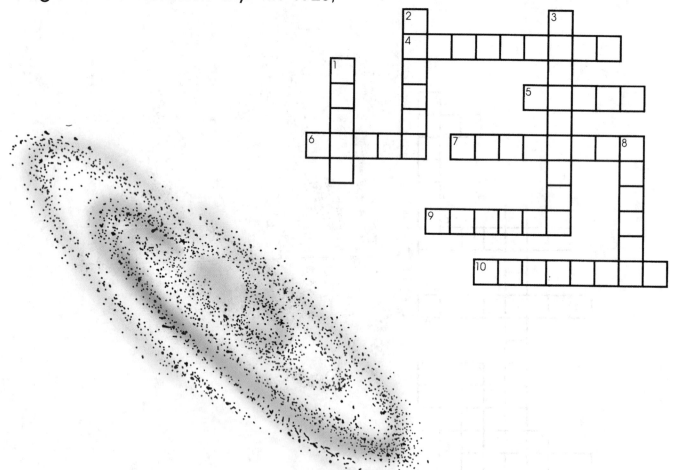

**ACROSS**
4. The most distant galaxy that you can see with the naked eye.
5. The Andromeda galaxy is at least two million light-____from Earth.
6. First word in the name of the Earth's galaxy
7. The Andromeda galaxy has a____center.
9. Name of the man who proved Andromeda's distance from Earth
10. The Andromeda galaxy is faintly seen in the____sky.

**DOWN**
1. It has arms made of billions of stars that ____around its galactic center.
2. The Andromeda galaxy is outside our own____.
3. You do not need a____to see the Andromeda galaxy in the night sky.
8. Location from which stars spiral out of the Andromeda galaxy

# A Black Hole

Have you ever heard of a mysterious black hole? Some scientists believe that a **black hole** is an invisible object somewhere in space. Scientists believe that it has such a strong pull toward it, called gravity, that nothing can escape from it!

These scientists believe that a black hole is a star that has collapsed. The collapse made its pull even stronger. It seems invisible because even its own starlight cannot escape! It is believed that anything in space that comes near the black hole will be pulled into it forever. Some scientists believe there are many black holes in our galaxy.

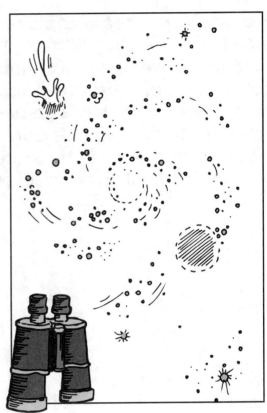

**Check:**
Some scientists believe that:

☐ a black hole is an invisible object in space.
☐ a black hole is a collapsed star.
☐ a black hole is a path to the other side of the Earth.
☐ a black hole has a very strong pull toward it.
☐ a black hole will not let its own light escape.

**Write:**

| A - gravity |
| B - collapse |

_____ To fall or cave in

_____ A strong pull toward an object in space

Draw what you think the inside of a black hole would look like.

# Black Hole

A black hole is really a place where gravity is so strong that it traps everything, even the star's light. Since no light can escape from the compressed star, the star becomes invisible. Since scientists cannot see black holes directly because they give out no light, they discover them by looking for their effects on nearby objects that can be seen. Scientists believe they are formed by very massive stars that explode in supernova blasts. There are no known black holes close to our solar system, and they do not appear to be a danger to Earth or our astronauts.

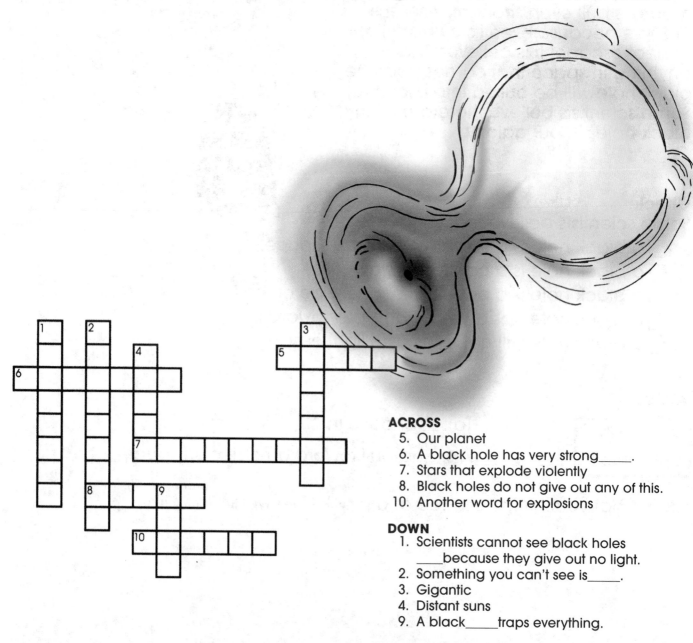

**ACROSS**

5. Our planet
6. A black hole has very strong_____.
7. Stars that explode violently
8. Black holes do not give out any of this.
10. Another word for explosions

**DOWN**

1. Scientists cannot see black holes _____because they give out no light.
2. Something you can't see is_____.
3. Gigantic
4. Distant suns
9. A black_____traps everything.

# Space Snowballs

Planets and moons are not the only objects in our solar system that travel in orbits. Comets also orbit the Sun.

A **comet** is like a giant, dirty snowball that is $\frac{1}{2}$ to 3 miles wide. It is made of frozen gases, dust, ice, and rocks.

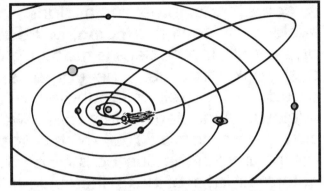

As the comet gets closer to the Sun, the frozen gases melt and evaporate. Dust particles float in the air. The dust forms a cloud called a **coma**. The "wind" from the Sun blows the coma away from the Sun. The blowing coma forms the comet's tail.

There are more than 800 known comets. Halley's Comet is the most famous. It appears about every 76 years. The last scheduled appearance in this century was in 1985. When will it appear next?

Find the words from the Word Bank in the word search. When you are finished, write down the letters that are not circled. Start at the top of the puzzle and go from left to right.

**Word Bank**

| | |
|---|---|
| dust | orbit |
| Halley | tail |
| coma | ice |
| snowball | sky |
| melt | shining |
| solar system | |

```
S P M E L T L A N H E
O T S S H A C O M A V
L E N O R D B I T L S
A L O I K U E C I L R
R C W L E S S C O E M
S E B T S T H A V Y E
Y O A R O R B I T B I
S T L S S H A P E D L
T I L K T A I L E A F
E O O T I C E B A L L
M S K Y S H I N I N G
```

_ _ _ _ _ _ _ _ _   _ _ _ _ _   _ _ _ _

_ _ _ _ _ _ _ .   _ _ _ _ _ _   _ _ _ _   _ _ _ _

_ _ _ _ _ _ _ _   _ _ _ _ _ _ _ _ _ _ .

# Comets

A comet has three main parts: a **nucleus**, or center; a **coma**, or head; and a **tail**. The nucleus is made up of dust, rock, and ice. The coma is a cloud of gases surrounding the nucleus. A nucleus a few miles wide can have a coma 50,000 miles across. The heat from the Sun boils away the outermost layer of ice on the nucleus to form the gas of the coma. Sunlight and the solar wind push the gas and dust particles of the coma back to form a long, filmy tail that can stretch millions of miles into space. The tail of a comet always points away from the Sun. A comet may spend most of its long orbit around the Sun where it is so cold that the nucleus is frozen solid and the comet has no coma or tail. Edmund Halley did not discover Halley's Comet but was the first to predict its return. It returns to Earth's vicinity about every 76 years. The last time it passed Earth was in 1986. Every time a comet visits the Sun, it loses a little more ice. After perhaps one thousand returns, there will be hardly anything left of the comet except rocks and dust.

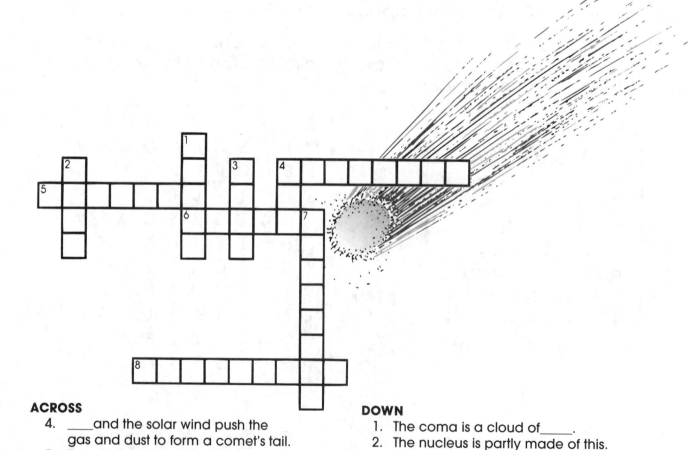

**ACROSS**
4. ____and the solar wind push the gas and dust to form a comet's tail.
5. The center of the comet
6. First name of the man who predicted the return of Halley's Comet
8. Gas and dust____form a long filmy tail.

**DOWN**
1. The coma is a cloud of____.
2. The nucleus is partly made of this.
3. The head of the comet
4. A comet may spend most of its long orbit around the____.
7. To uncover or find something new

# Here Comes a Comet!

Billions of comets travel through our solar system. A comet is a mass of rock and dust wrapped around a ball of ice like a dirty snowball! The comet's ball-like head can be from 1 to 100 kilometers in diameter. The heat from the center of the ball creates a cloud-like cover or coma. The coma can reach out as far as 100 million kilometers from the comet's center!

Comets can be pulled by the Sun's gravity into a pathway or orbit. As the comet nears the Sun, it often forms a long tail. A comet's tail may trail behind the coma for thousands or millions of miles. A comet can take several million Earth years to travel around the Sun just once!

Sometimes comets travel close enough to Earth to be seen.

## Make a Comet Kite!

1. Use a 6 or 7-inch paper plate to be the comet. Color it bright yellow.
2. Attach 3-foot paper streamers or ribbons to make a bright, long tail.
3. Cut a 6 x 2–inch strip of construction paper for a handle. Glue one inch of each end to the underside of your comet.
4. Hold on to the handle and let your comet fly!

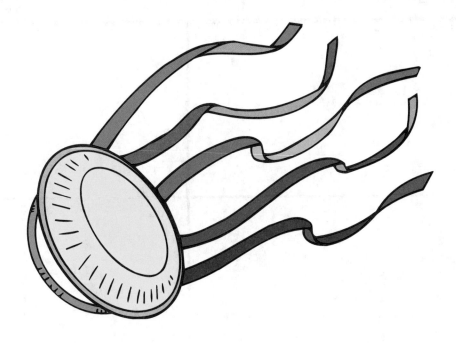

# Amazing Asteroids

**Asteroids** are extremely small bodies that travel mainly between the orbits of Mars and Jupiter. There are thousands of them, and new ones are constantly being discovered.

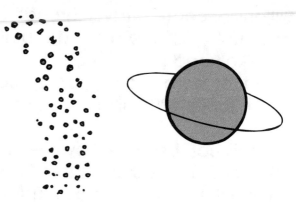

Many asteroids are made of dark, rocky material, have irregular shapes, and range widely in size. Ceres, the first-known asteroid, is about 600 miles in diameter. Hildago, another asteroid, is only about nine miles in diameter. Ceres is now known as a dwarf planet.

Because the asteroids' orbits change slowly due to the gravitational attraction of Jupiter and other large planets, asteroids sometimes collide with each other. Fragments from these collisions can cause other collisions. Any resulting small fragments that reach the surface of Earth are called meteorites.

Try your hand at personification. **Personification** means giving an inanimate, or non-living, object human qualities. Draw a cartoon below of two asteroids colliding with each other. Give the asteroids names and write what they might say to each other.

| | |
|---|---|
| 1 | 2 |
| 3 | 4 |

# The Mystery of Asteroids

Where did asteroids come from? We don't really know. Below are two different ways they could have been formed.

**A.** When the solar system formed billions of years ago, the largest asteroids, were formed at the same time as the planets. Some of the larger ones crashed together, breaking apart and becoming smaller asteroids.

**B.** Billions of years ago, the planets were formed from swirling gases in outer space. An extra planet was between Mars and Jupiter. Something crashed into this planet, breaking it into thousands of pieces, all different sizes and shapes.

Which story do you think could be true? Circle the letter: **A    B**

If you circled **B**, what do you think crashed into the planet?

_____

Can you think of more than one answer?

_____

**An Extra Planet?**

1. Here is how the extra planet might have looked. Use your imagination to design the planet.

2. Color it using brown, gray, and black.

3. Add more craters to the surface.

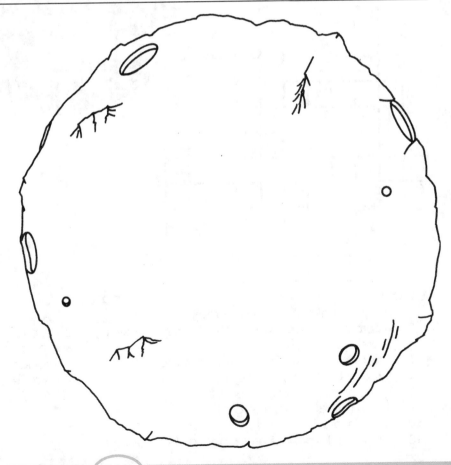

# Asteroids

Asteroids are large chunks of metal and rock orbiting the Sun like tiny planets. Most are about the size of small mountains. There are thousands of asteroids in the space between Mars and Jupiter. This area is generally known as the **asteroid belt**. It is more than 600 miles wide. Some asteroids, like Eros, Apollo, and Amor, travel close to the Earth as they orbit the Sun. Perhaps one day spacecraft will be able to mine the metal and important minerals of the asteroids.

**ACROSS**

4. Large chunks of metal and rock
5. Asteroids can be found in the space between Mars and_____.
6. Asteroids are like tiny planets that orbit the Sun and move through_____.
8. Perhaps someday spacecraft will_____ the minerals of the asteroids.
9. An asteroid
10. Once the largest asteroid, now a dwarf planet

**DOWN**

1. Asteroids are like tiny_____.
2. A planet in our solar system
3. The number of asteroids in the space between Mars and Jupiter
7. Name of an asteroid
9. An asteroid; its name means lover

The United States launched a spacecraft called Pioneer 10 in 1972. There were no human passengers, only special machines. Pioneer 10 traveled past Mars into the asteroid belt. Scientists feared the "little planets" might hit Pioneer 10 and stop it from working.

The scientists were partially right. Small asteroids hit Pioneer 10 over 40 times, but the spacecraft kept working. It continued on its way to the next planet, Jupiter.

## Pioneer 10 Meets the Asteroids!

1. Color and cut out Pioneer 10 below.
2. Glue your Pioneer 10 to the top of a popsicle stick or any 5-inch long flat piece of wood.
3. Color a large piece of cardboard black.
4. Collect small rocks to be asteroids. Press them into the cardboard and glue them into place.
5. Use a crayon or marker to trace a pathway for Pioneer 10 through the asteroids. Make sure your path stays at least 2 inches away from the edges of the cardboard. Also, keep your path from crossing itself.
6. Ask an adult to help you cut along the path all the way through the cardboard.
7. Insert your flat stick in the pathway. Let Pioneer 10 travel through the asteroids!

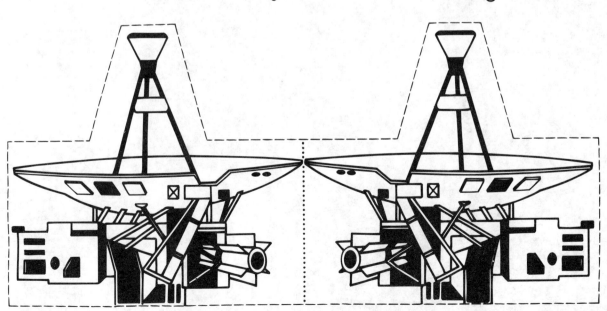

# Meteoroids, Meteors, and Meteorites

**Meteoroids** are small chunks of rock that travel through space orbiting the Sun and have entered the Earth's atmosphere. Some meteoroids have come from the Asteroid Belt and entered Earth's atmosphere. Some are pieces of leftover comets. When a meteoroid falls toward Earth, it travels very fast. The speed of the meteoroid through the air causes friction, which heats the meteoroid until it and the air around it glow white-hot. The streak of light is called a **meteor**. From Earth you can sometimes see meteors shooting through the sky. Most meteoroids burn up before they hit Earth, but some large ones hit the ground. Once the meteoroid hits the ground, it is called a **meteorite**. Meteorites come in all sizes and shapes. If a giant meteoroid, as big as a building or bigger, hits the ground, it can land with enough force to blast out a hole, called a crater.

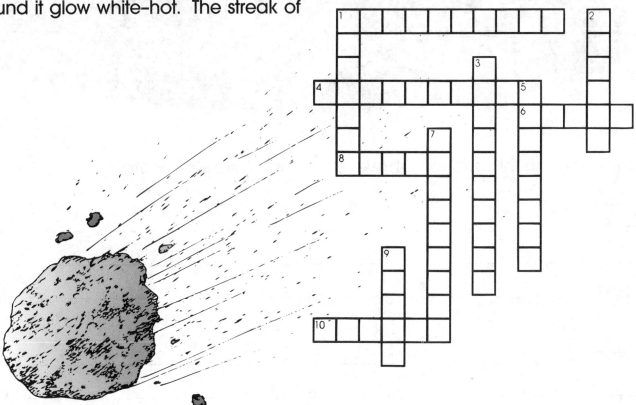

## ACROSS

1. They are small chunks of rock that travel through space.
4. Meteors that hit Earth's surface are called_____.
6. Sometimes meteorites can make _____in the ground.
8. They twinkle in the sky at night.
10. Some meteoroids are leftover_____.

## DOWN

1. The streaks of light are called_____.
2. Meteorites come in all sizes and___.
3. Meteoroids are chunks of rocks that have floated through space and entered Earth's_____.
5. From Earth you can sometimes see meteors_____through the sky.
7. Some meteoroids are really_____from the Asteroid Belt.
9. The_____of the meteoroid causes friction.

273

A small bit of rock or metal out in space, orbiting the Sun, is called a meteoroid. If it collides with the Earth, it will be seen as a glowing spot of light, a meteor rushing across the sky. If it survives its fiery plunge through the air and lands on the ground, it is then called a meteorite. Some meteorites are small chunks that have broken off of asteroids. About 26,000 meteorites land on Earth a year. Most of them land in the oceans. They usually weigh about 3.5 ounces, about the weight of an apple.

Now using the information above, define the following words.

Meteoroid:_____

_____

_____

Meteor:_____

_____

_____

Meteorite:_____

_____

_____

# Space Exploration and Travel

275

The first American to walk in space was astronaut Ed White, orbiting the Earth aboard Gemini 4 on June 3, 1965.

On July 20, 1969, Neil Armstrong and Edwin "Buzz" Aldrin landed on the Moon's surface. They set up an American flag and left a plaque that read:

*Here Men From Earth First Set Foot Upon the Moon*
*July 1969 AD*
*We Came in Peace for All Mankind*

Humans aren't the only earthlings who have traveled into space. Since the beginning of space exploration, animals, called **animalnauts**, have been sent in hopes of teaching scientists about outer space.

What did Commander Alan B. Shepard do to commemorate his historical trip to the Moon aboard Apollo 14? After completing his official duties, Shepard took a golf ball from his pocket and with a makeshift golf club hit it miles out into space!

The National Aeronautics and Space Administration, NASA, has erected a monument to honor all of America's astronauts who have died tragically. The monument, called the Space Mirror, can be viewed at the Kennedy Space Center in Florida.

# An Interesting Word

In the old Greek language, *astro* meant "star" and *naut* meant "sailor." So, the modern word *astronaut* really means "sailor of the stars." Today's astronauts are men or women trained to explore outer space. Astronauts use rockets to fly around the Earth, to the Moon, and to other planets in space.

1. What kind of trip is a nautical voyage? Do you take a plane, a boat, a train, or a car? _____

   _____

   _____

2. What do you think scientists called *astronomers* study? _____

   _____

   _____

3. What special clothing does an astronaut wear in outer space?

   _____

   _____

   _____

4. When a rocket is launched into space, there is a countdown until blast-off. What does this mean? _____

   _____

   _____

5. What kinds of food do astronauts eat while in their rocket ships?

   _____

   _____

   _____

   _____

   _____

# Amazing Astronauts

Read the passages below to find out about some of the astonishing individuals who have taken part in the space program. Then use the information on the next page.

### Laika
The first living creature to go into outer space was a dog named Laika! Laika rode aboard Sputnik 2, launched by the USSR in 1957. She helped prove that space travel would be possible for human beings.

### John H. Glenn, Jr.
John Glenn was the first American to orbit the Earth. Aboard Friendship 7, Glenn circled the Earth three times in almost five hours. After being a U.S. Senator, Glenn returned to space in 1998 at the age of 77 to become the oldest space traveler!

### Alan B. Shepard, Jr.
Alan Shepard was the first American to go into outer space. His first flight aboard Mercury-Redstone 3 reached 117 miles high, traveled 304 miles, and lasted 15 minutes.

### Neil A. Armstrong
Remembered most for saying "That's one small step for man, one giant leap for mankind," Neil Armstrong became the first human to step foot on the Moon on July 20, 1969.

### Edwin E. "Buzz" Aldrin, Jr.
During the Gemini 12 mission, Buzz Aldrin walked in space for $5\frac{1}{2}$ hours! He also joined Neil Armstrong on the Moon's surface during the Apollo 11 mission in 1969.

### Judith Resnik
Judith Resnik was among the first group of women to become astronauts in 1978. She was the second American woman to fly in space and studied for her pilot's license. Tragically, Resnik died in the Challenger space shuttle explosion in 1986.

### Sally Ride
Sally Ride was the first female astronaut in the U.S. and third woman ever in space. Ride served on the commission to investigate the Challenger disaster and has since become a college professor and children's book author.

Draw a line to match each astronaut on the left to the correct fact about his or her life on the right.

Laika

                            At age 77, became the oldest space traveler.

John H. Glenn, Jr.

                            First living creature to go into outer space.

Alan B. Shepard, Jr.

                            Said, "That's one small step for man, one giant leap for mankind."

Neil A. Armstrong

                            Walked in space for $5\frac{1}{2}$ hours.

Edwin E. "Buzz" Aldrin, Jr.

                            Second U.S. woman to fly in space.

Judith Resnik

                            First American to go into outer space.

Sally Ride

First U.S. woman astronaut.

# What It Takes to Become an Astronaut!

When NASA, the National Aeronautics and Space Administration, began its astronaut selection program in 1959, all qualifying candidates were military jet pilots with extensive knowledge of engineering. Soon after, NASA expanded the range of qualified candidates, accepting applications from civilian pilots with many hours of flying experience. Later, the requirements changed again to allow nonpilots with academic expertise in biology, medicine, and other sciences into the astronaut program.

Today, the requirements are fairly simple. All Mission Specialist candidates must be American citizens between 4'10" and 6'4" tall. Pilot candidates must be between 5'4" and 6'4" tall. Candidates must pass a routine physical test and have a bachelor's degree in math, science, or engineering.

Of course, since astronaut requirements have changed in the past, they will probably change again in the future! For more information on becoming an astronaut, write to:

Astronaut Selection Office
NASA Johnson Space Center
Houston, TX 77058

Pretend that you are going to write a letter to the Astronaut Selection Office. List the top five reasons why you think you would make a good astronaut.

1._____

2._____

3._____

4._____

5._____

# What Do Astronauts Eat?

In the early days of the space program, providing astronauts with delicious meals was a low priority. Most food was liquefied and squeezed out of tubes, and nothing tasted good. Today's shuttle astronauts eat food not too different from what we eat on Earth. Even better, each astronaut can sample the available menu and choose his or her own favorite meals before liftoff!

Space shuttle astronauts are able to select their meals from a wide range of available foods. A typical day's menu might include:

**Breakfast**
strawberries
oatmeal with brown sugar
granola with raisins
granola bar
breakfast roll
orange juice
coffee with cream and sugar

**Lunch**
shrimp cocktail
spaghetti with meat sauce
green beans
tapioca pudding
brownie
lemonade

**Dinner**
shrimp cocktail
smoked turkey
chicken and noodles
green beans
peach dessert
lemonade

If you were an astronaut for a day, what would you choose to eat? List your

favorite foods below.

**Breakfast**

_____

_____

_____

_____

_____

**Lunch**

_____

_____

_____

_____

_____

**Dinner**

_____

_____

_____

_____

_____

# Did You Know?

Read the passages below to learn more interesting facts about astronauts!

## Training for Weightlessness

An important part of an astronaut's training program is learning how to float in space. Here on Earth, however, there's one main way to imitate weightlessness: flying in an airplane nicknamed "The Vomit Comet." The Vomit Comet is actually an ordinary airplane with all the seats removed. The pilot flies steeply upward, and then changes direction and races back toward the ground, making everything—and everybody—inside the plane float in the air for a brief period of time. Before reaching the ground, the pilot changes direction again, racing upward and repeating the maneuver. It's something like a roller coaster ride in the sky, and many astronauts have found the experience sickening enough for the plane to earn its name!

## An Instant Way to Grow!

One of the more unusual aspects of weightlessness is its effect on an astronaut's height. In space, the spine spreads farther apart, making a person one or two inches taller! The back muscles attached to the spine don't grow any longer, however, so the extra stretching sometimes gives the astronauts a backache!

The extra height is temporary. Once the astronauts return to Earth, the effects of gravity collapse the spine again, and the astronauts return to their normal size.

# Zero G

"Zero G" is an abbreviation for "zero gravity," which is sometimes called weightlessness. It means not being able to sense or feel the pull of gravity. The Earth's gravity pulls us toward the center of our planet. We do not fall to the center of the Earth because the structure of our planet resists our falling through it. We call this resistance to gravity weight. We feel weight because the ground supports us when we sit or a bed supports us when we lie down. When you fall, you feel weightless until you hit something that resists gravity. A spacecraft in orbit is falling continually. It does not crash because its sideways velocity, or motion, keeps it from hitting the ground. The astronauts inside an orbiting spacecraft are also falling and so feel weightless. Some astronauts find that Zero G makes them feel sick, so they cannot work as well as they did on Earth. Others adjust to weightlessness very well, though they need to exercise a lot to stay healthy while in Zero G.

**ACROSS**
2. Resistance to gravity
3. Not weakly, but_____
6. The structure of our planet_____our falling through it.
7. The ground helps____us when we stand.
8. Velocity
9. Spaceship

**DOWN**
1. Zero G
4. A force that is constantly pulling on us
5. Sometimes astronauts feel____in Zero G.

# Designing Mission Patches

For an astronaut, every trip into space is special! To help commemorate each mission, flight crews are allowed to design their own "mission patch." Sometimes the astronauts draw their own patches, and sometimes they use designs offered by artists around the country. All mission patches are four inches wide and are sewn onto the suits that are worn during the spaceflight.

In the space below, design your own mission patch!

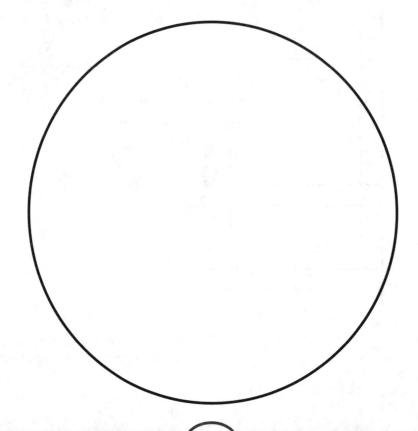

# An Astronaut for a Day!

Even if you don't qualify to join NASA's astronaut training program, you can still experience what it's like to be a space person—at the U.S. Space Camp, Space Academy, and Aviation Challenge. These private programs are available to children, adults, and teachers, with sessions scheduled in Alabama and Florida.

For more information, contact:

U.S. Space Camp, Space Academy, and Aviation Challenge
U.S. Space and Rocket Center
One Tranquility Base
Huntsville, Alabama 35807

1-800-63-SPACE

Or check out this Web site:

www.spacecamp.com

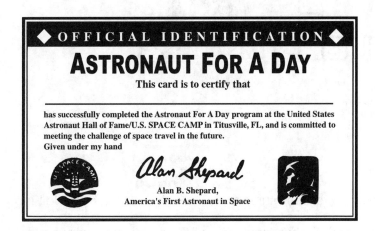

◆ OFFICIAL IDENTIFICATION ◆
ASTRONAUT FOR A DAY
This card is to certify that

has successfully completed the Astronaut For A Day program at the United States Astronaut Hall of Fame/U.S. SPACE CAMP in Titusville, FL, and is committed to meeting the challenge of space travel in the future.
Given under my hand

Alan Shepard
Alan B. Shepard,
America's First Astronaut in Space

# Spacesuit

Human beings can survive in space only with the protection of a spacesuit or space vehicle. A spacesuit has tanks of heated oxygen. Inside the spacesuit the person is surrounded with oxygen, which is a vital gas for human life. To survive in space, human beings have had to find ways to recreate the surroundings that they are used to on Earth. They need oxygen, air pressure, and comfortable temperatures. When astronauts leave the spaceship, they carry oxygen tanks on their backs and other life-support equipment. They can leave the ship for only short periods of time because the tanks run out of oxygen.

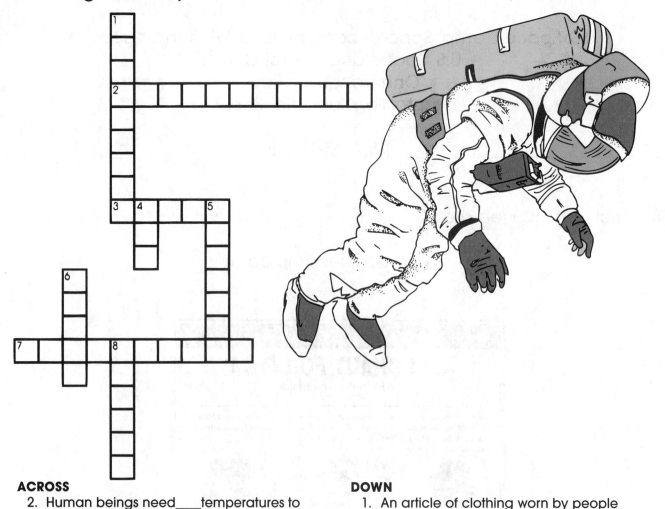

**ACROSS**

2. Human beings need____temperatures to survive in space.
3. When astronauts leave their ship, they carry oxygen____on their backs.
7. Inside a spacesuit, a person is ____with oxygen.

**DOWN**

1. An article of clothing worn by people traveling in space
4. Human beings need____pressure.
5. Human beings cannot____in space without a spacesuit.
6. Period of time that an astronaut can leave his or her ship
8. A gas that human beings breathe

# John Kennedy and the Space Program

By the time John Kennedy became president, the space race already had begun. This was more than just a race to get a human being into space and safely back to Earth again. This was a race between two great, powerful nations. The two nations were the United States and the Soviet Union. The race was to show the world which country was smarter and stronger.

In 1957, the Soviet Union stunned the world by putting its first satellite into space. A month later it sent a dog into space. In1959, the Soviet Union sent a probe all the way to the Moon. And in 1961, at the beginning of John Kennedy's presidency, the Soviet Union sent the first person into space. His name was Yuri A. Gagarin, and he went all the way around the Earth one time.

President Kennedy knew the United States was losing the space race. So, he decided to set a goal for the nation that, if met, would put the United States firmly in front of the Soviets. On May 21, 1961, the president announced his plan to Congress.

*Above: Neil A. Armstrong was the first person to walk on the Moon. Below: This photograph is a portrait of astronaut John H. Glenn, the first American to orbit Earth. Pg. 288: President John F. Kennedy and John Glenn inspect the spaceship that took John Glenn into space.*

He said, "I believe that this nation should commit itself to achieving the goal, before this decade is out, of landing a man on the Moon and returning him safely to Earth. No single space project in this period will be more impressive to mankind, or more important for the long-range exploration of space; and none will be so difficult or expensive to accomplish."

President Kennedy did not live to see whether the United States could rise to the challenge of landing a man on the Moon. On July 20, 1969, an American spaceship touched down on the Moon's surface. All over the world, televisions broadcast pictures of astronaut Neil Armstrong taking humankind's first steps on the Moon. Millions also heard him speak the first words ever spoken on the Moon: "That's one small step for man, one giant leap for mankind."

## Show what you know!

On a separate sheet of paper, write what you think President Kennedy would have said about the landing on the Moon.

# Apollo Moon Mission

On July 20, 1969, Neil Armstrong became the first person to set foot on the Moon. Between 1969 and 1972, eleven other astronauts landed on the Moon. The astronauts set up science experiments on the Moon, and they brought back 843 pounds of moon rocks for scientists to study. Studying the moon rocks, scientists found out that they contained the same chemical elements that are found in Earth rocks. These chemical elements also make up living things. The proportions of the elements found in the Moon rocks were slightly different from those found in Earth rocks. The astronauts did not find life on the Moon.

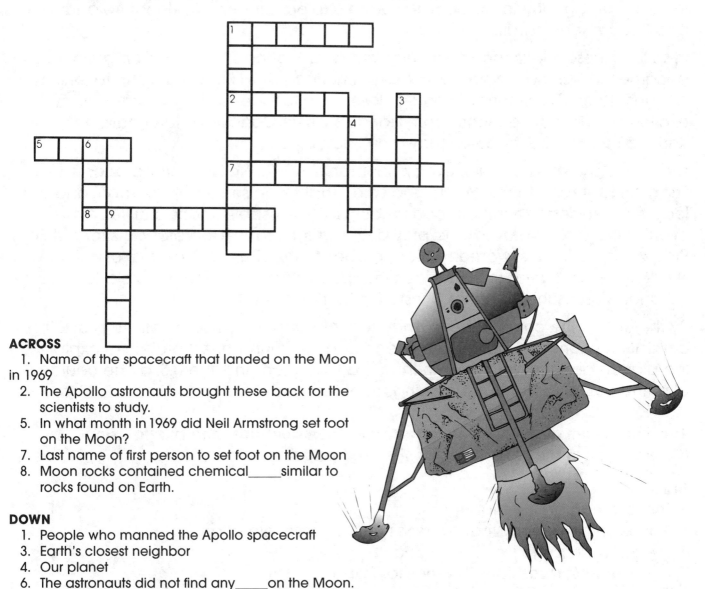

**ACROSS**

1. Name of the spacecraft that landed on the Moon in 1969
2. The Apollo astronauts brought these back for the scientists to study.
5. In what month in 1969 did Neil Armstrong set foot on the Moon?
7. Last name of first person to set foot on the Moon
8. Moon rocks contained chemical_____similar to rocks found on Earth.

**DOWN**

1. People who manned the Apollo spacecraft
3. Earth's closest neighbor
4. Our planet
6. The astronauts did not find any_____on the Moon.
9. Between 1969 and 1972, eleven other astronauts_____on the Moon.

# Into Outer Space

The United States first sent ships into outer space as a result of the Cold War rivalry with the Soviet Union. Both nations were working on rocket ships as an outgrowth of rocketry research begun by Germany during World War II. The U.S. was shocked, though, when the Soviets sent Sputnik, the first satellite, into orbit in 1957. Sputnik inspired work that allowed the first American satellite, Explorer, to be launched just four months later. The government also began a program of stronger science education, and founded an agency to overlook its space exploration—the National Aeronautics and Space Administration, or NASA.

In spite of these efforts, the Soviet Union remained "ahead," when Yuri Gagarin became the first man in space in 1961. American Alan Shepard went up less than a month later. Americans at home followed the fortunes of the first astronauts with excitement. Rocket launches from Florida's Cape Canaveral, later called the Kennedy Space Center, were shown on television.

The U.S. space program achieved a triumph in 1969. Neil Armstrong became the first man to step onto the Moon, and said, "That's one small step for man, one giant leap for mankind." After the moon landings, the reusable space shuttle was developed to save money and provide an outer space laboratory. Astronaut Sally Ride became the first woman in space aboard the shuttle. The worst disaster in NASA history occurred in 1986, when the space shuttle Challenger exploded with six astronauts and schoolteacher Christa McAuliffe aboard.

By the end of the century, the U.S. had launched many useful satellites, providing communications around the world, and had sent unmanned probes to explore the planets and the galaxy. With the Cold War at an end, the U.S. alone could plan the next steps for human beings in outer space.

**Read the clues about space exploration. Then complete the puzzle using the words from the Word Bank on the next page.**

**Across**
2. The first man on the Moon
4. Initials of the agency that oversees U.S. space exploration
6. The first man to go into outer space
7. A reusable spaceship with wings for flying
8. The second phrase of the first sentence spoken on the Moon: "...one giant _____ for mankind"

10. The first woman in space
11. Name of the first satellite in outer space
12. Research in this field made reaching outer space possible.

**Down**

1. Original name of the cape where rockets are launched for outer space
3. Course of a ship or satellite around a planet
5. Name of the Florida space center today
6. An astronaut who returned to space over 30 years after his first trip
7. The first American in outer space
9. Term for an unmanned space exploring machine

## Word Bank

| | | | |
|---|---|---|---|
| ARMSTRONG | GLENN | ORBIT | SHEPARD |
| CANAVERAL | KENNEDY | PROBE | SHUTTLE |
| GAGARIN | LEAP | RIDE | SPUTNIK |
| | NASA | ROCKETRY | |

# What a Trip!

On July 20, 1969, Neil Armstrong and Edwin Aldrin, Jr. became the first human beings to walk on the Moon. Imagine that you were with these two astronauts on this history-making journey. Write about your experience below.

_____
_____
_____
_____
_____
_____
_____
_____
_____
_____
_____
_____
_____
_____
_____
_____
_____
_____

# The Challenger and the Columbia

The Space Shuttle program began in the late 1970's to create reusable spacecraft for exploring outer space. Before this, space capsules could only be used once, and then they were discarded. The Columbia, the Challenger, the Discovery, and the Atlantis were the four space shuttles in this fleet.

On January 28, 1986, the Challenger lifted off on its ninth mission into space. This flight gained special attention because one crew member, Christa McAuliffe, won a contest to become the first teacher in space. She was to have given lectures from the shuttle to students across the country. However, about one minute after takeoff, the Challenger exploded. Tragically, its seven-member crew—Francis "Dick" Scobee, Michael Smith, Judith Resnik, Ronald McNair, Ellison Onizuka, Gregory Jarvis, Christa McAuliffe—was killed. Experts concluded that the extremely low temperature at the time of liftoff caused the rubber o-rings around its main boosters to break down.

Saturday, February 1, 2003, was another sad day in the history of the space program. That morning, the Columbia space shuttle exploded high over Texas as it reentered the atmosphere. The tragedy occurred 39 miles above the Earth, 16 minutes before the shuttle was scheduled to land at the Kennedy Space Center in Florida.

Numerous teams of officials and investigators gathered from all over the country to investigate what went wrong with the Columbia mission. Aboard the Columbia was a seven-member crew. Rick Husband, Michael Anderson, David Brown, Kalpana Chawla, Laurel Clark, William McCool, and Ilan Ramon were extraordinary individuals who dedicated their lives to the space program.

After these tragic events, special memorial services were held nationwide to remember and pray for the astronauts, and American flags were flown at half-staff to honor them. They will be remembered as the brave heroes of the space shuttles Challenger and Columbia.

# Liftoff

"3-2-1, liftoff!" With a mighty roar, the Saturn V **rocket** leaves the **launch pad**.

Riding high on top of the Saturn V in the **Command Module** are the three Apollo astronauts. Below their Command Module is a Lunar Landing Module which will land two of the astronauts on the Moon's surface.

Below this, the Saturn V has three parts, or **stages**. It takes a lot of power to escape the Earth's pull, called **gravity**. The spacecraft must reach a speed of almost 25,000 miles per hour. The bottom, or first stage, is the largest. After each stage uses up its **fuel**, it drops off, and the next stage starts. Each stage has its own fuel and **oxygen**. The fuels need oxygen, otherwise they will not burn.

The astronauts are now on their 3-day journey to the Moon. Using the color key, color each Saturn V section a different color.

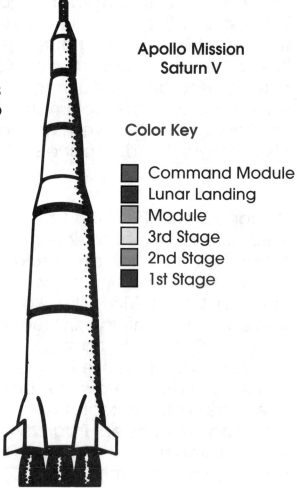

**Apollo Mission
Saturn V**

**Color Key**

| | |
|---|---|
| ■ | Command Module |
| ■ | Lunar Landing |
| ▨ | Module |
| □ | 3rd Stage |
| ▨ | 2nd Stage |
| ■ | 1st Stage |

Fill in the spaces with the highlighted words from above.

**1.** The Saturn V __ __ __ __ __ __ has three main parts, or __ __ __ __ __ __.

**2.** Rocket engines burn __ __ __ __ and __ __ __ __ __ __.

**3.** The Earth's pull is called __ __ __ __ __ __ __.

**4.** "Liftoff." The Saturn V leaves the __ __ __ __ __ __ __ __ __.

**5.** The Apollo astronauts ride in the __ __ __ __ __ __ __ __ __ __ __ __ __.

# The Space Shuttle

Read the short story below. Then answer the questions.

The space shuttle takes astronauts into space. Rockets launch the shuttle. The shuttle orbits the Earth. The astronauts work in space—they set up satellites or conduct experiments. When it is time to return to Earth, the shuttle lands on a runway like an airplane.

1. What takes astronauts into space?

_____

2. What launches the shuttle into space?

_____

3. What kinds of work do astronauts do in space?

_____

4. Where does the shuttle land when it returns to Earth?

_____

# A Super Space Shuttle

Space shuttle systems began to operate in the early 1980's. They greatly reduce the cost of space flights, as they are reusable.

A space shuttle has three main parts: 1) an orbiter, which has three main engines, 2) an external tank, and 3) two solid rocket boosters.

Thinking about the description above, design your very own space shuttle in the space below!

# Astro-Flier

**You will need:**

a hole punch
scissors
coffee-can size lids
ruler
colored felt-tip pens
wire or string
pencils
short, clear plastic drinking glasses
stencils
paper
tape
bottom of styrofoam egg carton
colored pipe cleaners
glue
colored toothpicks
colored ribbon
glitter
colored yarn

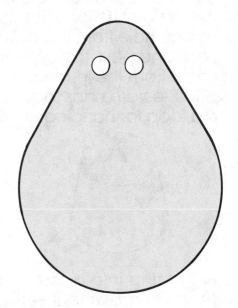

You will need an adult to help you. Make a stencil by tracing around the pattern above on paper, cutting it out, and punching two holes in it where the small circles are drawn. Put the stencil on a plastic lid. Using a pencil, draw around its outline and holes. Cut out the lines you have made on the lid and punch holes. Run a string or a wire across the room. Tie pieces of yarn from which to hang the astro-flier.

**Directions:**

1. Divide a plastic lid into quarters. Cut it apart. On each of the quarters, cut off the rim of the lid.

2. Use a stencil to mark the holes with a pencil in each pointed end. Punch out the holes.

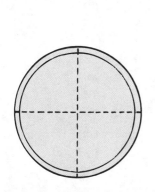
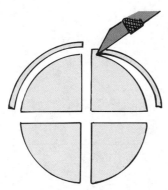

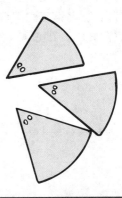

3. Using scissors, make two holes in the bottom of the plastic glass. Cut a piece of yarn 10" long. Put the yarn in one hole from the outside of the glass, and put it through the other hole from the inside of the glass. Tie the yarn ends together to make a loop for hanging.

4. Set the plastic glass upside-down over the middle of the plastic lid. Trace around the glass using a pencil. Cut out the inner circle, cutting just inside the circle you traced.

5. Divide the ring into quarters. Use the stencil to make four sets of holes on the ring. Punch them out.

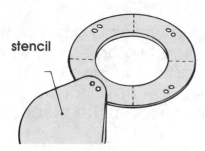

stencil

6. Cut out six $\frac{1}{4}$" x $2\frac{1}{4}$" strips from the plastic lid. Make sure the strips are a little wider than the holes on the stencil. Otherwise, they won't hold the pieces described on page 299 together.

actual size $\longrightarrow$

7. Use four plastic strips to attach the wings under the ring at the holes. Set the other two strips aside. Match up a pair of holes in the wings with a pair on the ring. Put one end of the strip through one hole and the other end through the other hole of the pair.

8. Pull the glass up from the bottom through the big center hole. Tape the glass to the ring underneath.

# Astro-Flier

9. Use the stencil to mark two sets of holes in the ring between wings BC and wings AD. Punch them out.

10. Cut off the rim of another plastic lid, the same size as the one that made the ring. Place it under the first ring and mark the two sets of holes in the ring on it. Punch them out. Set this ring aside.

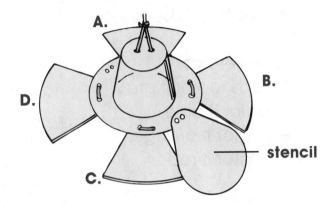

A.

B.

D.

stencil

C.

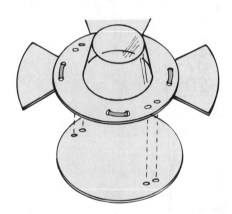

11. Cut out one egg section from a carton. Cut around it so that it is flat on the bottom. Draw a face on it.

12. Tape the astronaut (face) onto the center of the flat ring you set aside.

13. Put the ring with the astronaut under the first ring. Line up the holes. Use the last two plastic strips to fasten the circle to the plastic ring.

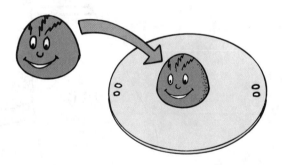

14. Use pipe cleaners for antennae, ribbons for streamers, toothpicks for decorations or antennae, glitter for sparkle, etc. You can glue them on or poke very small holes in the glass in which to stick the decorations.

15. Tie your finished astro-flier to the piece of string or wire hanging across the room or in an open doorway.

# BLAST OFF!

Add or subtract. Use the code to color the space rocket.

**If the answer has:**
9 hundreds, color it gray.
7 tens, color it blue.
5 ones, color it orange.
4 ones, color it red.

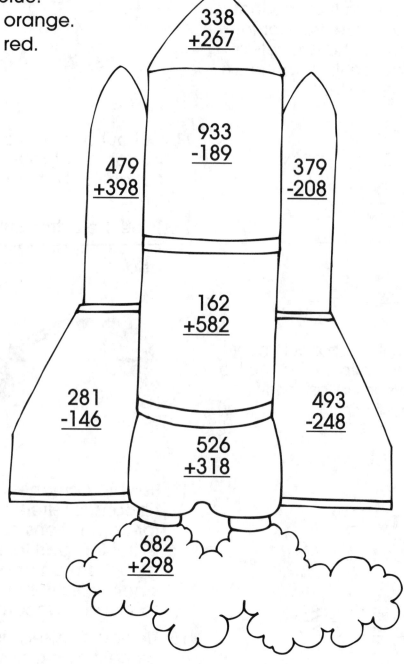

$$\begin{array}{r} 338 \\ +267 \\ \hline \end{array}$$

$$\begin{array}{r} 933 \\ -189 \\ \hline \end{array}$$

$$\begin{array}{r} 479 \\ +398 \\ \hline \end{array}$$

$$\begin{array}{r} 379 \\ -208 \\ \hline \end{array}$$

$$\begin{array}{r} 162 \\ +582 \\ \hline \end{array}$$

$$\begin{array}{r} 281 \\ -146 \\ \hline \end{array}$$

$$\begin{array}{r} 493 \\ -248 \\ \hline \end{array}$$

$$\begin{array}{r} 526 \\ +318 \\ \hline \end{array}$$

$$\begin{array}{r} 682 \\ +298 \\ \hline \end{array}$$

Space Exploration and Travel

# Telescopes

The first telescope was invented in about 1600. In 1609, the Italian astronomer Galileo used his hand-made telescope to observe craters on the Moon, sunspots, the moons of Jupiter, and the stars of the Milky Way. The early telescopes were **refracting telescopes**. They collected light by refracting or bending it to produce an image. A different kind of telescope, called a **reflecting telescope**, uses a curved mirror to collect light and produce an image. An eyepiece lens allows scientists to magnify the image made by either type of telescope. The reflecting telescope was invented by Sir Isaac Newton in 1668. Because it gathers more light than the human eye, a telescope will make faint objects appear brighter. One of the largest telescopes is a six-meter reflector in the Soviet Union. Another large one is a reflector telescope at the Mt. Palomar Observatory in California. These giant telescopes allow us to see objects nearly a million times fainter than anything we can see with our eyes alone. New telescopes under construction will gather even more light and allow us to see even further into space.

## ACROSS
3. Place were a large telescope is located
4. Early_____collected light by bending it.
8. Scientist who observed sunspots in 1609
9. Building
10. Not made by machine

## DOWN
1. One of the largest telescopes in the world is a six-meter_____in the Soviet Union.
2. The opposite of dark
5. An_____lens allows us to magnify an image.
6. Planet whose moons Galileo was able to see
7. Sir_____Newton

# Live Via Satellite

"This program is brought to you live via satellite from halfway around the world." Satellites are very helpful in sending TV messages from the other side of the world. But this is only one of the special jobs that satellites can do.

Most satellites are placed into orbit around the Earth by riding on top of giant rockets. More recently some satellites have been carried into orbit by a space shuttle. While orbiting the Earth, the giant doors of the shuttle are opened, and the satellite is pushed into orbit.

**This satellite relays TV signals from halfway around the world.**

Satellites send information about many things. Use the code to find the different kinds of messages and information satellites send.

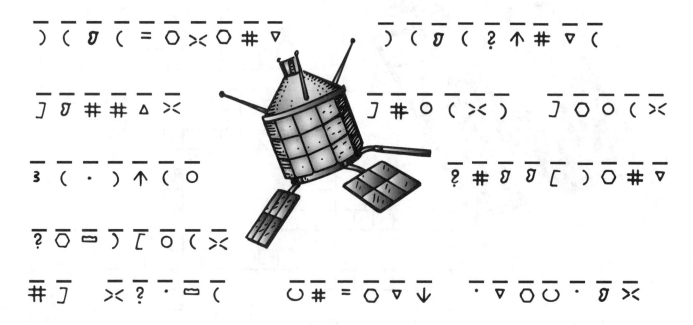

**Code**

· ! ▭ △ ( ⅃ ↓ ↑ O + : ♂ ∪ ▽ # ? ▢ ο ⤬ ) [ = з 𝒪 ⊣⋔
A B C D E F G H I J K L M N O P Q R S T U V W X Y Z

# Skylab 1

Skylab 1 was the first United States space station. It was launched in 1973. In it, astronauts lived and worked for as long as 84 days before returning to Earth. Before being launched to Skylab 1, the astronauts had to prepare for almost three months of living away from Earth.

Living in a small space away from Earth for that long a period of time took some careful planning. The astronauts had to think about how their daily routine would change when they were in space. When packing and preparing for their trip, the astronauts considered two main areas.

Look at the areas below and list or draw pictures of what you think you would need to survive in a space station for twelve weeks.

**Life's Necessities:**

**Life's Pleasures:**

# Space Station Word Search

Below are hidden words that have something to do with a space station. Can you find them all? Use the Word Bank to help you, and circle the words as you find them.

## Word Bank

| telerobotic | solar | battery |
| heat | modular | light |
| skylab | laboratory | |
| generator | astronauts | |

```
T  E  L  E  R  O  B  O  T  I  C  F
B  S  I  K  L  J  A  P  A  N  U  R
O  D  G  R  D  P  U  A  C  V  N  E
O  V  H  E  A  T  L  S  V  U  F  E
M  U  T  S  H  O  K  T  I  Y  T  D
T  S  K  Y  L  A  B  R  B  T  E  O
G  Q  C  R  Q  I  A  O  N  R  L  M
N  E  U  O  W  U  T  N  M  A  S  D
C  A  N  A  D  A  T  A  Q  R  T  S
A  S  A  E  P  Y  E  U  W  R  W  V
S  K  R  L  R  T  R  T  E  A  T  B
T  R  U  S  S  A  Y  S  T  Y  R  N
R  P  T  I  E  R  T  E  R  S  S  M
O  N  A  U  T  S  S  O  L  A  R  L
K  W  M  O  D  U  L  A  R  T  J  K
L  B  L  A  B  O  R  A  T  O  R  Y
```

# Look at This!

Imagine that you have access to the biggest telescope ever invented. You are able to see the planets and everything on them perfectly. Choose one of the planets to focus on. Draw what you see below!

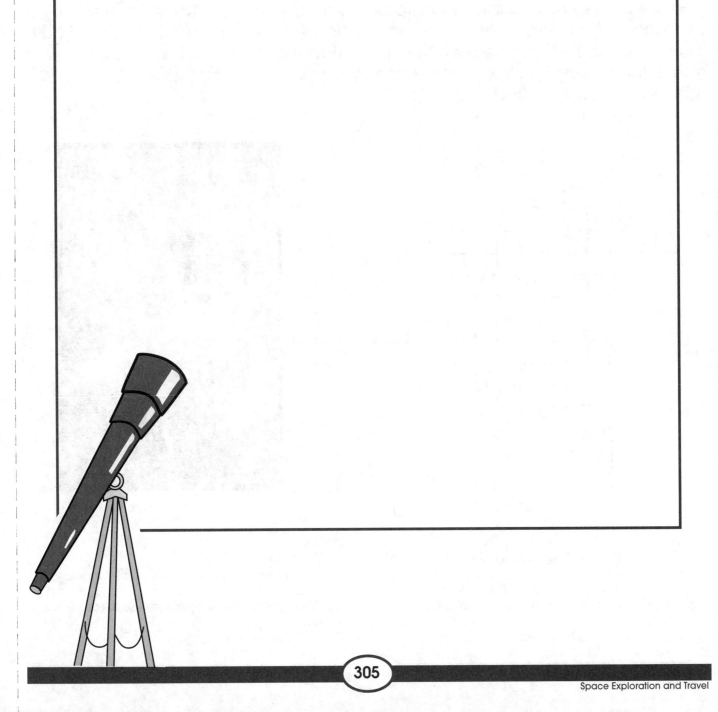

# Observatories

An observatory is a place with telescopes and other scientific instruments used for studying the sky. Most observatories are located far from cities and high up in the mountains. To get a clear view of the sky, it is important for telescopes to be far away from city lights with as dark and clear a sky as possible. Hundreds of years ago astronomers sat and looked through their telescopes to make their observations. Now most telescopes are used like giant cameras. Some observatories are used for special kinds of work. One of the telescopes at Kitt Peak National Observatory, near Tucson, Arizona, is designed only to study the Sun. The Lowell Observatory, near Flagstaff, Arizona, specializes in the study of the planets. There are observatories all over the world. There are some in Australia, South America, and South Africa that are located in places with very good views of space.

**ACROSS**
2. A place with telescopes and other scientific instruments
4. Kangaroos come from this nation.
6. Scientists who study the stars and outer space
9. Tucson is in this state.

**DOWN**
1. The opposite of near
3. Instruments used to see objects in space
5. A continent
7. Observatory telescopes are used like giant_____.
8. _____Peak is near Tucson.

# Is There Anybody Out There?

*Belleville, Wisconsin, 1987*—Reports of a strange sausage-shaped object moving across the night sky were made by many people from scattered locations around the Belleville area. The Illinois Air Traffic Control also verified an unidentified object at the same time and location. No one had an explanation for the unidentified flying object (UFO).

Between the years 1952 and 1969, more than 12,000 similar investigations were made as part of a secret project called Project Bluebook. Usually, investigators found that people had just seen bright planets or stars, strange clouds, aircraft, birds, balloons, kites, aerial flares, meteors, or satellites. None of the investigations clearly proved the existence of visitors from another world.

However, the universe is so immense that it is hard to positively say whether or not life exists in other worlds. Scientists have carefully considered many factors to guess the likelihood of extraterrestrials, or life from another planet. It is guessed that perhaps as few as one of every 100,000 stars has a planet with some kind of life. This means that there could be a million planets with life just within our own Milky Way galaxy! How many of these planets have intelligent life? That is even harder to guess.

What do you think about life on other planets? Do you think it is possible?

_____

_____

_____

_____

_____

# What Would Extraterrestrials Look Like?

Do other worlds have intelligent beings, plants, and animals? Possibly, but it is very unlikely that they would look anything like the ones on Earth. What do you think extraterrestrials would look like? Draw an example of what you think an extraterrestrial person, plant, and animal would look like in the spaces below.

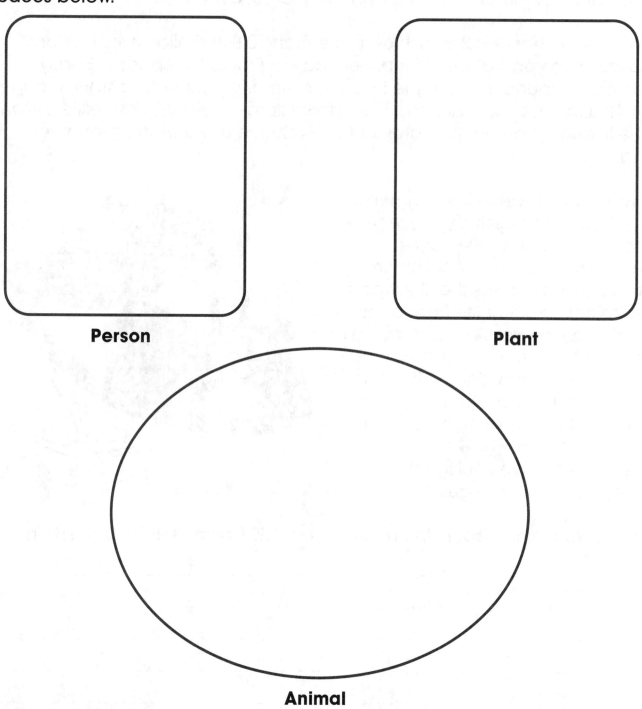

**Person**

**Plant**

**Animal**

# Space Friends

Look at the letters on the spaceships below. They spell out the word **space**. How many lines do you need to draw to connect each spaceship to all the other spaceships?

Try writing the letters **S**, **P**, **A**, **C**, and **E** on a sheet of paper to match the positions in the picture. Then draw lines to find the answer.

# What's That I Hear?

SETI, the Search for Extraterrestrial Intelligence, listens for life from outer space with radio telescopes. The telescopes pickup radio wave signals from outer space. A constant stream of natural radio waves comes from space. Astronomers hope that some day the telescopes will pick up a special signal or a message sent to Earth from other life forms!

Pretend that you are able to pickup radio waves signaling life on another planet. Use the space below to write an imaginary radio commercial or advertisement that you might hear. Be creative!

_____

_____

_____

_____

_____

_____

_____

_____

# Gorf's Word Game

Gorf is from a faraway planet. While traveling to Earth, he played a game to pass the time. He wrote the word **planet** on a piece of paper. Gorf erased the letter **e** from the word, and he was left with the word **plant**. Then he erased another letter, and he was left with a word again. Gorf kept erasing the letters one by one. Each time he was left with a word. Even the last letter that was left was a word! In what order did Gorf erase the letters? Use the area below Gorf's spaceship to work the problem out.

# Venusian

## The Venusian's three suctioned feet help it maneuver around its planet, Venus!

Follow the steps below to draw the imaginary space creature. Use the following page for your artwork.

1. To begin, draw a half-circle for the top of its head. Add two rounded horns. Then insert its eyes and big, open mouth.

2. Add three more horns of varying sizes. Then sketch eyebrows.

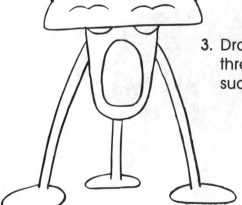

3. Draw the Venusian's three legs with suctioned feet.

4. Erase the unneeded lines, add finishing details, and color.

**See that cool-looking eyepiece the Gordo is wearing?
With it, this alien can see through anything—
water, walls...even you!**

Follow the steps below to draw the imaginary space creature. Use the following page for your artwork.

1. Create the Gordo's body by drawing a four-sided shape with a rounded bottom. Sketch its two small arms, and then draw its special eyepiece.

2. Detail the eyepiece by adding a thin rectangle. This is the lens. Now draw two small circles for the palms of the Gordo's hands and a wide, slightly down-turned mouth. Don't forget to draw the small dimple beneath the mouth.

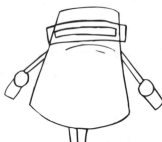

3. Complete the outline of its hands with rectangular shapes on the ends of the circles. Add two short legs.

4. Detail each hand with fingers and a thumb. Draw two long, rectangular feet.

5. To finish, add antennae on top of the Gordo's head, spots on its body, and toe lines on its feet. Shade the eyepiece, erase the unneeded lines, and color.

# Spaceship Search

Gus Galactic needs help in identifying these alien spaceships. Use the compass to write a ship's letter in each blank to solve these riddles.

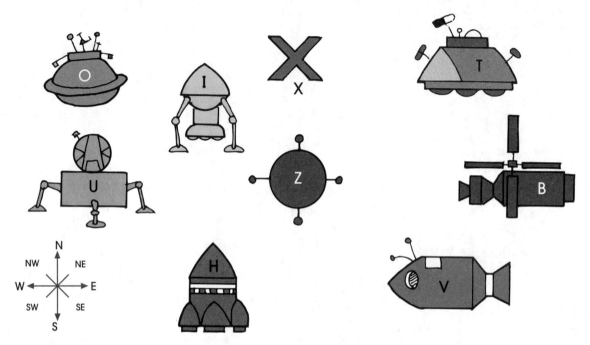

1. I am **N** of Ship **H**. _____

2. I am **E** of Ship **Z**. _____

3. I am **SE** of Ship **Z**. _____

4. I am **S** of Ship **O**. _____

5. I am **NW** of Ship **Z**. _____

6. I am **SW** of Ship **B**. _____

7. I am **NE** of Ship **Z**. _____

8. I am **NE** of Ship **I**. _____

9. I am **SE** of Ship **U**. _____

10. I am **NW** of Ship **B**. _____

## Cosmic Challenge!

Start at Ship **H**. Travel in the orbit given. Which ship will you dock with?

1. Go **NW** to Ship _____.

2. Go **NE** to Ship _____.

3. Go **NE** to Ship _____.

4. Go **S** to Ship _____.

5. Go **SE** to Ship _____.

6. Go **NE** to Ship _____.

7. Go **NW** to Ship _____.

This is your docking station. Congratulations!

# Googlies and Winkles

The Space Fantasy Theater invited aliens from all over the galaxy to the opening of a new movie. Some Googlies and Winkles waited in line to get into the movie theater. Googlies are creatures with two legs. Winkles are creatures with three legs. Read the clues below.

How many Googlies and Winkles waited in line?

Only Winkles and Googlies waited in line.

There were more Winkles than Googlies.

There were 18 legs in the line.

The Zops and Snarfs are watching an exciting ball game. Look at the fans. See if you can tell one way that the Zops are alike and one way that the Snarfs are alike.

Now look at the players. Draw a circle around the ones that are Zops.
Draw a square around the ones that are Snarfs.

A          B          C          D

# Space Trek
# Game Directions

**You will need:**
- The game board on pages 321 and 323
- The game cards on pages 325 and 327
- Markers for each player, such as coins or paper clips
- Dice

**Directions:**

1. Carefully tear out the two game board sheets and tape them together.

2. Ask an adult to help you cut out the game cards. Place the cards next to the game board.

3. Each player should choose an object to use as a marker.

4. When you are setup, chose someone to go first. That person rolls the dice and moves his or her marker that number of spaces on the game board. Another player draws a card and reads the question to the player. The player must answer correctly to stay on that space. If the player answers incorrectly, he or she must go back to the space he or she came from.

5. If a player lands on a space with directions, he or she must follow whatever the directions say.

6. The first person to reach the end wins!

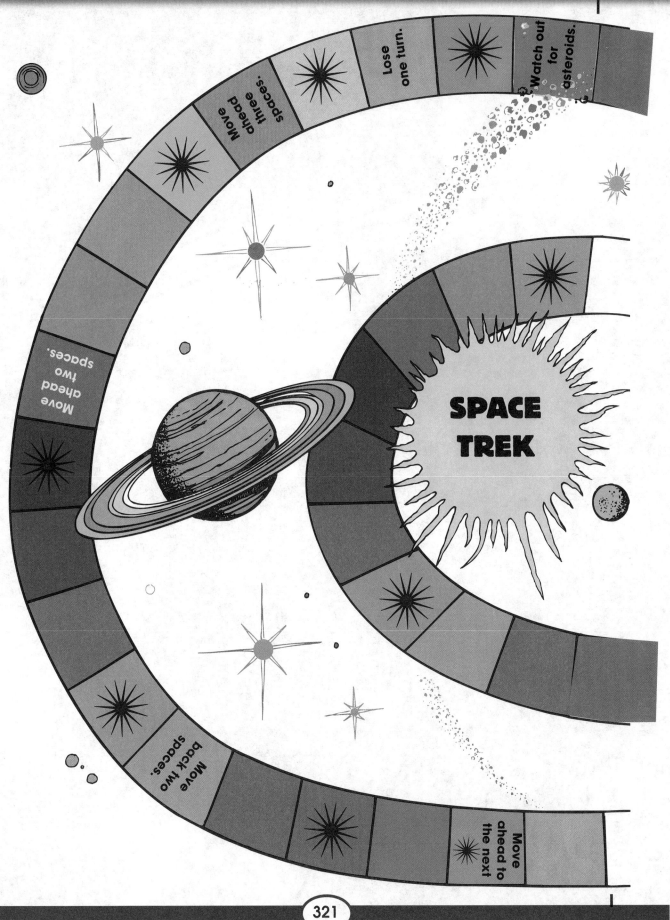

SPACE TREK

Move ahead three spaces.

Lose one turn.

Watch out for asteroids.

Move ahead two spaces.

Move back two spaces.

Move ahead to the next

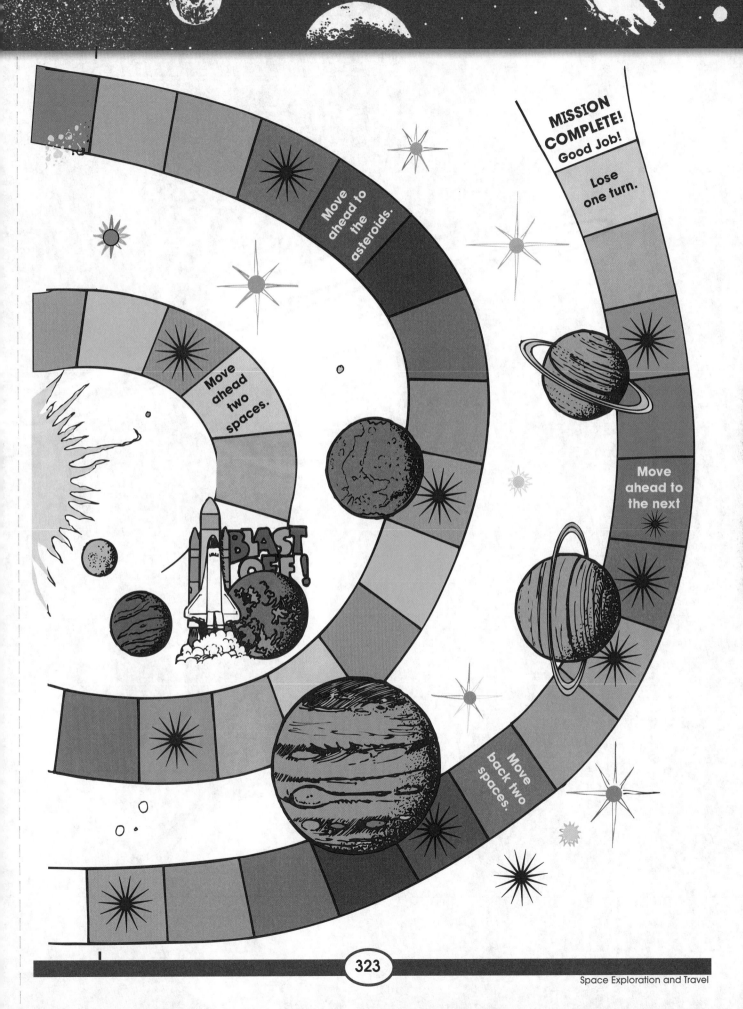

MISSION
COMPLETE!
Good Job!

Lose
one turn.

Move ahead to
the asteroids.

Move
ahead
two
spaces.

BLAST
OFF!

Move
ahead to
the next

Move
back two
spaces.

Space Exploration and Travel

# Space Trek Game Cards

| | | |
|---|---|---|
| Name the four inner planets.<br><br>(Mercury, Venus, Earth, Mars) | Name the four outer planets.<br><br>(Jupiter, Saturn, Uranus, Neptune) | Name the planet farthest from the Sun.<br><br>(Neptune) |
| Which planet is difficult to see with a telescope because it is so close to the Sun?<br><br>(Mercury) | Name the two planets that have orbits between Earth and the Sun.<br><br>(Mercury and Venus) | How long is the Sun's rotation?<br><br>(about one month) |
| On which planet is the surface about 70 percent water?<br><br>(Earth) | Name one reason why you cannot live on Mars.<br><br>(Examples: no air, no water) | Which star is closest to the Earth?<br><br>(the Sun) |
| Which planet is commonly called the "Red Planet?"<br><br>(Mars) | As this planet rotates, its moon's gravitational pull causes the ocean tides.<br><br>(Earth) | Which planet rotates while it is tipped on its side?<br><br>(Uranus) |
| Name the largest planet.<br><br>(Jupiter) | Dust storms change the landscape on which planet?<br><br>(Mars) | Name the force that keeps the planets in their orbits.<br><br>(gravity) |

# Space Trek Game Cards

| | | |
|---|---|---|
| Name the two planets that have orbits between Jupiter and Uranus.<br><br>(Mars, Saturn) | Name the planet closest to the Sun.<br><br>(Mercury) | Name two kinds of energy we receive from the Sun.<br><br>(heat and light) |
| What is it called when a planet spins around on an imaginary axis?<br><br>(rotation) | The Earth's moon has no atmosphere.<br>True or false?<br><br>(true) | Surface water has been found on Earth's moon.<br>True or false?<br><br>(false) |
| Name the planet with the warmest surface temperature.<br><br>(Venus) | Name the four planets that have rings.<br><br>(Jupiter, Saturn, Uranus, Neptune) | Which planet has something called the "Great Red Spot?"<br><br>(Jupiter) |
| Which planet has the shortest rotation, or day?<br><br>(Jupiter) | Which planet is about half the size of Earth?<br><br>(Mars) | Describe our solar system.<br>(Example: it consists of eight planets which revolve around the Sun, asteroids, comets, etc.) |
| Name the planets in order from the Sun<br><br>(Mercury, Venus, Earth, Mars, Jupiter, Saturn, Uranus, Neptune) | Which planet's rings can be viewed through a telescope or even some binoculars?<br>(Saturn) | Which planet is commonly referred to as the "Green Planet?"<br><br>(Uranus) |

# ANSWER KEY

## Science Essentials: Solar System
## Grades 1-3

---

### Space

Space is what separates one thing from another. When objects are close together, there is not much space between them. When they are far apart, there is a lot of space. The space between planets is called **interplanetary space**. The space between stars is **interstellar space**. The space between galaxies is **intergalactic space**. There is more space between stars than between planets. Space is everywhere. Look around, and you will see that there is space between you and other people and objects. There is a lot of space in the universe. Space is not empty. It can be filled with air. Air is made of different gases. Earth's air is made of mainly nitrogen, oxygen, and carbon dioxide. The air on other planets is made of gases, but some are poisonous for human beings to breathe.

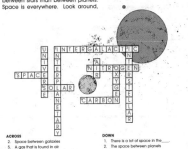

Crossword answers: UNIVERSE, INTERGALACTIC, NITROGEN, SPACE, SOLAR, INTERPLANETARY, OXYGEN, INTERSTELLAR, CARBON

**ACROSS**
2. Space between galaxies
5. A gas that is found in air
7. There is more ___ between the stars than between the planets.
8. The system we live in (first word)
9. ___ dioxide is a gas.

**DOWN**
1. There is a lot of space in the ___.
2. The space between planets
3. The space between stars
4. It is made of different gases.
6. Another gas that is part of Earth's air

**7**

---

### The Solar System

Our **solar system** is made up of the Sun and all the objects that orbit, or go around, the Sun.
The Sun is the only star in our solar system. It gives heat and light to the eight planets in the solar system. The planets and their moons all orbit the Sun.
The time it takes for each planet to orbit the Sun is called a **year**. A year on Earth is 365 days. Planets closer to the Sun have shorter years. Their orbit is shorter. Planets farther from the Sun take longer to orbit, so their years are longer.
Asteroids, comets, and meteors are also part of our solar system.

Draw the eight planets around the Sun.

**Underline:**
The solar system is: the Sun without the nine planets.
the Sun and all the objects that orbit it.

**Check:**
☑ is the center of our solar system.
☑ is the only star in our solar system.
☐ is a planet in our solar system.
☑ gives heat and light to our solar system.

**Write:**
A _____ year _____ is the time it takes for a planet to orbit the Sun.
month   year

**Match:**
Planets closer to the Sun . . . have a longer year.
Planets farther from the Sun . . . have a shorter year.

**8**

---

### What's in Our Solar System?

An **astronomer**, or scientist who studies the universe, might make this list if you asked her what is in our solar system.

- one **star**, or hot glowing ball of gases, called the Sun
- all the planets' moons
- small chunks of rock or ice called **meteoroids**
- lots of empty space

- nine worlds called **planets** that travel around the Sun
- chunks of rock and metal called **asteroids**
- frozen balls of dirty ice called **comets**

Now write a definition for each of these words.

1. astronomer _a scientist who studies the universe._

2. star _a hot glowing ball of gases._

3. planets _nine worlds that travel around the Sun._

4. asteroids _chunks of rock and metal._

5. meteoroids _small chunks of rock or ice._

6. comets _frozen balls of dirty ice._

**9**

---

### Solar System

Solar means anything having to do with the Sun or something that uses or operates with energy from the Sun. Our solar system consists of the nine known planets, their moons, asteroids, meteor-oids, and comets orbiting the Sun. A **meteoroid** is a small piece of rock or metal traveling through space. A **meteor** is the name of a meteoroid that falls to Earth, producing a streak of light in the sky. A **comet** is a mass of ice and rock that orbits the Sun. **Asteroids** are large pieces of rock and metal that are mostly found between Mars and Jupiter. There are 101 known moons, or satellites, that orbit the planets. The Sun is by far the biggest and heaviest celestial body in our solar system.

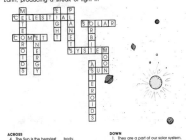

Crossword answers: CELESTIAL, METEOROIDS, COMET, SOLAR, ORBIT, ENERGY, SYSTEM, MOONS, SUN, ASTEROIDS, FLIGHT, PLANET

**ACROSS**
4. The Sun is the heaviest ___ body.
5. Pertaining to the Sun
7. A mass of ice and rock that orbits the Sun
9. Earth is part of the solar ___.
12. Earth orbits the ___.

**DOWN**
1. They are a part of our solar system.
2. Number of planets in our solar system
3. Earth and Mars are ___.
6. To repeatedly move around a star or planet in the same path
8. Earth uses ___ from the Sun.
10. Earth's closest neighbor
11. They are large pieces of rock and metal.

**10**

---

### Space Words

Find the space words in the puzzle below. The words go across and down. Use the Word Bank to help you, and circle the words as you find them.

**Word Bank**

| Moon | Shuttle | Land | Orbit |
|------|---------|------|-------|
| Flight | Comet | Astronaut | Star |
| Rocket | Planet | Space | Sun |

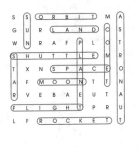

Word search grid with answers: ORBIT, LAND, SHUTTLE, SPACE, MOON, FLIGHT, ROCKET, ASTRONAUT

**11**

---

### Solar System Scramble

Unscramble the name of each numbered object below. Write the name on the correct line below.

**Word Bank**

| Neptune | Asteroids | Mars | Earth |
|---------|-----------|------|-------|
| Jupiter | Sun | Saturn | Uranus |
| | Venus | Mercury | |

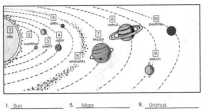

1. _Sun_
2. _Mercury_
3. _Venus_
4. _Earth_
5. _Mars_
6. _Asteroids_
7. _Jupiter_
8. _Saturn_
9. _Uranus_
10. _Neptune_

**12**

---

## A Strip of Space

Compare the positions of the planets from the Sun.

1. Color:
- the Sun yellow
- Mercury brown
- Venus yellow
- Earth green
- Mars red
- Jupiter orange
- Saturn yellow
- Uranus and Neptune blue

2. Cut out the four strips below.

3. Glue:
- strip 2 to the right end of strip 1
- strip 3 to the right end of strip 2
- strip 4 to the right end of strip 3

(Distances are to approximate scale.)

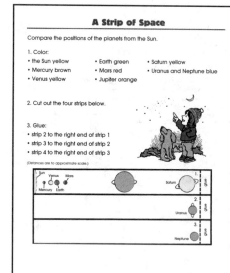

**13**

## Found in Space

Read each riddle. Then write the answer using one of the scrambled words from the Word Bank.

**Word Bank**

| | | |
|---|---|---|
| ttfoa | nuS | htlesut |
| srast | rEath | nruSat |
| rMas | erscrat | |

1. This huge star lights the day. S u n
2. These shine at night. s t a r s
3. These are on the Moon. c r a t e r s
4. This is our home planet. E a r t h
5. This flies into space. s h u t t l e
6. This planet is red. M a r s
7. This planet has rings. S a t u r n
8. Astronauts do this in space. f l o a t

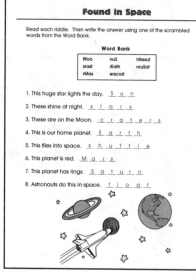

**16**

## Beyond Our Solar System

Astronomers know that much lies beyond our solar system. In fact, in the drawing on this page our solar system is just a tiny speck in a larger group of objects in space. This larger group is called the **Milky Way galaxy**. The Milky Way is made up of all the stars you can see in the night sky and many more beyond those. It also contains large clouds made of gas and dust. But that's not all! Beyond our Milky Way, astronomers have seen millions of other galaxies. Each of these has billions of stars. Astronomers call space and everything in it the **universe**.

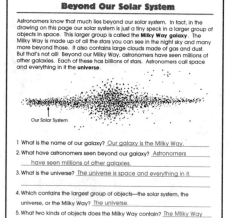

Our Solar System

1. What is the name of our galaxy? Our galaxy is the Milky Way.
2. What have astronomers seen beyond our galaxy? Astronomers have seen millions of other galaxies.
3. What is the universe? The universe is space and everything in it.
4. Which contains the largest group of objects—the solar system, the universe, or the Milky Way? The universe
5. What two kinds of objects does the Milky Way contain? The Milky Way contains stars and large clouds made of gas and dust.

**21**

## Where in the World Is...

What is your global address? It's more than your street, city, state, and ZIP code.

What would your address be if you wanted to get a letter from a friend living in outer space?

Use an atlas, encyclopedia, science book, or other source to complete your global address.

**Inter-Galactic Address Book**

Name Answers will vary.
Street _____
County or Parish _____
State or Province _____
Country _____
Continent _____
Hemisphere _____
Planet The Earth.
Galaxy The Milky Way.

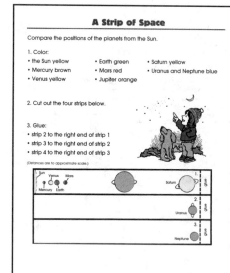

Draw an X to mark the approximate place where you live.

**22**

## A Space Riddle

Find a word in the Word Bank that matches each clue below. Write the word on the blanks.

**Word Bank**

atmosphere   axis   revolve   planets
rings   star   orbit   astronomer
astronaut   rotate   craters

1. person who travels in space a s t r o n a u t
2. deep holes c r a t e r s
3. eight worlds p l a n e t s
4. to spin r o t a t e
5. to travel around r e v o l v e
6. scientist who studies the objects in space a s t r o n o m e r
7. imaginary line through the center of a planet a x i s
8. a planet's path around the Sun o r b i t
9. ball of hot glowing gases s t a r
10. Saturn, Jupiter, and Uranus have these r i n g s
11. a blanket of gases a t m o s p h e r e

Answer this riddle! Write the circled letters on the blanks below.
**What is another name for our solar system?**

o u r   p l a c e   i n   s p a c e
8  4   11  3  9  2  5  7   8   10  11  9  2  5

**23**

## Mystery Picture

Use the clues below to find the mystery picture! Read each sentence and then cross out the picture that does not belong. Which picture is left?

1. It is not Earth.
2. It is not an astronaut.
3. It is not a space shuttle.
4. It is not the Sun.
5. It is not a satellite.
6. It is not a rocket ship.
7. It is not a telescope.

What is the mystery picture?

The mystery picture is the Moon.

**26**

## The Universe

The universe contains everything you could see, or touch, or measure that exists, no matter how close or how far away. All the galaxies and the space between them are part of the universe. All the stars and planets in the galaxies are part of the universe. Some of the planets are much larger than Earth, some are smaller. Almost all the stars are big.

The Sun is a star. Did you know that more than a million planets the size of Earth would fit into the Sun? The Sun is only a medium-sized star. There are stars much larger than the Sun in the universe. Even though there are large planets and giant stars in the universe, there is more space than anything else.

**ACROSS**
2. There is ___ space that anything else in the universe.
5. Earth, Mars, and Venus are all ___.
6. Size of some planets
7. It includes all the galaxies and the space between galaxies.
9. The Sun is one.

**DOWN**
1. Size of some planets in comparison to Earth
3. The planet we live on
4. The universe includes all the ___ and space between them.
8. Empty area

Crossword answers: LARGE, MORE, PLANETS, SMALL, UNIVERSE, STAR

**29**

## Hunt for It!

Now that you know more about the solar system, see if you can find the hidden words from the Word Bank in the puzzle below. Circle the words as you find them.

**Word Bank**

| | | | |
|---|---|---|---|
| Planet | Meteor | Oort Cloud | Sun |
| Asteroid | Space | Milky Way | Solar System |
| Comet | Galaxy | Astronomer | Universe |

```
M E T E O R Q G W E R T Y S U N
S D T F G F R A P L I K M N N S
A C Z B N M I L K Y W A Y W I S
S B N M O P R A W E R S P R V A
T X N O A T Y X W G H P A W E A
R A S T R R T Y P O R S C R S L
O R T O E A E P L J R G O O S D
N S S O L A R S Y S T E M S E F
O L K R J H G F S D D R E R S G
M F G T S D E R S L K T T P O H
E T R C S T O P P I O S D O P J
R A S L D F S G A P P L A N E T
T Y R O E W F S C D S A G H R K
S A Q U W A S T E R O I D E R L
Z X C D V B N M L K J H G F D P
```

**30**

## ABC Planets

Unscramble the names of the nine planets in our solar system. Then write the names of the planets in ABC order.

1. Earth
2. Jupiter
3. Mars
4. Mercury
5. Neptune
6. Saturn
7. Uranus
8. Venus

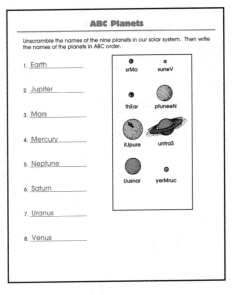

srMa    suneV
thEar    ptuneeN
itJpure    untraS
Uusnar    yerMruc

**35**

## How Big?

Planets vary greatly in size. Look at the list of planets and their diameters rounded to the nearest hundred miles.

| Planet | Diameter |
|---|---|
| Mercury | 3,000 miles |
| Venus | 7,500 miles |
| Earth | 7,900 miles |
| Mars | 4,200 miles |
| Jupiter | 88,700 miles |
| Saturn | 74,900 miles |
| Uranus | 31,600 miles |
| Neptune | 30,200 miles |

**Diameter** means distance through the middle.

Write the names of the planets in order by size, starting with the planet that has the **largest** diameter.

1. Jupiter
2. Saturn
3. Uranus
4. Neptune
5. Earth
6. Venus
7. Mars
8. Mercury

**36**

## Nine Planets Orbit Our Sun

Cut out the eight planets below and paste them in their correct order from the Sun.

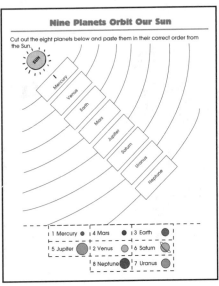

SUN, Mercury, Venus, Earth, Mars, Jupiter, Saturn, Uranus, Neptune

| 1 Mercury ● | 4 Mars ● | 3 Earth ● |
| 5 Jupiter ● | 2 Venus ● | 6 Saturn ● |
| 8 Neptune ● | 7 Uranus ● | |

**37**

## The Planets Are Moving!

Each of the planets in our solar system **revolves**, or travels, around the Sun. The planets circle the Sun along paths called **orbits**. Because the planets are at different distances from the Sun, each one takes a different length of time to revolve once.

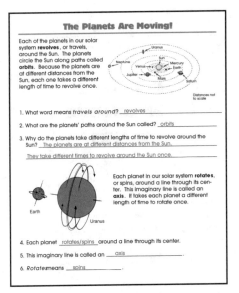

Distances not to scale

1. What word means *travels around*? __revolves__
2. What are the planets' paths around the Sun called? __orbits__
3. Why do the planets take different lengths of time to revolve around the Sun? __The planets are at different distances from the Sun.__
__They take different times to revolve around the Sun once.__

Each planet in our solar system **rotates**, or spins, around a line through its center. This imaginary line is called an **axis**. It takes each planet a different length of time to rotate once.

Earth    Uranus

4. Each planet __rotates/spins__ around a line through its center.
5. This imaginary line is called an __axis__.
6. *Rotates* means __spins__.

**39**

## So Far Apart

Mercury · Venus · Earth · Mars · Jupiter · Saturn · Uranus · Neptune

Sizes of planets not to scale

### Planets and Their Average Distances From the Sun

| Mercury | 36 million miles | Mars | 142 million miles | Uranus | 1,781 million miles |
| Venus | 67 million miles | Jupiter | 484 million miles | Neptune | 2,788 million miles |
| Earth | 93 million miles | Saturn | 885 million mile | | |

Use the chart and diagram to answer these questions.

1. What is Neptune's average distance from the Sun? __2,788 million miles__

2. Which planet has an average distance from the Sun of 142 million miles?
   __Mars__

3. Which planet is closest to the Sun—Saturn, Mars, or Neptune?
   __Mars__

4. How much farther from the Sun is Venus than Mercury?
   __31 million miles__

5. How much farther is the fourth planet from the Sun than the third planet
   from the Sun? __49 million miles__

**47**

---

## The Planets' Names

Match each symbol in the puzzle to a clue below. Write the planet's name across or down in capital letters.

(crossword: NEPTUNE, VENUS, MARS, EARTH, URANUS, MERCURY, JUPITER, SATURN)

### Across

♆ Neptune was named after the Roman god of the sea.

♀ Venus was named after the Roman goddess of love and beauty.

♂ Mars was named after the Roman god of war.

♅ Uranus was named after the Greek god of the sky.

### Down

☿ Mercury was named after the Roman messenger of the gods.

♃ Jupiter was named after the Roman king of the gods and ruler of the universe.

♄ Saturn was named after the Roman god of farming.

⊕ Earth was named after the Greek Earth goddess.

**48**

---

## Read My Mind

Pretend you have been contacted by NASA to serve as an astronaut on a secret mission. Because of its secrecy, NASA cannot give you your destination. Instead, you must figure it out using the clues below. After each clue, check the possible answers. The planet with the most clues checked will be your destination.

| Destination Clues | Mercury | Venus | Earth | Mars | Jupiter | Saturn | Uranus | Neptune |
|---|---|---|---|---|---|---|---|---|
| It is part of our solar system. | ✓ | ✓ | ✓ | ✓ | ✓ | ✓ | ✓ | ✓ |
| It is a bright object in the sky. | | ✓ | | ✓ | ✓ | ✓ | | |
| It is less than 2,000,000,000 miles from the Sun. | ✓ | ✓ | ✓ | ✓ | ✓ | ✓ | | |
| It orbits the Sun. | ✓ | ✓ | ✓ | ✓ | ✓ | ✓ | ✓ | ✓ |
| It has less than 15 known satellites. | ✓ | ✓ | ✓ | | | | | ✓ |
| There is weather there. | | ✓ | ✓ | ✓ | ✓ | ✓ | ✓ | |
| It rotates in the opposite direction of Earth. | | ✓ | | | | | | |
| It is the hottest planet. | | ✓ | | | | | | |
| Its years are longer than its days. | ✓ | | ✓ | ✓ | ✓ | ✓ | ✓ | |
| It is called "Earth's twin." | | ✓ | | | | | | |
| It is closest to Earth. | | ✓ | | | | | | |

Secret Mission Destination is ____Venus____
I know this because ___It is the planet with the most check marks.___

**49**

---

## Space Trips

Mr. Ward asked his students this question: *What planet would you most like to visit?*
The children made a graph to show their answers.

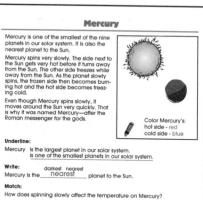

Saturn
Mars
Jupiter

1 2 3 4 5 6 7 8 9

Which planet did the most students choose?

Saturn   (Mars)   Jupiter

Which planet did the fewest students choose?

(Saturn)   Mars   Jupiter

Which planet would you choose? Why? __Answers will vary.__

**50**

---

## Mercury

Mercury is one of the smallest of the nine planets in our solar system. It is also the nearest planet to the Sun.

Mercury spins very slowly. The side next to the Sun gets very hot before it turns away from the Sun. The other side freezes while away from the Sun. As the planet slowly spins, the frozen side then becomes burning hot and the hot side becomes freezing cold.

Even though Mercury spins slowly, it moves around the Sun very quickly. That is why it was named Mercury—after the Roman messenger for the gods.

Color Mercury's:
hot side - red
cold side - blue

**Underline:**
Mercury _is the largest planet in our solar system._
_is one of the smallest planets in our solar system._

**Write:**
Mercury is the __nearest__ planet to the Sun.
(darkest   nearest)

**Match:**
How does spinning slowly affect the temperature on Mercury?

The side next to the Sun — is freezing cold.
The side away from the Sun — is burning hot.

**Circle:**
Mercury moves (quickly) around the Sun.   Mercury spins very (slowly.)
    quietly                                     lightly.

**Check:**
Mercury was named for the ☐ famous Roman speaker.
☑ Roman messenger for the gods.

**55**

---

## Closest to the Sun

Mercury is the planet closest to the Sun. That is why Mercury travels around the Sun faster than any other planet. It takes Mercury 88 days to revolve once around the Sun.
Little was known about Mercury before 1974. Scientists have a hard time studying Mercury with telescopes because of the Sun's great light. In 1974 and 1975, an unmanned spacecraft named Mariner X flew by Mercury three times and sent scientists new information about the planet. The surface of Mercury is much like the Moon's surface. It has high cliffs and deep craters, or holes. Mercury has almost no atmosphere, or gases, surrounding it. Temperatures on the planet range from over 750°F to -300°F! Mercury does not have a moon.

Write each answer in a sentence.

1. Which planet is closest to the Sun? __Mercury is the planet__
   __closest to the Sun.__

2. How long does it take Mercury to revolve around the Sun? __It takes__
   __Mercury 88 days to revolve once around the Sun.__

3. Why do scientists have a hard time studying Mercury with telescopes? ___
   __Scientists have a hard time because of the Sun's great light.__

4. What did Mariner X do? __Mariner X flew by Mercury three times__
   __and sent scientists new information.__

5. Describe Mercury's surface. __It is like the Moon's surface.__
   __It has high cliffs and deep craters.__

**56**

## A Short Year!

You know that Mercury is the planet located closest to the Sun, right? This little planet, less than half the size of Earth, orbits around the Sun quickly because it is so close to that star.

What is a year? Circle your answer.

(A) The time it takes a planet to go around the Sun once.

B  The time it takes for a star to stop shining.

C  The time it takes for a moon to orbit a planet.

*The answer is A!* Mercury's year is the shortest of all the planets—88 Earth days.

A year on Earth is how many days? __365 days__

**Now Try This:** Answers will vary.

1. How old would you be on Mercury if you had been there for 440 days?

    _____

2. Write your age: _____

    How many days would you have to be on Mercury to reach your present age? _____

    _____

**57**

---

## Mercury

Mercury is the closest planet to the Sun. It is about 36 million miles from the Sun. Half the size of Earth, Mercury is just a little larger than our Moon. It circles the Sun very fast. It takes Earth 365 days, or one year, to complete one orbit around the Sun. It takes Mercury only 88 Earth days to orbit the Sun. Mercury spins slowly. It takes Earth 24 hours, or one day, to make one complete turn on its axis. Mercury turns once every 59 Earth days. Because this is close to the length of one Mercury orbit, Mercury has a "day" from one sunrise to the next, of 176 Earth days. Mercury's "day" is twice as long as its year! The surface of Mercury is desertlike, with rocks and giant holes, or craters. Its biggest crater is called *caloris bash.* These craters make Mercury look like our moon. Because of its nearness to the Sun, Mercury is extremely hot — twice as hot as a pizza oven — about 800° F.

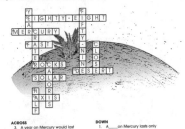

**ACROSS**
3. A year on Mercury would last ___-___ Earth days.
4. The closest planet to the Sun
6. Mercury circles the Sun very___.
8. These are found on Mercury.
10. The surface of Mercury is like a___.
11. Mercury is part of our___system.
13. Mercury spins on its___slowly

**DOWN**
1. A___on Mercury lasts only 88 Earth days.
2. Mercury turns once every__days.
5. Giant holes on Mercury
7. Mercury is very hot because it is so___to the Sun.
9. First word in name of Mercury's largest crater
12. Size of Mercury in comparison with the Earth

**59**

---

## More About Mercury

Do you think you could ever live on Mercury? The side facing the Sun is over 800 degrees! The side away from the Sun is almost -305 degrees!

If you want to know what Mercury looks like, just think of the Moon. Mercury has almost no atmosphere or air mass surrounding it. Without an atmosphere, if you stood on the planet and looked up, the sky would seem black. The Sun looks 2 ½ times larger from Mercury than Earth.

**Mercury Word Search**
Circle the words you find.

**Word Bank**
meteorite
Mercury
bang
punching
bag
planet
hole
crater
hits
surface
rock
moon
land
air
atmosphere
stop

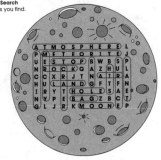

**60**

---

## Venus

Venus is the planet nearest to Earth. Because it is the easiest planet to see in the sky, it has been called the Morning Star and Evening Star. The Romans named Venus after their goddess of love and beauty. Venus is sometimes called "Earth's twin."

Venus is covered with thick clouds. The Sun's heat is trapped by the clouds. The temperature on Venus is nearly 900°F!

Space probes have been sent to study Venus. They have reported information to scientists. But they can only last a few hours on Venus because of the high temperature.

Venus turns in the opposite direction from Earth. So, on Venus, the Sun rises in the west and sets in the east!

West | East

Draw the Sun rising on Venus.

**Unscramble and Circle:**

__Venus__ is the __friendliest__ (nearest) planet to Earth.
e s V u n
2 5 1 4 3

**Check:**
It is called the ☐ Evening Sun
☑ Morning Star    because it is so easy to see.
☑ Evening Star

**Circle:**
The Romans named Venus for their:

(goddess of love and beauty)    god of light    goddess of truth

**Circle Yes or No:**

Half of Venus is frozen with ice and snow.    Yes  (No)
Space probes have reported information from Venus.    (Yes)  No
On Venus, the Sun rises in the east and sets in the west.    Yes  (No)

**63**

---

## Earth's Twin

Use the words in the Word Bank to complete the story.

**Word Bank**

| light | against | lightning | size |
|---|---|---|---|
| closest | higher | atmosphere | melt |

Venus has been called Earth's twin because it is about the same __size__ as Earth. Venus is the second planet from the Sun and is the planet __closest__ to Earth. Venus was also the first planet to be studied by spacecraft. Venus has no moon.

Venus has an interesting __atmosphere__, or blanket of gases around it. It reflects, or bounces off, so much of the Sun's __light__ that Venus is easier to see than any other planet. The atmosphere also lets some sunlight in and traps heat __against__ the planet's surface. Therefore, temperatures on Venus are high enough to __melt__ some metals. Clouds move at high speeds in Venus's atmosphere, and bolts of __lightning__ streak across the sky.

Venus has volcanoes on its surface and a mountain __higher__ than the highest on Earth. There is no liquid water on Venus. Earth's plants and animals could not live on Venus.

**64**

---

## Sparkling Venus

Beautiful Venus is the second planet from the Sun. Why do you think it is brighter than any other planet? Circle the best answer.

A. Its surface is almost as hot as the Sun.

B. Its surface is covered with millions of diamonds.

C. Its thick clouds reflect the Sun's light.

Venus is covered by very thick clouds, so C is correct. Sometimes we can see Venus as a bright, sparkling, starlike object in the morning or the evening sky.

**Something's Wrong!**
There is something wrong with these facts about Venus. Circle the wrong word in each sentence. Write the correct word on the line.

1. Venus is the second planet from the (Earth.) __Sun__

2. Venus looks (dull) in the sky. __bright__

3. Venus has a (thin) cloud cover. __thick__

4. At night, (Mercury) sparkles in the sky. __Venus__

**65**

## Venus

Venus is the second planet away from the Sun in our solar system. With a diameter of 7,521 miles, it is almost as large as Earth. The diameter of the Earth is 7,927 miles. Venus, the brightest planet seen from Earth, was named after the Roman goddess of love and beauty. It is covered with clouds that reflect the Sun's light. After Earth's moon, Venus is the second brightest light in the night sky. Look for Venus in the western evening sky just after sunset or the eastern morning sky just before sunrise. Some people call Venus the evening star when it is in the evening sky because it looks like a very bright star. Venus is a rocky desert with high mountains and valleys. Maxwell Mountain on Venus is seven miles high. We could not survive on Venus without lots of protection because it is so hot. It takes Venus 225 Earth days to circle the Sun. It turns on its axis slowly. A day on Venus from one sunrise to the next lasts 117 Earth days.

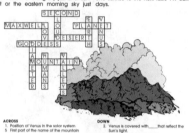

**ACROSS**
1. Position of Venus in the solar system
5. First part of the name of the mountain on Venus
7. Venus is a _____.
8. Venus is a rocky _____.
9. Venus was named after the Roman _____ of love.
13. Maxwell is one.

**DOWN**
2. Venus is covered with_____ that reflect the Sun's light.
3. Venus is almost as large as_____.
4. Second planet in our solar system
6. Venus is the name of the Roman goddess of _____ and beauty.
10. The _____ of Venus is 7,625 miles.
11. It is too hot on Venus for_____.
12. There are mountains and_____.

**66**

---

## Hot Stuff!

Venus is not only beautiful, but it is also the hottest planet in our solar system. Space probes like Mariner 2 and the Russian Veneras probes discovered that the thick clouds that surround Venus are not like the clouds we have on Earth. They are made of carbon dioxide gas and hold in the Sun's heat.

Temperatures on Venus reach 900 degrees Fahrenheit. Think how hot you feel when it's only 90 degrees outside!

The sky of Venus seems to be a reddish-orange color. Violent lightening and terrible winds blow across the planet.

Space explorers landing on this planet would have a difficult time. Besides the heat and the poisonous atmosphere, the air pressure on Venus is about 100 times greater than on Earth. That means it would be much harder to move around on Venus. It would be like trying to walk underwater.

The carbon dioxide gas makes the air very dense. The clouds are filled with sulfuric acid droplets. The atmosphere around Venus is thick and deadly.

**Feel the Heat**
1. Get an empty glass jar with a lid. Screw the lid on and set the jar in the sunlight for two hours.
2. Carefully unscrew the jar—it's hot!
3. Put your hand inside the jar. Do you feel the heat?
4. What kept the heat inside? _the lid_
5. The lid kept the heat inside like Venus's clouds hold in the Sun's warmth causing very high temperatures.

**Circle the different conditions that space travelers might face on Venus.**
swampy areas
(active volcanoes)
hail storms
90° temperatures
black ice
(thick dense air)
(dangerous lightening)
storms
snowstorms
(900° temperatures)
cool rain showers
muddy roads
(terrible winds)

**67**

---

## Our Planet Earth

Earth is the planet where we live. Earth has land and water. It gets light and heat from the Sun. Earth has one moon. Earth is the only planet that we know has life. Many people think there is life on other planets. Do you think there is life on other planets?

**Unscramble:**
Earth is the _____ _planet_
where we live. l e t p n a

**Check** the sentences about the Earth that are true.

☑ I have land and water.
☑ I get light and heat from the Sun.
☐ I have five moons.
☑ I have one moon.
☑ I am a planet.

**Circle:** Earth is the only planet that we know has ~~stars.~~ (life.)

**Color:** Draw one yellow moon in the picture.

**Draw** and color a picture of the Earth.

**71**

---

## The Earth

Although you can't tell from where you are, the Earth is round, like an orange. You can see this by looking at pictures of Earth taken from space.

We cannot feel it, but the Earth moves around the Sun. There are eight big, round planets that all move around the Sun.

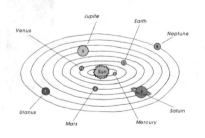

Look at the nine planets in the picture.

Which planet is closest to the Sun? _Mercury is the planet closest to the Sun._

Which planet is farthest from the Sun? _Neptune is the planet farthest from the Sun._

**72**

---

## Earth

Earth is about 93 million miles from the Sun. Earth is the only planet in the solar system that has plants, animals, and human beings living on it. Earth is a giant ball of rock and metal about 8,000 miles across. Its crust is made of rock. On top of the Earth's crust are oceans and land. Oceans store heat from the Sun and help keep Earth from becoming too hot or too cold for human life. Earth orbits around the Sun in about 365 days, or one year. As Earth orbits the Sun, it also spins on its axis. One complete spin takes 24 hours, or one day. As it spins on its axis, we experience day and night. When our side of the Earth is turned toward the Sun, the Sun lights up our sky and we experience day. When our side of the Earth is turned away from the Sun, we cannot see its light and we experience night. When our part of the Earth is tipped toward the Sun, the Sun is high in the sky, the days are long and the nights are short, giving us warm summer weather. When our part of the Earth is tipped away from the Sun, the Sun is low in the sky, the days are short and the nights are long, giving us cold winter weather.

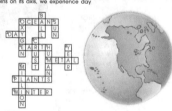

**ACROSS**
2. They help keep the Earth cool.
4. It is made up of 24 hours.
6. The planet we live on
9. Earth is a giant ball of rock and_____.
11. They grow on Earth.
12. Opposite of summer

**DOWN**
1. Earth is a giant_____.
2. A colorless, odorless gas found on Earth
3. Earth orbits this star.
5. On top of the Earth's_____ are oceans and land.
7. They live on Earth.
8. It is made up of 365 days.
10. Earth is 93_____ miles from the Sun.

**73**

---

## Spinning Top

Whir-r-r-ling! Matt's top is spinning very fast. Just like Matt's top, the Earth is also spinning.

The Earth spins about an imaginary line that is drawn from the North **Pole** to the South Pole through the center of the Earth. This line is called Earth's **axis**. Instead of using the word "spin," though, we say that the Earth **rotates** on its axis.

The Earth rotates **one** time every 24 hours. The part of the Earth facing the Sun experiences **day**. The side that is away from the Sun's light experiences **night**.

Draw a line from each picture of Matt to the correct day or night picture of the Earth.

**Directions:**
Use the highlighted words above to solve the puzzle.
1. The part of the Earth not facing the Sun experiences _____.
2. Earth's axis goes from the North to the South _____.
3. The Earth spins, or _____.
4. Number of times the Earth rotates in 24 hours.
5. Imaginary line on which the Earth rotates.

**74**

## Our Rotating Planet

Try the experiments below to discover firsthand how our planet rotates and revolves around the Sun.

**Around the Axis**
1. Use a large thread spool for the planet.
2. Use a thin round stick for the axis. Sometimes a pencil will work if the hole in the spool is big enough.
3. With a pencil or marker, put a dot on the top of the spool near the edge.
4. Put the stick through the hole in the spool so the spool will spin.
5. Hold the bottom of the stick with one hand so the spool won't fall off.
6. Use your other hand to spin or rotate the spool.
7. Rotate the spool so the dot goes around the stick or axis once. This is called one rotation. It didn't take very long to rotate your planet once, did it?

It takes 24 hours for Earth to rotate once. We call this amount of time a day. Other planets take different amounts of time to rotate on their axis.

While Earth is spinning, it is also revolving or moving around the Sun. We usually say that it takes 365 days for the Earth to orbit the Sun once. Remember, it really takes 365 and $\frac{1}{4}$ days, but to make it easier we say a year is just 365 days.

**Once Around the Sun**
1. Put a chair in the middle of the room. Pretend it's the Sun.
2. Start spinning your planet around its axis. At the same time, begin orbiting or walking in a circle around the Sun. Be sure to keep spinning your planet.
3. Stop at the place you started. You have completed one revolution of the Sun.
4. Do this one foot away from the Sun. Then move four feet away from the Sun.

Which orbit took more time to go around the Sun?
The orbit four feet away from the Sun should take more time.

Did your planet rotate more times with the longer orbit?
Yes, the planet should rotate more times with a longer orbit.

**75**

## A Day's Work

It takes 24 hours, or one full day, for the Earth to rotate completely.

Circle the picture of the Earth that belongs with the last Sun. Color the suns yellow.

**76**

## A Big Ball

Earth is like a big ball.

Most of the Earth is covered by
water ~~~~~ The rest of the Earth is
land ▒▒▒

Color the ~~~~~ blue.
Color the ▒▒▒ green

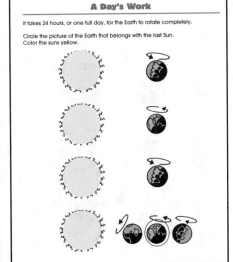

Why do you think the Earth is called the water planet?
The Earth is called the water planet because most (nearly three-fourths) of the Earth's surface is covered by water.

**77**

## The Earth's Layers

Now you know that oceans and continents cover the Earth. But what's inside the Earth?

The Earth has three layers — the crust, the mantle, and the core. Unscramble the words below to discover where each layer is located. Write the new words on the lines.

eorc
core

tanmle
mantle

struc
crust

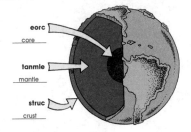

**78**

## What's Inside?

The **core** of the Earth is its hardest and hottest part. Around the core lies a thick layer, called the **mantle**, which is hot and rocky. The outside layer of the Earth is the **crust**. This is where the oceans and the continents are. People, plants, and animals live on the Earth's crust.

Color the rocky, hot part of the Earth red. What is it called?
It is called the mantle and should be colored red.

Find the layer that is hot and hard. Color it black. What is it called?
It is called the core and should be colored black.

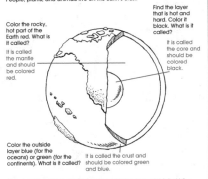

Color the outside layer blue (for the oceans) or green (for the continents). What is it called?
It is called the crust and should be colored green and blue.

There is nothing alive below the Earth's crust. Why do you think that is?
Sample answer: Nothing lives below the Earth's crust because it is too hot and there is no air.

**79**

## Atmosphere

The air that surrounds the Earth is called Earth's **atmosphere**. The atmosphere is made up of gases that contain tight bundles of atoms called **molecules**. Gravity holds Earth's atmosphere close to the surface of Earth. Near the surface of Earth the atoms are tightly packed together. When the atoms are packed close together, the atmosphere is said to be dense. Feel the air around you. It has high density. On top of a high mountain, the air density is lower because atoms in the gases are not tightly packed. Most airplanes cannot fly more than 20 miles above the Earth because the density of the air is too low.

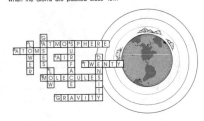

**ACROSS**
3. The air that surrounds Earth
5. The atmosphere is made up of gases that contain tight bundles of ____ called molecules.
6. It is called the atmosphere
8. Most airplanes can't fly higher than ____ miles up in the sky.
10. The gases in the atmosphere are made of bundles of atoms called ____.

**DOWN**
1. What the atmosphere is made of
2. On the top of a high mountain the air density is ____
4. Earth's atmosphere is held closely to Earth's ____ by gravity.
7. Measurement of the atmosphere
9. Opposite of high

11. It holds Earth's atmosphere close to the surface of Earth.

**80**

## The Earth's Four Seasons

1. Write the season words from the Word Bank under the correct boxes below.
2. Color the clothes for autumn blue.
3. Color the clothes for winter red.
4. Color the clothes for spring green.
5. Color the clothes for summer yellow.

**Word Bank**

| Spring | Summer |
|--------|--------|
| Autumn | Winter |

Winter    Spring

Summer    Autumn

**82**

## Day or Night?

Pretend you live on the continent or continents in each picture. Would it be day or night there? Circle the picture to the right that shows what it would be like.

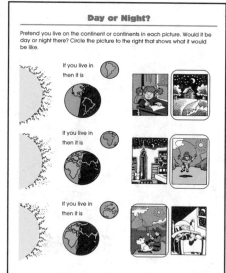

If you live in ___ then it is ___

If you live in ___ then it is ___

If you live in ___ then it is ___

**84**

## LO-O-O-NG Trip

What is the longest trip you have ever taken? Was it 100 miles? 500 miles? Maybe it was more than 1,000 miles. You probably didn't know it, but last year you traveled 620 million miles.

The Earth travels in a path around the Sun called its **orbit**. Earth's orbit is almost 620 million miles. It takes 1 year, or 365 days, for the Earth to orbit or **revolve** around the Sun.

Earth's orbit is not a perfect circle. It is a special shape called an **ellipse**.

1. How long does it take for the Earth to revolve around the Sun? __365 days or 1 year__

2. How many times has the Earth revolved around the Sun since you were born? __Answer will vary.__

3. How many miles has the Earth traveled in orbit since you were born? __multiply child's age by 620 million miles.__

4. Draw an **X** on Earth's orbit to show where it will be in six months.
   See picture above.

**Experiment:**

You can draw an ellipse. Place two straight pins about 3 inches apart in a piece of cardboard. Tie the ends of a 10-inch piece of string to the pins. Place your pencil inside the string. Keeping the string tight, draw an ellipse.

Make four different ellipses by changing the length of the string and the distance between the pins. How do the ellipses change?

**86**

## Model Earth

Imagine you are flying around in space. You look down and see a big round ball. It is the Earth.

green

blue

A model of the Earth is called a **globe**. It is a round map that shows land and water. It uses colors to show which is the land and which is the water.

Unscramble the letters below to find out the colors that are used on the globe.

Land is __green__ . e r g e n

Water is __blue__ . l u e b

**Colo**r the land on the globe green.
**Colo**r the water on the globe blue.

**88**

## It's a Round World

The picture of the globe on page 89 shows both halves of the Earth. It shows the large pieces of land called **continent**s. There are seven continents. Find them on the globe.

**Directions:** Write the names of the seven continents.

1. North America
2. South America
3. Europe
4. Africa
5. Asia
6. Australia
7. Antarctica

There are four bodies of water called **oceans**. Find the oceans on the globe. Write the names below.

1. Atlantic
2. Pacific
3. Indian
4. Arctic

**90**

## A Global Guide

Use the globe on page 89. Read the clues below. Write the answers on the lines. Then, use the numbered letters to solve the riddle at the bottom of the page.

1. This direction points up.  n o r t h
2. This direction points down.  s o u t h
3. This direction points right.  e a s t
4. This direction points left.  w e s t
5. This ocean is west of North America.  P a c i f i c  O c e a n
6. This ocean is south of Asia.  I n d i a n  O c e a n
7. This ocean is east of South America.  A t l a n t i c  O c e a n

Riddle: What does a globe do?  It spins us "around" our planet.

**91**

# ANSWER KEY

## Our Home Planet

Use the words from the Word Bank to complete the story.

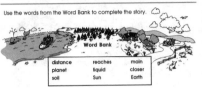

**Word Bank**

| distance | reaches | main |
| planet | liquid | closer |
| soil | Sun | Earth |

The third planet from the __Sun__ is our home planet Earth. Earth has something no other __planet__ is known to have—living things.

Earth is at the right __distance__ from the Sun to have the liquid water necessary to support life. Mercury and Venus are too hot because they are __closer__ to the Sun. The other planets are too far from the Sun to have __liquid__ water. Not much heat or light __reaches__ them, so the water would be in the form of ice.

Earth has a lot of water. Most living things need water. Water helps to control the Earth's weather and climate. Water also breaks rock into __soil__ which plants need to grow.

Earth is surrounded by a blanket of air called the atmosphere. Oxygen is one of the __main__ gases in the atmosphere. Most animals breathe oxygen.

__Earth__ is a special planet!

**92**

## Why Can't We Fall off the Earth?

Everything is held on the Earth by a force called **gravity**. Gravity causes things to fall down toward the center of the Earth. All objects, including planets, stars, and moons, are made up of stuff called matter. The more matter something has in it for its size, the stronger its gravity is. Some objects, like the Sun, have lots of matter. The Sun's gravity is much stronger than the Earth's. The Moon's gravity is weaker than the Earth's. You would weigh a lot less on the Moon than you do on Earth!

1. What brings a rocket ship back down to Earth?
   __Gravity__

2. Why is it so difficult to walk up a very steep hill? __Because gravity__ __keeps trying to pull us down.__

3. Why is it so easy to go downhill? __Because gravity causes us to move__ __down.__

4. Why is the Sun's gravity stronger than the Earth's gravity? __Because the__ __Sun is made up of more matter__ __than the Earth__

5. Would things weigh more or less on the Sun than on the Earth? __More, because the Sun has more__ __matter and stronger gravity.__

6. Can smaller objects have strong gravity? __Yes, sometimes__ __even smaller objects (like some__ __kinds of stars) can be made up of__ __lots and lots of matter squeezed__ __together into a small space__

**95**

## Gravity

Have you ever wondered why the Earth orbits the Sun and why it doesn't fly off into space? A force called gravity keeps Earth from flying off into space. Everything in the universe has gravity. Every galaxy, every star, every planet and moon, every building, every tree, every person, every bug, every atom has gravity. The gravity of a thing pulls on every other thing in the universe.

Gravity pulls much harder on nearby things than on faraway things, but even the tiniest flower tugs on the farthest galaxy. The more massive the object, the harder it pulls at other things. Since the Sun is the greatest mass in our solar system, it has the strongest pull. The Sun's gravitational pull on Earth and other planets keeps them from flying off into space.

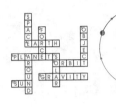

**ACROSS**
4. The planet we live on
5. There are nine ___ in our solar system.
8. To move around another planet
9. A force of nature that keeps everything from flying off into space
10. Earth orbits the ___.

**DOWN**
1. The area all around Earth, the planets, galaxies, and stars
2. Gravity is a ___ that keeps Earth orbiting the Sun.
3. The more massive the ___ the harder it pulls at other things.
6. Earth moves ___ the Sun.
7. Everything in the ___ system has gravity.

**97**

## Fast Fall

**One Step Further:**
Try the experiment with a pencil and a flat piece of paper. Now crumble up the paper and try it again. Do the two objects hit the floor at the same time in both cases? Why or why not? The force of gravity on the pencil and the __paper is equal. Air molecules, or particles, bump into falling objects and__ __slow them down. The air slows down the light, flat piece of paper more than__ __it does the pencil. When the paper is crumbled into__ a ball, the air doesn't slow it down as much.
**Questions:**
1. Why do objects fall down instead of up?
   __Objects fall down because they're pulled to__ __Earth by gravity.__

2. If you wanted to travel to Mars, how would you overcome Earth's gravity?
   __You would need a very fast spaceship to__ __overcome Earth's gravity.__

3. Gravity is stronger on bigger planets. Pluto is the smallest planet in our solar system. Can you name a planet that has stronger gravity than Pluto?     Answers will vary.
   __All the other planets in the solar system have stronger gravity.__

4. Earth is larger than the Moon. Could you jump higher on the Moon or on Earth? Explain your answer.
   __You could jump higher on the Moon. The Moon is smaller than Earth, so__ __gravity is weaker there. The Moon wouldn't "pull" on you as hard as Earth__ __does, so you could jump higher.__

5. The gravity of a black hole is so strong that nothing can escape it, not even light. What do you think happens to things that are pulled into a black hole?
   __Answers will vary. Scientists guess that objects pulled into a black hole__ __are crushed into extremely fine, very heavy specks.__

**99**

## A Riddle Review

Fill in the blanks below to find out how much you have learned about your home planet, Earth!

1. Three-fourths of the Earth is covered by __w a t e r__.

2. Earth is the only planet that can support __l i f e__.

3. The Earth has one __m o o n__.

4. 365 days make up one Earth __y e a r__.

5. It takes 24 hours for the Earth to rotate the __S u n__.

6. The Earth has four __s e a s o n s__.

7. This keeps us from falling off the Earth __g r a v i t y__.

**100**

## The Red Planet

Mars, the fourth planet from the Sun, is half the size of Earth. Mars has two moons. It has been called the Red Planet because of its red color. Parts of this planet's surface are covered with sand dunes and dry, reddish deserts. Other areas look like dried up riverbeds. Some scientists believe water may once have flowed on Mars. Mars also has two polar caps made up of frozen water and dry ice. Pink, blue, and white clouds move through the Red Planet's sky.

For a long time, some people thought there might be life on Mars. When two U.S. spacecraft landed on the planet in 1976, they sent back photographs of Mars and did experiments to find out if life exists there. Scientists now believe that Mars does not have plant or animal life like that on Earth.

Finish each sentence below with details from the story.

1. Mars is the __fourth__ planet from the Sun, and it has __two__ moons.

2. Mars is nicknamed the __Red Planet__.

3. Two U.S. spacecraft landed on Mars in __1976__, sent back photographs, and did __experiments__.

4. Mars has dry, reddish __deserts__ and what looks like dried up __riverbeds__.

5. Mars has two __polar caps__ made of frozen water and dry ice.

**105**

## Mars (113)

Mars is a planet half the size of Earth. In some ways, Mars resembles Earth. It has ice caps at its North and South Poles, and some of its surface was shaped long ago by running water and streams. A day on Mars is also very different from Earth. It takes Mars 687 Earth days to circle the Sun. The air on Mars is too thin for human beings to breathe. The rivers that once crossed Mars have dried up, leaving a planet that is covered with deserts and ice caps. During the day, the temperature can be comfortable at 72 degrees Fahrenheit, but at night, it can drop to about 200 degrees below zero! Mars looks red to us because its surface soil is rich in minerals that are like rust. The sky around Mars is pink from the rusty dust that floats in the atmosphere. There are huge wind storms on Mars. Mars has two moons, Phobos and Deimos. It also has huge mountains and deep canyons. Mons Olympus, a giant volcano, is three times higher than Mt. Everest. Robots from the Viking spaceship tested the air and soil of Mars for signs of life. These studies found no trace of life as we know it.

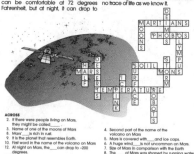

**ACROSS**
2. If there were people living on Mars, they might be called _____.
5. Name of one of the moons of Mars
8. Mars _____ is rich in rust.
9. It is the planet that resembles Earth.
10. First word in the name of the volcano on Mars
12. At night on Mars, the _____ can drop to -200 degrees.

**DOWN**
1. The name of one of the moons that orbits Mars
2. Phobos and Deimos are _____ of Mars.
4. Second part of the name of the volcano on Mars
5. Mars is covered with _____ and ice caps.
6. A huge wind _____ is not uncommon on Mars.
7. Size of Mars in comparison with the Earth
11. The _____ of Mars was shaped by running water.
12. Type of caps on Mars
13. Color of sky around Mars
14. They tested the air and soil of Mars.

## Marvelous Mars (114)

Can you find the hidden words about Mars in the puzzle below? Use the Word Bank to help you, and circle the words as you find them.

**Word Bank**

| red | dusty | craters | seasons |
| windy | lifeless | volcanoes | stable temperature |
| dry | mountainous | polar ice caps | frozen |

## Jupiter (117)

Jupiter is the largest planet in our solar system. It has thirty-nine moons. Jupiter is the second-brightest planet—only Venus is brighter.

Jupiter is bigger and heavier than all of the other planets together. It is covered with thick clouds. Many loose rocks and dust particles form a single, thin, flat ring around Jupiter.

One of the most fascinating things about Jupiter is its Great Red Spot. The Great Red Spot of Jupiter is a huge storm in the atmosphere. It looks like a red ball. This giant storm is larger than Earth! Every six days it goes completely around Jupiter.

**Unscramble the words below:**

1. Jupiter is the _____largest_____ planet in our solar system.
   etsirga
2. Jupiter has _____thirty-nine_____ moons.
   htriyt-ienn
3. Jupiter is covered with thick _____clouds_____.
   dsoclu
4. Loose rocks and dust form a _____ring_____ around Jupiter.
   girn
5. The Great Red _____Spot_____ of Jupiter is a huge storm.
   tSop

**Circle and Write:**
Jupiter is the second (largest/brightest) planet.

Jupiter is _____bigger_____ and _____lighter_____ than all of the planets together.
(bigger/redder)  (lighter/heavier)

## The Great Red Spot (118)

Jupiter has a famous "beauty mark" called the Great Red Spot, or GRS for short. The GRS is a football-shaped globe of gases, first seen in 1664.

What year is it now? _____

How many years ago was the GRS first discovered? _____
subtract 1664 from the current year.

The United States spacecraft Pioneer 10 and Pioneer 11 flew past Jupiter in 1973 and 1974. They took pictures of the planet and its moons. They recorded much new information. Scientists learned that the GRS is a huge storm, like a hurricane, big enough to hold two Earth-sized planets. Winds blow at hundreds of miles per hour, causing swirling gases.

Scientists also discovered that Jupiter had a thin, flat ring of particles orbiting it just like Saturn and Uranus.

**Jupiter—The True Story**

1. Read the facts about Jupiter. Some are true, others are false.
2. Draw a line to connect the true facts to the planet Jupiter.

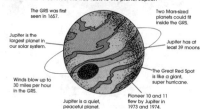

The GRS was first seen in 1657.

Jupiter is the largest planet in our solar system.

Winds blow up to 30 miles per hour in the GRS.

Jupiter is a quiet, peaceful planet.

Two Mars-sized planets could fit inside the GRS.

Jupiter has at least 39 moons.

The Great Red Spot is like a giant, super hurricane.

Pioneer 10 and 11 flew by Jupiter in 1973 and 1974.

## The Giant Planet's Moons (119)

Jupiter has many more moons than Mars and Earth! At least 39 moons have been discovered orbiting Jupiter.

How do we decide if something is a moon? Scientists in the United States have a rule: A spacecraft must record the potential moon moving around the planet two separate times before it is counted as a moon. As spacecraft get closer to distant planets, we learn more about them and new moons continue to be discovered.

The surfaces of Jupiter's four largest moons are very different from other moons in our solar system.

**Europa** is bright and smooth like a billiard ball. Scientists think it is covered with a frozen ocean of ice. There are dark streaks and lines all over the surface. It is about the size of our moon.

The moon, **Io**, is the only moon with active volcanoes. Volcanic lava shoots onto its surface. It is a very dry moon with high mountains and cliffs. It is bright orange in color.

**Callisto** is covered with craters. It has more craters than anything else in the solar system—even Mercury. Callisto has been called a ball of frozen slush.

**Ganymede** is the largest of Jupiter's moons. It is bigger than Mercury. It is half ice and half rock. Scientists discovered that the deep grooves in the moon were really mountains, valleys, and craters.

**Jupiter's Moon Facts**
Complete the following sentences.
1. Jupiter has at least _____thirty-nine_____ moons.
2. _____Volcanic lava_____ shoots onto the surface of Io.
3. The largest of Jupiter's moon is _____Ganymede_____.
4. Callisto is covered with _____craters_____.
5. Ganymede's dark grooves are really mountains, valleys, and craters.
6. _____Europa_____, the brightest moon, is covered with ice.

## Jumbo Jupiter (120)

Jupiter is the largest of the nine planets. It is more than 11 times larger than Earth. Jupiter is the fifth planet from the Sun, and it travels once around the Sun every 12 years. This jumbo planet rotates in just ten hours—faster than any other planet! Thick clouds surround Jupiter. Most scientists believe that the belts of color in Jupiter's atmosphere are caused by different gases. The planet is a giant ball of liquids and gases with, perhaps, a small rocky core. Its famous Great Red Spot is a huge storm.

Lightning streaks across Jupiter's sky. Jupiter has a thin dust ring around its middle and 39 know moons.

**Jupiter's Great Red Spot**

Write **true** or **false**.

_false_ 1. Jupiter is the smallest planet in our solar system.
_false_ 2. Earth is larger than Jupiter.
_true_ 3. It takes 12 years for Jupiter to travel around the Sun.
_true_ 4. Jupiter rotates faster than any other planet.
_true_ 5. Jupiter's Great Red Spot is a huge storm of swirling gases.
_false_ 6. Jupiter has a thick ice ring around its middle.
_true_ 7. Jupiter has more than ten moons.
_false_ 8. Jupiter is the sixth planet from the Sun.

## Jupiter

Jupiter is the largest planet and the fifth out from the Sun. Named after the king of the Roman gods, Jupiter is easy to see in the night sky. It shines almost as brightly as Venus does. It is 1,300 times the volume of Earth. Jupiter takes about twelve Earth years to circle the Sun. It spins so rapidly on its axis that its day is only about ten hours long. There is no solid ground on Jupiter. It is a giant ball of liquid and gas. It is made of the same elements as the Sun. Jupiter is called a gas giant because it is a giant planet made mostly of hydro- gen and helium rather than rock and metal like the Earth. Storms and swirling clouds continually move through Jupiter's atmosphere that scientists call the Great Red Spot, big enough to hold two Earth's. They have discovered 39 moons orbiting around Jupiter and there are probably lots more. The moon Io has active volca- noes. The moon Ganymede is the largest moon in the solar system, even larger than Pluto and Mercury. There is also a ring around Jupiter made of dust.

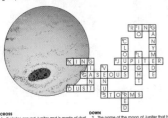

**ACROSS**
1. It circles around Jupiter and is made of dust.
2. Jupiter was named after the ___ of the Roman gods.
8. The largest planet and fifth out from the Sun
10. Jupiter is called a "gas giant" because of its ___ surface.
11. What Jupiter's ring is made of
12. Jupiter's atmosphere is very violent and full of ___.

**DOWN**
2. The name of the moon of Jupiter that has an active volcano
4. Name of the largest moon in the solar system
5. Storms and swirling ___ move through Jupiter's atmosphere.
6. The ___ from Jupiter shines brightly in the night.
7. Jupiter is often called a gas ___.
9. A planet that shines brighter than Jupiter
13. The place on Jupiter that never seems to change is called the Great ___ Spot.

121

## The Large Planets

Jupiter is about 88,733 miles at its equator. Named after the king of the Roman gods, it is the fifth-clos- est planet to the Sun at about 483,600,000 miles away. Jupiter travels around the Sun in an oval- shaped, elliptical, orbit. Jupiter also spins faster than any other planet and makes a complete rota- tion in about 9 hours and 55 minutes.

The surface of Jupiter cannot be seen from Earth because of the layers of dense clouds surrounding it. Jupiter has no solid surface but is made of liquid and gases that are held together by gravity.

One characteristic unique to Jupiter is the Great Red Spot that is about 25,000 miles long and about 20,000 miles wide. Astronomers believe the spot to be a swirling, hurricane- like mass of gas.

Saturn, the second-largest planet, is well known for the seven thin, flat rings encircling it. Its diameter is about 74,898 miles at the equator. It was named for the Roman god. Saturn is the sixth planet closest to the Sun and is about 888,200,000 miles away from it. Like Jupiter, Saturn also travels around the Sun in an elliptical orbit, and it takes the planet about 10 hours and 39 min- utes to make one rotation.

Scientists believe Saturn is a giant ball of gas that also has no solid surface. They believe it also may have an inner core of rocky material, like Jupiter. Whereas Saturn claims 30 satellites, Jupiter has 39 known satellites.

Fill in the chart below to compare Jupiter and Saturn. Make two of your own categories.

| Categories | Jupiter | Saturn |
|---|---|---|
| 1. diameter | 88,836 miles | 74,898 miles |
| 2. origin of name | Roman mythology | Roman mythology |
| 3. distance from Sun | 483,600,000 miles | 888,200,000 miles |
| 4. rotation | 9 hrs. 55 minutes | 10 hrs. 39 minutes |
| 5. surface | no solid surface | no solid surface |
| 6. unique characteristics | Answers will vary | Answers will vary |
| 7. | | |
| 8. | | |

122

## Saturn

Saturn is probably most famous for its rings. These rings are made of billions of tiny pieces of ice and dust. Although these rings are very wide, they are very thin. If you look at the rings from the side, they are almost too thin to be seen.

Saturn is the second-largest planet in our solar system. It is so big that 758 Earths could fit inside it!

Saturn is covered by clouds. Strong, fast winds move the clouds quickly across the planet.

Saturn has 30 moons! Its largest moon is called Titan.

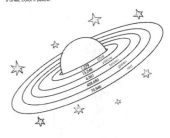
Positions will vary.
Draw 30 moons around Saturn!

**Circle:**
Saturn is most famous for its ___ spots.  (rings).

**Write:**
Saturn's rings are made of __ice__ and __dust__.
mud ice        dust moons

**Check:**
Saturn's rings are ☐ red, yellow, and purple.
☑ wide, but thin.

**Underline:**
Saturn...  is the second-largest planet in our solar system.
is big enough to hold 758 Earths inside it.
is farther from the Sun than any other planet.
is covered by fast, strong winds.
has 30 moons.

**Unscramble:**
Saturn's largest moon is called ___Titan___.
i T a n t

125

## Stunning Saturn

Saturn is the sixth planet from the Sun and is best known for the beautiful rings around its middle. The rings are thin and flat and made of pieces of rock and ice. They stretch more than 100,000 miles across!

Some scientists believe the rings are made of particles left over from the time when Saturn first became a planet. Others believe the rings are made of pieces of a moon that was torn apart when it came too close to Saturn.

Saturn is the second largest planet. Since Saturn is more than nine times farther than Earth is from the Sun, it is much colder than Earth. The planet is a giant ball of spinning gases. Saturn has at least 30 moons.

**Write each answer in a sentence.**

1. For what is Saturn best known? _Saturn is best known for the beautiful rings around its middle._

2. What is one idea scientists have about how Saturn's rings were made? _Answers vary._

3. How does Saturn compare in size with the other planets? _Saturn is the second largest planet._

4. Why is Saturn colder than Earth? _Saturn is more than nine times farther than Earth is from the Sun._

5. How many moons does Saturn have? _Saturn has at least 30 moons._

126

## Moons, Moons, And More Moons!

Saturn has many, many, many moons! Scientists know that more than 30 moons orbit Saturn. They do not know the exact number. They are still studying information sent back to Earth from the Pioneer and Voyager spacecraft. Remember the sci- entists' rule: A moon must be seen two dif- ferent times orbiting a planet before it can be called a moon. Perhaps even more moons will be found orbiting Saturn!

One moon is named Titan. The word titan means "very big," and that's the perfect name for Saturn's biggest moon. Titan is larger than the planet Mercury, but smaller than Ganymede, Jupiter's moon. Scientists believe that Titan is the only moon in the solar system with an atmosphere. The surface may have oceans and lakes of methane ice. Other areas are filled with methane ice. The nitrogen in the atmosphere gives the sky a red-orange color.

**Watch Out—Moons Ahead!**
You are in a spacecraft visiting all of Saturn's moons.
Use a pencil or a crayon to draw a path through the moon maze.

129

## Saturn's Rings

Use the code to color Saturn's rings.

If the number has:
7 ten thousands, color it red.
1 thousand, color it blue.
4 hundred thousands, color it green.
6 tens, color it brown.
8 ones, color it yellow.

130

## Saturn (131)

Saturn, the sixth planet out from the Sun, is often called the "ringed planet" because it has bright rings around it. Saturn is a gas giant planet like Jupiter. It's 758 times the volume of Earth. It takes Saturn nearly 30 Earth years to circle the Sun, but only ten hours and fourteen minutes to turn once on its axis. The center of Saturn is very hot, and the tops of the clouds are very cold. The rings around Saturn look solid, but they actually are not. They are made of billions and billions of pieces of ice and rock. The ring particles orbit Saturn like tiny moons. Saturn also has 30 moons. Its largest moon is called Titan. Titan has an atmosphere, but it is poisonous to human beings.

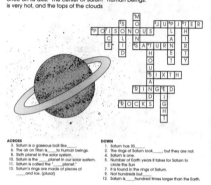

**ACROSS**
3. Saturn is a gaseous ball like ____.
6. The air on Titan is ____ to human beings.
8. Sixth planet in the solar system.
10. Saturn is the ____ planet in our solar system.
11. Saturn is called the "____ planet."
13. Saturn's rings are made of pieces of ____ and ice. (plural)

**DOWN**
1. Saturn has 30 ____.
2. The rings of Saturn look ____, but they are not.
4. Saturn is one.
5. Number of Earth years it takes for Saturn to circle the Sun
7. It is found in the rings of Saturn.
9. Not hundreds but ____.
12. Saturn is ____ hundred times larger than the Earth.

## What Is Missing? (132)

As you know, Saturn is most famous for its beautiful rings. Saturn is the only gas planet whose rings are visible through a telescope and can even be seen with some binoculars!

This picture of Saturn is missing something. Use crayons or markers to draw what is missing from the picture below.

Position of rings can vary slightly.

## Uranus (135)

Did you know that Uranus was first thought to be a comet? Many scientists studied the mystery comet. It was soon decided that Uranus was a planet. It was the first planet to be discovered through a telescope.

Scientists believe that Uranus is made of rock and metal with gas and ice surrounding it.

Even through a telescope, Uranus is not easy to see. That is because it is almost two billion miles from the Sun that lights it. It takes Uranus 84 Earth years to orbit the Sun!

Scientists know that Uranus has twenty moons and is circled by ten thin rings. But there are still many mysteries about this faraway planet.

○ position will vary

Draw ten thin rings around Uranus.

**Circle:**
Uranus was first thought to be a (comet). moon.

**Write:**
Uranus was the first planet to be discovered through a ___telescope___.
telescope   TV

**Check:**
Scientists believe that Uranus is made of:
☑ rock   ☐ oil   ☑ metal   ☐ oceans   ☑ gas   ☑ ice

**Match:**
two billion miles — the number of Uranus's moons
84 Earth years — the distance of Uranus from the Sun
twenty — the number of Uranus's rings
ten — the time it takes Uranus to orbit the Sun

## The Green Planet (136)

Uranus, a frozen dim world, is the seventh planet from the Sun. Uranus takes 84 Earth years to orbit the Sun one time! If you were 42 Earth years old, how old would you be on Uranus?
You would be two years old.

Can you figure out the nickname for Uranus? Unscramble each of the two words below.

NEGRE    LPNAET

Write Uranus's nickname: Green Planet

**Add the Rings!**
Remembering its nickname, color the picture of Uranus below. Then add Uranus's rings with a pencil or crayon.

Rings should be drawn vertically around the planet

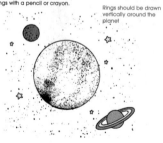

## Uranus (138)

Uranus, the seventh planet out from the Sun, is also a gas giant. It is too distant to be seen without a telescope and was discovered in 1781 in England. It is 60 times the volume of Earth. It is a blue-green color. It is probably very hot at the center, but the tops of its clouds are cold. It has thousands of rings that are very dark and thin compared to those of Saturn. Scientists believe that the rings are made of dark dust. It also has 20 known moons. Most of them were discovered in photographs of Uranus sent back by the Voyager spacecraft that flew by in 1986. Uranus orbits the Sun once every 84 Earth years. It takes Uranus 17 hours to complete one turn on its axis.

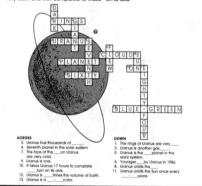

**ACROSS**
2. Uranus has thousands of ____.
4. Seventh planet in the solar system
7. The tops of the ____ on Uranus are very cold.
9. Uranus is one.
10. It takes Uranus 17 hours to complete ____ turn on its axis.
12. Uranus is ____ times the volume of Earth.
13. Uranus is a ____-____ color.

**DOWN**
1. The rings of Uranus are very ____.
3. Uranus is another gas.
5. Uranus is the ____ planet in the solar system.
6. Voyager ____ by Uranus in 1986.
8. Uranus orbits the ____.
11. Uranus orbits the Sun once every ____ ____ years.

## Unusual Uranus (140)

Uranus is almost four times larger than Earth. Scientists think it has a thick, cloudy atmosphere made of hydrogen and helium gases. Deep inside is probably a solid core.

How many Earth years does Uranus take to orbit the Sun once? 84 Earth years

While orbiting the Sun, Uranus turns on its axis very quickly, one turn every 17 hours.

How many hours are there in one Earth day? 24 hours in one Earth day

Uranus has two days for every day on Earth. Scientists know the Green Planet is very cold. Temperatures probably drop lower than 240 degrees below zero.

**A Crossword Puzzle About Uranus**

**Across**
2. The atmosphere is made of hydrogen and ____.
4. Nicknamed the "____ planet."
5. A day on Uranus is almost 17 ____ long.
7. The atmosphere is ____ and thick.
8. Uranus doesn't spin on its axis. It ____.

**Down**
1. An axis is an imaginary ____.
3. Uranus is four times larger than this planet.
6. The seventh planet from the Sun.
7. Temperatures on Uranus are very ____.

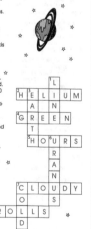

# ANSWER KEY

## The Twin Planets

1. Uranus and Neptune are similar in size, rotation time, and temperature. Sometimes they are called twin planets. Uranus is about 1,786,400,000 miles from the Sun. Neptune is about 2,798,800,000 miles from the Sun. What is the difference between these two distances? **1,012,400,000 miles**

2. Neptune can complete a rotation in 18 to 20 hours. Uranus can make one in 16 to 18 hours. What is the average time it takes Neptune to complete a rotation? **19 hours** Uranus? **17 hours**

3. Can you believe that it is about -353°F on Neptune and about -357°F on Uranus? Brrr! That's cold! What is the temperature outside today in your town? **answer will vary**
How much warmer is it in your town than on Neptune? **Uranus?**

4. Uranus has at least five small satellites moving around the planet. One, Triton, is large and rocky and almost as big as Miranda, Ariel, Umbriel, Tatania, and Oberon. They are 292, 721, 727, 982, and 945 miles in diameter, respectively. What is the average diameter of Uranus's satellites? **733.4 miles**

5. Neptune was first seen in 1846 by Johanna G. Galle. Uranus was first discovered by Sir William Herschel in 1781. How many years ago was Neptune discovered? **Answers will vary.** About how many years later was Uranus discovered than Neptune? **65 years**

6. Both Uranus and Neptune have names taken from Greek and Roman mythology. Use an encyclopedia to find their names and their origins.
**Uranus was named for "Ouranos," a Greek mythological figure person-ifying Heaven and the ruler of the world.**
**Neptune was the ancient Roman god of the sea.**

142

## The Blue-Green Giants

Uranus and Neptune are giant planets more than a billion miles from the Sun and Earth. They are about the same size. Each is more than 3½ times larger than Earth. They look blue-green in photos because both have a gas called methane in their atmospheres. Uranus and Neptune are very cold planets where life probably doesn't exist.

Uranus is the seventh planet from the Sun. It is known to have at least 20 moons and 11 thin rings. Uranus rotates in the direction opposite of Earth. It can be seen from Earth without a telescope.

Neptune is farther from the Sun than Uranus. It has eight known moons and also has rings. Neptune cannot be seen without a telescope.

Decide which planet or planets each fact describes. If it describes Uranus, write *Uranus*. If it describes Neptune, write *Neptune*. If it describes both Uranus and Neptune, write *both*.

1. rotates in the opposite direction **Uranus**
2. called a blue-green giant **both**
3. cannot be seen without a telescope **Neptune**
4. is more than a billion miles from Earth **both**
5. has methane in its atmosphere **both**
6. has at least 11 rings **Uranus**
7. can be seen without a telescope **Uranus**
8. has eight known moons **Neptune**

145

## Neptune

Neptune is the eighth planet from the Sun. It is difficult to see Neptune—even through a telescope. It is almost three billion miles from Earth.

Scientists believe that Neptune is much like Uranus—made of rock, iron, ice, and gases. Neptune has eight moons. Scientists believe that it may also have several rings.

Neptune is so faraway from the Sun that it takes 164 Earth years for it to orbit the Sun just once!

Scientists still know very little about this cold and distant planet.

Eight moons should be drawn. Positions will vary.

**Draw 8 moons around Neptune.**

**Write, Circle, or Unscramble:**

**N**eptune is the **sixth** (**eighth**) planet from the Sun.
**E**arth is almost three **billion** (million **billion**) miles from Neptune.
**P**eople know **very little** (very little / very much) about Neptune.
**T**elescopes are used to see Neptune. (**Yes**) No
**U**ranus and Neptune are made of: (**rock**) soap gases (**ice**)
**N**eptune is a **cold** (warm **cold**) and **distant** (**distant** near) planet.
**E**very orbit around the **Sun** takes Neptune 164 Earth years.

146

## How Many Moons?

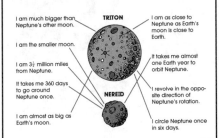

Neptune's moons are a mystery! Scientists know at least eight moons move around the planet. One, Triton, is large and rocky and almost as big as Earth's Moon. It is almost as close to Neptune as our Moon is to Earth. Triton circles Neptune one time every six Earth days. Triton is the only moon in our solar system which revolves around a planet in the opposite direction that the planet rotates.

One of Neptune's other moons is called Nereid. It is very small and is 3½ million miles from Neptune! Tiny Nereid takes 360 Earth days to go around Neptune once. That is almost one year on Earth.

**Know the Moons**
1. Read the facts about Neptune's moons below.
2. Draw a line from the fact to the moon it describes.

I am much bigger than Neptune's other moon.
I am the smaller moon.
I am 3½ million miles from Neptune.
It takes me 360 days to go around Neptune once.
I am almost as big as Earth's moon.

**TRITON**
**NEREID**

I am as close to Neptune as Earth's moon is close to Earth.
It takes me almost one Earth year to orbit Neptune.
I revolve in the opposite direction of Neptune's rotation.
I circle Neptune once in six days.

147

## Neptune

Neptune, the eighth planet out from the Sun, is another gas giant. It is about the same size as Uranus. It is blue in color. Scientists know that Neptune gives off more heat than it gets from the Sun. It takes 165 Earth years for Neptune to orbit the Sun. It completes one turn on its axis every 16 to 18 hours. Neptune can only be seen in the night sky with a telescope.

Scientists do not yet know if Neptune has any rings, but they know it has eight moons including Triton and Nereid.

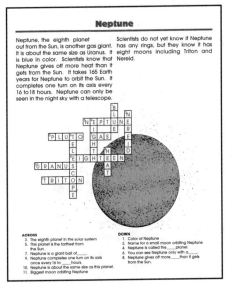

**ACROSS**
3. The eighth planet in the solar system
5. This planet is the farthest from the Sun.
7. Neptune is a giant ball of____.
9. Neptune completes one turn on its axis once every 16 to ____hours.
10. Neptune is about the same size as this planet.
11. Biggest moon orbiting Neptune

**DOWN**
1. Color of Neptune
2. Name for a small moon orbiting Neptune
4. Neptune is called the____planet.
6. You can see Neptune only with a____.
8. Neptune gives off more____than it gets from the Sun.

148

## Pluto

Pluto used to be considered the ninth planet. Now, along with Ceres and Eris, it is considered a dwarf planet.

If you stood on Pluto, the sun would look just like a bright star in the sky. Pluto is so far away that it gets little of the sun's heat. That is why it is freezing cold on Pluto.

Some scientists think that Pluto was once one of Neptune's moons that escaped from orbit and drifted into space.

Pluto is so far away from the sun that it takes 247 Earth years just to orbit the sun once!

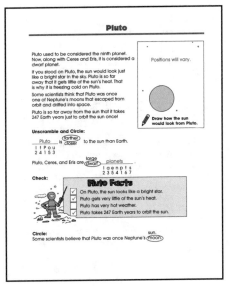

Positions will vary.

**Draw how the sun would look from Pluto.**

**Unscramble and Circle:**
**Pluto** is (**farther** closer) to the sun than Earth.
l t P o u
2 4 1 5 3
Pluto, Ceres, and Eris are (**dwarf**) **large** **planets**
l a e n p t s
2 3 5 4 1 6 7

**Check:**

### Pluto Facts
☑ On Pluto, the sun looks like a bright star.
☑ Pluto gets very little of the sun's heat.
☐ Pluto has very hot weather.
☑ Pluto takes 247 Earth years to orbit the sun.

**Circle:**
Some scientists believe that Pluto was once Neptune's (**moon**) sun.

151

341

## Faraway Pluto

At Pluto's farthest point, it is more than four billion miles from Earth!

Pluto is smaller than the Earth's moon.

Scientists know very little about Pluto because it is so faraway. It is believed to be like a rocky snowball in space. Charon is Pluto's only moon. Scientists don't think any life exists on faraway Pluto.

Earth

Pluto

Greatest distance: 4,670,000,000 miles

Unscramble each sentence so it tells one fact about Pluto. Write the fact.

1. farthest Sun Pluto travels from the
   Pluto travels farthest from the Sun.

2. has moon one Pluto
   Pluto has one moon.

3. travels billion more four than Earth from miles Pluto
   Pluto travels more than four billion miles from Earth.

4. Pluto's named is Charon moon
   Pluto's moon is named Charon.

**152**

## A Discovery!

An exciting discovery was made in 1978! An astronomer in Washington, D.C. discovered a moon orbiting tiny Pluto. Until 1978, scientists did not think Pluto had any moons.

This moon is called Charon. Even with a telescope this moon is difficult to see because it is so close to Pluto. Scientists think Charon is very small, only 840 miles in diameter.

Charon does not weigh very much. Like planet Jupiter, this moon may not have a lot of heavy matter inside. Scientists think it may be as light as a comet!

It takes little Charon 6 days, 9 hours, and 17 minutes to go around Pluto one time. This is exactly the same amount of time it takes Pluto to spin once on its axis. So, during one day on Pluto, Charon orbits the planet once.

Charon orbits close to Pluto. The pull of gravity from Charon is very strong. The pull causes **geysers**, jet sprays of water, to burst up from inside Pluto. The moment the water hits the surface, it freezes. This occurs all the time, causing Pluto to be continuously covered by new coats of frozen ice.

**Pluto Quiz**

1. What would you have named Pluto's moon?
   answers will vary.

2. How long is one day on Pluto?
   6 days, 9 hours, 17 minutes

3. What is an astronomer? A scientist who studies the planets and stars
   Would you like to be an astronomer? Tell why or why not.
   answers will vary.

4. How big is Charon?
   840 miles in diameter

5. Do you remember what "diameter" means? Draw where the diameter would be on this planet.

6. Why do you think no one had found Charon before 1978?
   answers will vary

7. What is a jet spray of water called?
   a geyser

**157**

## The Spectacular Sun

The Sun is the center of our solar system. The Earth and all the other planets travel around the Sun.

The Sun is made up of gases. Hydrogen makes up most of the Sun, but it also contains a lot of helium. There are small amounts of many other gases.

Use the information on this page and on the page that follows to help you complete the crossword puzzle below.

**Across**

3. The Sun is the center of the _____ system.
4. The Sun is mostly made of _____.
6. The Sun also contains lots of _____.

Crossword answers: STAR, SOLAR, PLANETS, HYDROGEN, EARTH, SUN, HELIUM, LIGHT

**Down**

1. The _____ travels around the Sun.
2. The Sun is a _____.
3. This puzzle is about the __SUN__.
4. The Sun gives off _____.
5. The Sun is the nearest star to _____.
7. The Sun makes its own _____.

**183**

## Our Sun

When you see the Sun shining during the day, you are seeing a star. A star is a huge glowing ball of gases. The Sun is the only star in our solar system. It looks much larger than the stars we see at night because it is closer to us than the others. Even so, the Sun is 93 million miles from Earth.

Our Sun is really only a medium-sized star. Some other stars in the universe are much bigger, and many stars are much smaller. The Sun is a yellow star. Hotter stars are blue, and cooler stars are red.

Copy the sentence from the story that answers each question.

1. What is a star?  A star is a huge glowing ball of gases.

2. Which star is in our solar system?  The Sun is the only star in our solar system.

3. How far is the Sun from Earth?  The Sun is 93 million miles from Earth.

4. What color is the Sun?  The Sun is a yellow star.

5. Why does the Sun look larger to us than other stars?  It looks much larger than the stars we see at night because it is closer to us than the others.

**185**

## Sunny News

The Sun is the closest star to Earth. How close? The Sun is 93,000,000 miles away. This great distance is fairly close when you think of the vast distances in outer space.

How long does light from the Sun take to travel 93 million miles to Earth? Circle your answer.

8½ days     8 years     (8 minutes, 20 seconds)

In just 8 minutes and 20 seconds, light from the Sun travels all that distance and lands on you!

Why is sunlight so important? Place your hand on a window where sunlight is shining in. You will feel the Sun's heat. The Sun's heat keeps the ground and air warm.

Plants need sunlight to make food that keeps them growing. When plants make food they give off oxygen, a gas people and animals breathe. We also eat plants to live.

The Sun helps you when you are lost! If you face the Sun in the morning, your direction is east. In the afternoon, you face the Sun to the west. How can this help if you are lost?

**Sun Talk**

People talk about the Sun all the time! Look at the words and pictures below. Draw a line connecting the picture with the "sun" word that matches it. Then color the pictures in a way that makes sense.

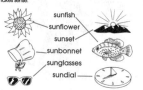

sunfish
sunflower
sunset
sunbonnet
sunglasses
sundial

Can you think of three more "sun" words? Write them here.

Answers may include: sundeck, sunroom, sunrise, suntan, Sunday, sundae, sunburn, sundress

**186**

## Sun-sational Puzzle

If we could travel from the Sun's core, or center, to the surface we would be at the **photosphere**, which is the surface part of the Sun seen from Earth. Flashes of light seen by scientists on the surface of the Sun are called **flares**, and dark patches are called **sunspots**. Sometimes eruptions of gas, called **prominences**, can also be seen during a solar eclipse. Just above the Sun's surface is a layer of bright gases called the **chromosphere**. The **corona**, the region beyond the chromosphere, consists of white concentric circles of light that radiate from the Sun.

Use words from the Word Bank to complete the crossword puzzle.

**Word Bank**
Sun
flares
sunspots
chromosphere
core
corona
photosphere
prominences

Crossword answers: PHOTOSPHERE, CHROMOSPHERE, CORE, CORONA, SUN, PROMINENCES, SUNSPOTS, FLARES

**Across:**

3. The part of the Sun you can see.
4. Huge glowing ball of gases at the center of our solar system
5. The region of the Sun's atmosphere above the chromosphere.
6. Big, bright eruptions of gas
7. Flashes of light on the Sun's surface

**Down:**

1. The middle part of the Sun's atmosphere
2. The center of the Sun
4. Dark patches that sometimes appear on the Sun

**189**

## Follow the Sunbeams

The Sun's rays provide the energy source for every living thing on Earth. Begin at the center of the Sun and find a path that allows the energy to beam toward Earth.

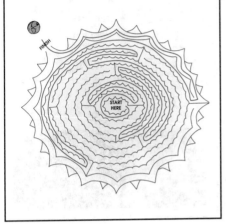

START HERE

**190**

## Sun

The Sun is a star. It is the only star in our solar system. Our Sun is just one of many billions of stars in the Milky Way galaxy. The Sun is a medium-sized star. It looks bigger than the other stars in the sky because it is closer to Earth than the stars we see at night. The Sun is a huge ball of hot, glowing gases that move and boil. The light from the hot gases of the Sun is so bright that you cannot look straight at it without hurting your eyes. The Sun is 93 million miles from Earth. If a spaceship could fly to the Moon in two days, it would take the same ship more than two years to fly to the Sun. The hottest part of the Sun is the center, or core. Nuclear energy from the core heats the outer parts of the Sun so they are hot enough to glow with light. It takes about eight minutes and twenty seconds for the Sun's light to travel across space and reach Earth.

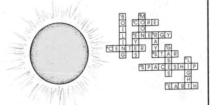

Crossword answers: BOILINGS (down), CORE, ENERGY, CENTER, STAR, SPACESHIP, EARTH, MOVING, RAYS, LIGHT

**ACROSS**
3. Center of the Sun
4. Nuclear___heats the outer parts of the Sun.
6. Core of the Sun
8. The Sun
10. If a___could fly to the Sun, the trip would take a long time.
11. The planet we live on.

**DOWN**
1. The gases of the Sun are always moving,___and spinning.
2. A satellite of the Earth
4. Looking straight at the Sun can hurt your___.
5. The Sun's___give us light; rhymes with days.
7. The Sun is made of hot, glowing___.
9. Waves of the Sun's___reach Earth in eight minutes and twenty seconds.

**191**

## A Matter of Time

The Sun can help you tell time with shadows. A **sundial**, or shadow clock, has something that sticks up from a flat surface, casting a shadow in the sunlight. During the day, the shadow moves. By watching the shadows, you can mark off hours and keep track of the time.

Why can't you tell time with a sundial at night? <u>Because the Sun doesn't shine at night to cast shadows on the sundial.</u>

**Make a Sundial**
1. Take a notebook-sized piece of cardboard.
2. Stick a 4-inch pencil into a small ball of clay.
3. Press the clay near one end of the cardboard as shown in the picture.
4. Take your cardboard outside early on a sunny morning. Lay it on a flat surface away from any possible shade.
5. Use a **compass**, an instrument for finding directions, to make sure the side of cardboard with the pencil is to the north.
6. Every hour trace the pencil's shadow on the cardboard. Write the time next to the point.
7. At day's end, connect the points of the shadows into a curve.
8. What time was the line the shortest? <u>Answers</u>
Why? <u>will vary.</u>

**From an Hour to a Year**
The shadows moved on your sundial. When we look in the sky, the Sun seems to move. We say that the Sun rises in the east and the Sun sets, or goes down, in the west. Sometimes this can be confusing. It seems the Sun moves, and we stand still. Actually, the Sun stays in one place and Earth rotates like a top. It takes 24 hours for Earth to rotate one time. We call this amount of time one day.

The Sun also helps us to tell time in another way. The time it takes for a planet like our Earth to travel around the Sun is called a year. It takes 365 and $\frac{1}{4}$ days for Earth to travel around the Sun once. The extra $\frac{1}{4}$ days add up to one full day every four years. That year is called a **leap year**.

How many days are in a leap year? <u>366 days</u>

**195**

## What Is a Light-Year?

A light-year is the distance that light travels in one year. Light travels at 186,282 miles per second. That's equal to about seven and a half times around the Earth in one second! In one year, light travels almost 6 trillion miles—or 6,000,000,000,000 miles!

Astronomers measure distances in space by light-years because most things in space are so faraway. **Proxima Centauri**, the nearest star to Earth after the Sun, is more than four light-years away.

1. Which is bigger, a billion or a trillion?
<u>A trillion is bigger. It's a thousand billion.</u>
2. What is an astronomer? <u>An astronomer is a scientist who studies space, stars, and planets.</u>
3. What instruments do astronomers use to study space? <u>Astronomers use telescopes, calculators, computers, and spectroscopes.</u>
4. Why is it important for scientists to continue investigating space? <u>Sample answer: To learn more about the solar system and the galaxy, things that can affect Earth, and what might happen to Earth in the future.</u>
5. Why is the Sun important to life on Earth? <u>It provides the warmth and light necessary for all life on Earth.</u>
6. What does the expression "Today's computers are light-years ahead of the first computers" mean? <u>Computers today can work much faster and do much more than the first computers, so we say they are "light-years" ahead of those machines.</u>

**196**

## Solar and Lunar Eclipses

A solar eclipse happens when the Moon passes directly between the Earth and the Sun. It blocks the sunlight to Earth and total darkness can happen in the middle of the day!

A lunar eclipse occurs when the Earth is lined up between the Sun and the Moon. The Moon shines by reflecting the Sun's light, but during a lunar eclipse, Earth is in the way. There is no moonlight during a lunar eclipse!

**Solar or Lunar?**

Read the facts below. Mark an **S** if the fact is describing a solar eclipse or an **L** if it is describing a lunar eclipse.

1. <u>L</u> The Earth lines up between the Sun and Moon, blocking the sunlight from the Moon.

2. <u>S</u> The Moon blocks the Sun's light from reaching Earth.

3. <u>S</u> Complete darkness occurs in the middle of the day.

4. <u>L</u> There is no moonlight at all.

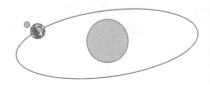

**197**

## We See Our Moon

Earth has one moon. It is the Moon that we see in the sky. The Moon is Earth's partner in space. It **orbits** the Earth. It also orbits the Sun along with the Earth.

The Moon looks large because it is closer to Earth than the Sun or planets. Four moons would stretch across the **diameter** of the Earth.

In 1969, **astronaut** Neil Armstrong took the first steps on the Moon. Scientists have studied rocks brought back from the Moon.

The surface of the Moon has many deep holes called **craters**. It has flat areas called **maria**. The Moon also has rocky mountain areas called **highlands**. There is no air, wind, or water on the Moon. No life exists there.

Write the boldfaced word from the story that matches each definition.

1. deep holes in the Moon's surface <u>craters</u>
2. to make a path around <u>orbits</u>
3. flat land on the Moon <u>maria</u>
4. the widest part of the Earth <u>diameter</u>
5. areas with rocky mountains <u>highlands</u>
6. a person who travels in space <u>astronaut</u>

Write two sentences about the Moon using two of the boldfaced words.

1. <u>Sentences will vary.</u>

2. _____

**201**

## That's a Fact!

Study the chart below.
Then answer the questions.

| The Moon at a Glance! | |
|---|---|
| Age: | about 4.6 billion years |
| Distance from Earth: | average of 237,083 miles |
| Diameter: | about 2,160 miles |
| Circumference: | about 6,790 miles |
| Surface Area: | about 14,670,000 square miles |
| Rotation Period: | about 27 days |
| Average Speed Around Earth: | 2,300 miles per hour |
| Length of One Day and Night: | about 15 Earth days |
| Temperature at Equator: | 260°F |

1. Write the number for 4.6 billion years.  4,600,000,000,000
2. What is the distance of the Moon from the Earth?  about 237,083 miles
3. About how many miles is the diameter of the Moon?  about 2,160 miles
4. How many days are in 5 rotation periods of the Moon?  about 135 days
5. How much hotter is the temperature at the Moon's equator than the
   temperature outside your house today?  260° - current temperature
6. How many Moon days equal 45 days on Earth?  about 3 Moon days

**203**

## Earth's Moon

Earth's closest neighbor is its moon. The Moon is about 240,000 miles from Earth. The Moon orbits Earth just as Earth orbits the Sun. Just as the Sun's gravity keeps Earth from spinning off into space, Earth's gravity keeps the Moon in place. The Moon is roughly a quarter the diameter of Earth. It would take about 81 moons to make up the same weight as Earth. The Moon's gravity is very weak, one-sixth as great as the Earth's gravity. The Moon's gravity is too weak to hold an atmosphere. The Moon is a stark, arid place, hot in the day and very cold at night. The surface of the Moon is a desert of rock and dust. The light that we see from the Moon is reflected sunlight. As the Moon orbits Earth, we see varying parts of the Moon lit up by sunlight. The changing appearance of the Moon is called its cycle of phases. The Moon spins on an axis, but it because it rotates and spins at the same rate. Astronauts learned from their trip to the Moon that people could live there if they brought their own water, air, and food.

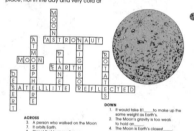

**ACROSS**
3. A person who walked on the Moon
7. It orbits Earth.
8. Planet that humans live on
10. The Moon is a _____ of Earth.
11. The Moon shines from _____ sunlight.

**DOWN**
1. It would take 81 _____ to make up the same weight as Earth's.
2. The Moon's gravity is too weak to hold an _____.
4. The Moon is Earth's closest _____.
5. Earth is a _____.
6. The Moon keeps its same face to Earth because it _____ and spins at the same speed.
9. The surface of the Moon is like a _____.

**207**

## Moon Facts

Write a word from "Origin of the Moon" on the previous page that matches each given detail.

1. capture — A theory that says the Moon originally had an orbit that was much like Earth's orbit.
2. formation — A theory that says Earth and the Moon were formed from gas and dust left by the Sun.
3. escape — A theory that says the Moon was pulled out of Earth by the pull from the Sun's gravity.
4. collision — A theory that says a piece of Earth broke off when a body from space smashed into it.
5. bulge — The escape theory explains that the Sun's gravity created this on one side of Earth.
6. impact — This word for a collision may have caused pieces of Earth to break off.
7. formation — Earth and the Moon were double planets in this theory.
8. satellite — This word describes what the Moon became after it was captured by Earth.

**213**

## Why Don't People Live on the Moon?

There is no air and no water on the Moon. It would be almost impossible to live there unless special places were built in which people could live. Since there is no air around it to protect it from the heat of the Sun, the Moon is boiling hot during the day, but at night it is freezing cold! You would need special gravity boots to help you walk on the Moon, because the Moon's gravity is not as strong as the Earth's.

1. How could you breathe on the Moon?  Only with a special air tank like the one the astronaut is wearing in the picture.
2. Could plants grow on the Moon? Why or why not?  No, because there is no water or air.
3. Where could you jump higher, on the Earth or on the Moon?  You can jump six times higher on the Moon.
4. Does the American flag that astronauts left on the Moon wave in the wind?  No, because there is no air to make wind.
5. Does the Moon always look the same to someone on the Earth?  No, it goes through four different phases (full, half, crescent, and new).
6. If you could build a city on the Moon, what would it look like? How would you get water and food?  Answers will vary.

**214**

## What Is the Temperature on the Moon?

The temperature on the Moon gets hotter or colder than any place on Earth. Temperatures as cold as –280 degrees Fahrenheit have been recorded during the Moon's lunar nights, the two-week period when the Moon is in darkness. The temperature is always near –400 degrees in some deep craters at the Moon's poles. But the Moon can also be very hot. At the Moon's equator, which is halfway between the poles, the temperature can go as high as 260 degrees.

1. If you wanted to warm up food on the Moon's surface, where would you put it?  On or near the equator.
2. How do spacesuits help to protect astronauts on the Moon?  They insulate, or protect, astronauts from extreme temperatures.
3. Why do you think it's so cold during the Moon's lunar nights?  The Moon is in darkness and receives less warmth from the Sun.
4. Would you like to explore the Moon? Why or why not?  Answers will vary.
5. Do you think there really is a "man in the Moon"?  Answers will vary.
6. How would you design a space station that would allow you to live on the Moon? Sketch a diagram and label all its parts on a separate piece of paper.

Answers will vary.

**216**

## Moonbeams

A **statement of fact** can be proven true or false. An **opinion** is what you believe or think.

**Examples: Fact:** An Apollo Mission landed a man on the Moon.
**Opinion:** My favorite astronaut is Neil Armstrong.

Write **F** if the sentence is a statement of fact. Write **O** if the sentence is an opinion.

1. O  The most beautiful object in the sky is the Moon.
2. F  The Moon is about 240,000 miles from our planet.
3. O  Plants would make the Moon a prettier place.
4. F  The surface of the Moon has mountains and craters.
5. O  Apollo 13 was the most exciting mission ever.
6. F  Astronauts first walked on the Moon in 1969.
7. F  The Moon is a satellite of Earth.
8. F  The Moon reflects light from the Sun.
9. F  People on Earth can only see one side of the Moon.
10. O  Neil Armstrong was the bravest of all the astronauts.
11. F  The force of gravity on the Moon's surface is weaker than that on Earth's surface.
12. O  Everyone should make a trip to the Moon someday.

**217**

## Interesting Moons

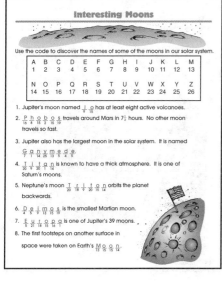

Use the code to discover the names of some of the moons in our solar system.

| A | B | C | D | E | F | G | H | I | J | K | L | M |
|---|---|---|---|---|---|---|---|---|---|---|---|---|
| 1 | 2 | 3 | 4 | 5 | 6 | 7 | 8 | 9 | 10 | 11 | 12 | 13 |

| N | O | P | Q | R | S | T | U | V | W | X | Y | Z |
|---|---|---|---|---|---|---|---|---|---|---|---|---|
| 14 | 15 | 16 | 17 | 18 | 19 | 20 | 21 | 22 | 23 | 24 | 25 | 26 |

1. Jupiter's moon named __I o__ has at least eight active volcanoes.

2. __P h o b o s__ travels around Mars in 7½ hours. No other moon travels so fast.

3. Jupiter also has the largest moon in the solar system. It is named __G a n y m e d e__.

4. __T i t a n__ is known to have a thick atmosphere. It is one of Saturn's moons.

5. Neptune's moon __T r i t o n__ orbits the planet backwards.

6. __D e i m o s__ is the smallest Martian moon.

7. __E u r o p a__ is one of Jupiter's 39 moons.

8. The first footsteps on another surface in space were taken on Earth's __M o o n__.

**218**

## Moon Sums

Add to find the sum on the moons. If the sum is 5, color the moon yellow. How many yellow moons are there? __6__

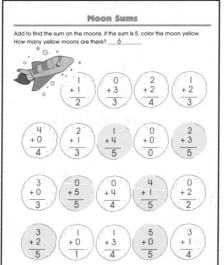

Row 1:
1 + 1 = 2 | 0 + 3 = 3 | 2 + 2 = 4 | 1 + 2 = 3

Row 2:
4 + 0 = 4 | 2 + 1 = 3 | 1 + 4 = 5 | 0 + 0 = 0 | 2 + 3 = 5

Row 3:
3 + 0 = 3 | 0 + 5 = 5 | 0 + 4 = 4 | 4 + 1 = 5 | 0 + 2 = 2

Row 4:
3 + 2 = 5 | 1 + 0 = 1 | 1 + 3 = 4 | 5 + 0 = 5 | 3 + 1 = 4

**220**

## Star Light, Star Bright

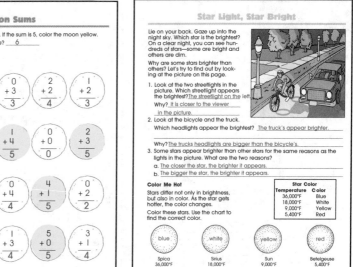

Lie on your back. Gaze up into the night sky. Which star is the brightest? On a clear night, you can see hundreds of stars—some are bright and others are dim.

Why are some stars brighter than others? Let's try to find out by looking at the picture on this page.

1. Look at the two streetlights in the picture. Which streetlight appears the brightest? The streetlight on the left.
Why? It is closer to the viewer in the picture.

2. Look at the bicycle and the truck. Which headlights appear the brightest? The truck's appear brighter.
Why? The trucks headlights are bigger than the bicycle's.

3. Some stars appear brighter than other stars for the same reasons as the lights in the picture. What are the two reasons?
a. The closer the star, the brighter it appears.
b. The bigger the star, the brighter it appears.

**Color Me Hot**

Stars differ not only in brightness, but also in color. As the star gets hotter, the color changes.

Color these stars. Use the chart to find the correct color.

| Star Color | |
|---|---|
| Temperature | Color |
| 36,000°F | Blue |
| 18,000°F | White |
| 9,000°F | Yellow |
| 5,400°F | Red |

blue — Spica 36,000°F | white — Sirius 18,000°F | yellow — Sun 9,000°F | red — Betelgeuse 5,400°F

**223**

## Stars

Stars are suns in the distant sky. Our Sun is a star of our solar system. Beyond the planet Pluto, beyond our solar system, are millions of other stars. Our Sun is a medium-sized star, but stars come in many sizes. Stars also range in color. There are red, blue, yellow, and white stars. Some stars circle each other like Earth and the Moon. Sometimes a rare giant star will explode, sending its energy into space and creating a giant cloud of gas.

Clouds of gas and dust in space are called **nebulae**. The Orion nebula is a huge glowing cloud where new stars are forming. A galaxy is a gigantic system of billions of stars held together by gravity. Our solar system is a tiny part of the spiral galaxy called the Milky Way. Scientists think that many other stars may have planets circling them, but the stars are too far away for scientists to know for certain.

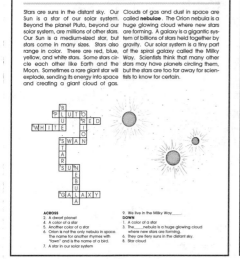

Crossword answers: PLUTO, BLUE, RED, WHITE, SWAN, STARS, SUN, NEBULA, GALAXY

**ACROSS**
2. A dwarf planet
4. A color of a star
5. Another color of a star
6. Orion is not the only nebula in space. The name for another rhymes with "town" and is the name of a bird.
7. A star in our solar system

9. We live in the Milky Way____.

**DOWN**
1. A color of a star
3. The ____ nebula is a huge glowing cloud where new stars are forming.
6. They are fiery suns in the distant sky.
8. Star cloud

**225**

## A Star Is Born!

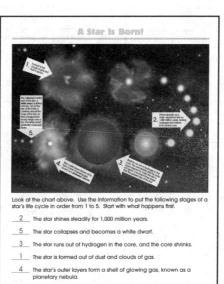

Look at the chart above. Use the information to put the following stages of a star's life cycle in order from 1 to 5. Start with what happens first.

__2__ The star shines steadily for 1,000 million years.

__5__ The star collapses and becomes a white dwarf.

__3__ The star runs out of hydrogen in the core, and the core shrinks.

__1__ The star is formed out of dust and clouds of gas.

__4__ The star's outer layers form a shell of glowing gas, known as a planetary nebula.

**226**

## Light-Years

Distance to the stars is measured in light-years. A light-year is the distance light travels in a year. Light travels at 186,282 miles per second. In one year, light will travel almost six trillion miles. The distance to our neighboring galaxy, Andromeda, is about two and a half million light years. This means that it would take a spaceship traveling at light-speed almost two and a half million years to get to the Andromeda galaxy.

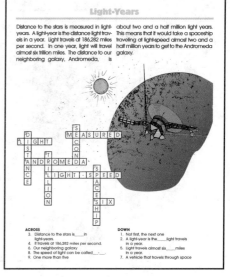

Crossword answers: LIGHT, MEASURED, DISTANCE, ANDROMEDA, LIGHT-SPEED, SPACESHIP, SIX, SECOND

**ACROSS**
3. Distance to the stars is____ in light-years.
4. If it travels at 186,282 miles per second.
6. Our neighboring galaxy
8. The speed of light can be called ____-____.
9. One more than five

**DOWN**
1. Not first, the next one
2. A light-year is the ____ light travels in a year.
5. Light travels almost six ____ miles in a year.
7. A vehicle that travels through space

**227**

## Seeing Stars!

Stars are divided into different categories according to their color, size, and temperature. Can you find the names of the different types of stars in the puzzle below? Use the Word Bank to help you, and circle the words as you find them.

**Word Bank**

| | | |
|---|---|---|
| Black Dwarf | Orange Giant | Red Giant |
| Blue Giant | Pulsating Star | White Dwarf |
| Brown Dwarf | Red Dwarf | Yellow Star |

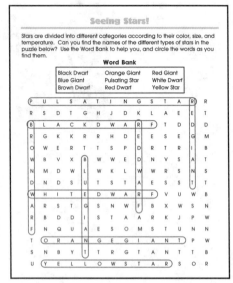

**228**

## Constellations

On a clear night, you can see about two thousand stars in the sky. Scientists can use giant telescopes to see billions of stars.

Stars in groups form pictures called **constellations**. These constellations have been recognized for years. Ancient people named many constellations for animals, heroes, and mythical creatures. Many of these names are still used.

Some constellations can be seen every night of the year. Others change with the seasons.

Since all stars are constantly moving, these same constellations that we now see will be changed thousands of years from now.

**Write:**

Stars in groups form pictures called ___constellations___

telescopes    constellations

**Check :**

Ancient people named many constellations for:

☑ animals ☑ heroes ☐ oceans ☑ mythical creatures

**Match:**

Billions of stars can be seen.
About two thousand stars can be seen.

**Circle Yes or No:**

Some constellations can be seen every night. **Yes** No
Some constellations change with the seasons. **Yes** No
In thousands of years, all constellations will be the same. Yes **No**

Connect the stars to form the constellation called the Little Dipper.

**229**

## Constellations

On a clear night, you can see constellations. A constellation is a group of stars named after a mythological character, inanimate object, or animal. There are 88 named constellations that astronomers use to divide the sky. The Big Dipper, in the constellation of Ursa Major, is an easy star pattern to spot. The Pleiades is a compact cluster of stars in the constellation Taurus. The Pleiades is also called the Seven Sisters because it is named after seven beautiful sisters in ancient Greek mythology. American Indians once used the Pleiades as a way of testing the keenness of a warrior's eyesight. There are about 400 stars in the Pleiades. In comparison with the Sun, the stars of the Pleiades are young. They are only a few tens of millions years old.

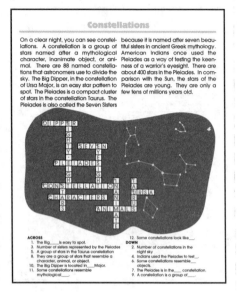

**ACROSS**
1. The Big___is easy to spot.
3. Number of sisters represented by the Pleiades
5. A group of stars in the Taurus constellation
8. They are a group of stars that resemble a character, animal, or object.
10. The Big Dipper is located in___Major.
11. Some constellations resemble mythological___.

**DOWN**
2. Number of constellations in the night sky
4. Indians used the Pleiades to test___.
6. Some constellations resemble___ objects.
7. The Pleiades is in the___constellation.
9. A constellation is a group of___.
12. Some constellations look like___.

**237**

## Star Struck

Use the Word Bank to unscramble the number words. Write them correctly on the lines in the box below. Answer the question by writing the letters from the boxes on the lines.

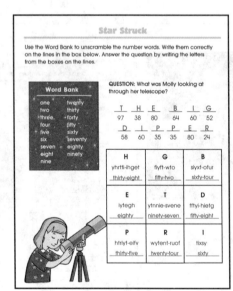

**Word Bank**

| | |
|---|---|
| one | twenty |
| two | thirty |
| three | forty |
| four | fifty |
| five | sixty |
| six | seventy |
| seven | eighty |
| eight | ninety |
| nine | |

QUESTION: What was Molly looking at through her telescope?

T H E   B I G
97 38 80   64 60 52

D I P P E R
58 60 35 35 80 24

| **H** | **G** | **B** |
|---|---|---|
| yhrtti-ihget | fiyft-wto | siyxt-ofur |
| thirty-eight | fifty-two | sixty-four |

| **E** | **T** | **D** |
|---|---|---|
| iytegh | ytnnie-svene | fftyi-hietg |
| eighty | ninety-seven | fifty-eight |

| **P** | **R** | **I** |
|---|---|---|
| htriyt-eifv | wytent-ruof | tixsy |
| thirty-five | twenty-four | sixty |

**242**

## Zodiac Puzzlers

Now test your knowledge of the zodiac! Fill in the blanks with the name of the constellation that matches the description. The first one has been done for you. Then, design a symbol for the last zodiac puzzler in the space below.

♈ the Ram   A R I E S
♒ the Water Carrier   A Q U A R I U S
♋ the Crab   C A N C E R
♊ the Twins   G E M I N I
♌ the Lion   L E O
♏ the Scorpion   S C O R P I U S
♑ the Sea-Goat   C A P R I C O R N U S
♍ the Young Maiden   V I R G O
♐ the Archer   S A G I T T A R I U S
♎ the Balance Scales   L I B R A
♉ the Bull   T A U R U S
♓ the Fishes   P I S C E S
Drawing will vary. the Serpent Bearer   O P H I U C H U S

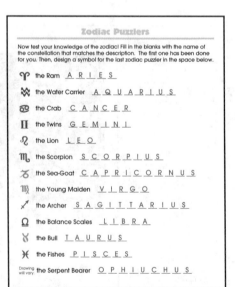

**253**

# ANSWER KEY

## Constellation Matchup

Look at the pictures of constellations below. Draw a line from each constellation to the picture on the next page that you think it represents.

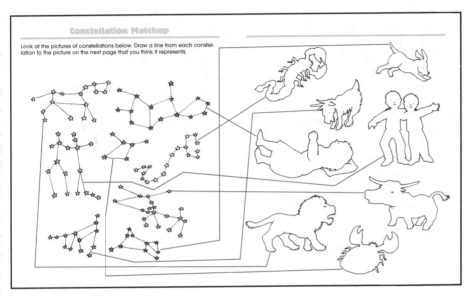

**254**

**255**

## Alpha Centauri

Alpha Centauri is the star system nearest to our solar system. Alpha Centauri is much farther away than the farthest planet in our solar system. How far is far? Let's pretend that you had a spaceship that could travel 100 thousand miles an hour. With that spaceship, you could reach the Moon in two and one-half hours. It would take you almost five years to reach Pluto. To reach Alpha Centauri would take about 30 thousand years! You can see that there is a lot of space between the stars.

Crossword grid:
P L A N E T (C, S O L)
S Y S T E M / A L P H A / A R
S T A R I / C E A R T H / H I
/ F I V E / P / I R T Y

**ACROSS**
2. Earth is one
6. First part of the name for the star system nearest to our solar system
7. The Sun is one
9. Planet we live on
10. Number of years it would take a spaceship to reach Pluto

**DOWN**
1. Second part of the name of the star system nearest to ours
3. System pertaining to the Sun
4. Alpha Centauri is a star____
5. A vehicle for traveling in space
8. From Pluto it would take you another___ thousand years to reach Alpha Centauri

**256**

## I See Stars!

We use the words **see** or **sees** to tell about something happening now. We use **saw** to tell about something that already happened. Write **see**, **sees**, or **saw** in the sentences about stars below.

1. Last night, we __saw__ the stars.
2. John can __see__ the stars from his window.
3. He __sees__ them every night.
4. Last week, he __saw__ the Big Dipper.
5. Can you __see__ it in the night sky, too?
6. If you __saw__ it, you would remember it!
7. John __sees__ it often now.
8. How often do you __see__ it?

**257**

## What Is a Galaxy?

A **galaxy** is a very large collection of stars, planets, moons, gas, and whatever other kinds of matter lurk in space. Galaxies come in many sizes. Small ones contain several billion stars, while the largest ones contain more than a trillion stars!

Galaxies also come in many shapes: round like a ball, oblong like a football, or flat like a pancake. Some of the flat ones have what look like huge arms spiraling outward. These are called spiral galaxies.

All galaxies spin, and the faster they spin, the flatter they are. We live in a pancake-shaped, spiral galaxy. Do you know its name?

Unscramble the letters below to discover the name of the galaxy in which we live.

T H E   M I L K Y   W A Y
E H T   L M K Y I   A W Y

**258**

## The Milky Way Galaxy

The Milky Way galaxy is made up of the Earth, its solar system, and all the stars you can see at night. There are over 100 billion stars in the Milky Way!

The Milky Way is shaped much like a c.d. It has a center which the outer part goes around.

The Milky Way is always spinning slowly through space. It is so large that it would take 200 million years for the galaxy to make one complete turn.

Many stars in the Milky Way are in clusters. Some star clusters contain up to one million stars!

**Check:**
The Milky Way galaxy is made up of
☑ Earth.
☐ no sun.
☑ our solar system.
☑ 100 billion stars.

**Circle Yes or No:**
The Milky Way is shaped like a pencil. Yes (No)
The Milky Way is always slowly moving in space. (Yes) No
Many stars in the Milky Way are in clusters. (Yes) No
Some star clusters have one million stars. (Yes) No

**Circle:**
It would take (200) 90 600 million years for the galaxy to spin once.

**Underline:**
Which object is the Milky Way shaped like?
c.d.     ruler

**260**

## Milky Way Galaxy

Our solar system is only a tiny part of the Milky Way galaxy. A galaxy is a giant collection of billions of stars. Our Milky Way galaxy contains over 100 billion stars including our Sun. On a clear night, we can see part of the Milky Way from Earth. It looks like a long, white cloud stretched across the sky. Beyond our galaxy, there are billions of other galaxies.

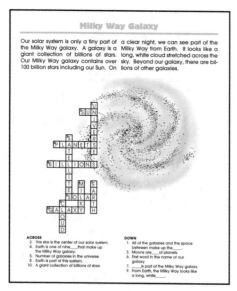

**ACROSS**
2. This star is the center of our solar system.
4. Earth is one of nine____that make up the Milky Way galaxy.
5. Number of galaxies in the universe
8. Earth is part of this system.
10. A giant collection of billions of stars

**DOWN**
1. All of the galaxies and the space between make up the____.
3. Moons are____of planets.
6. First word in the name of our galaxy
7. ____is part of the Milky Way galaxy.
9. From Earth, the Milky Way looks like a long, white____.

261

## The Andromeda Galaxy

The Andromeda galaxy is the closest big galaxy outside our own Milky Way. It is the most distant object in the sky that you can see without a telescope. It looks like a faint smudge of light in the northern sky. In 1923, Edwin Hubble proved that it was at least two million light-years from Earth. It is shaped like the Milky Way galaxy. It has "arms" made of billions of stars, which orbit around its galactic center.

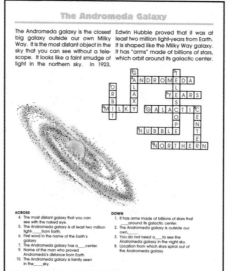

**ACROSS**
4. The most distant galaxy that you can see with the naked eye.
5. The Andromeda galaxy is at least two million light-____from Earth.
6. First word in the name of the Earth's galaxy
7. The Andromeda galaxy has a____center.
8. Name of the man who proved Andromeda's distance from Earth
10. The Andromeda galaxy is faintly seen in the____sky.

**DOWN**
1. It has arms made of billions of stars that____around its galactic center.
2. The Andromeda galaxy is outside our own____.
3. You do not need a____to see the Andromeda galaxy in the night sky.
9. Location from which stars spiral out of the Andromeda galaxy

262

## A Black Hole

Have you ever heard of a mysterious black hole? Some scientists believe that a **black hole** is an invisible object somewhere in space. Scientists believe that it has such a strong pull toward it, called gravity, that nothing can escape from it!

These scientists believe that a black hole is a star that has collapsed. The collapse made its pull even stronger. It seems invisible because even its own starlight cannot escape! It is believed that anything in space that comes near the black hole will be pulled into it forever. Some scientists believe there are many black holes in our galaxy.

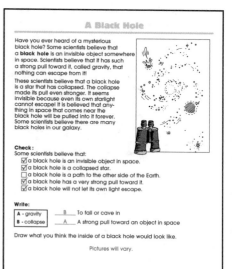

**Check:**
Some scientists believe that:
☑ a black hole is an invisible object in space.
☑ a black hole is a collapsed star.
☐ a black hole is a path to the other side of the Earth.
☑ a black hole has a very strong pull toward it.
☑ a black hole will not let its own light escape.

**Write:**
A - gravity    B    To fall or cave in
B - collapse    A    A strong pull toward an object in space

Draw what you think the inside of a black hole would look like.

Pictures will vary.

263

## Black Hole

A black hole is really a place where gravity is so strong that it traps everything, even the star's light. Since no light can escape from the compressed star, the star becomes invisible. Since scientists cannot see black holes directly because they give out no light, they discover them by looking for their effects on nearby objects that can be seen. Scientists believe they are formed by very massive stars that explode in supernova blasts. There are no known black holes close to our solar system, and they do not appear to be a danger to Earth or our astronauts.

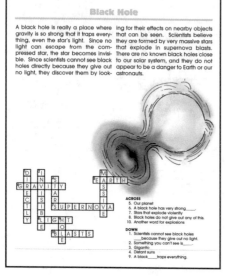

**ACROSS**
5. Our planet
6. A black hole has very strong____.
7. Stars that explode violently
8. Black holes do not give out any of this.
10. Another word for explosions

**DOWN**
1. Scientists cannot see black holes____because they give out no light.
2. Something you can't see is____.
3. Gigantic
4. Distant suns
9. A black____traps everything.

264

## Space Snowballs

Planets and moons are not the only objects in our solar system that travel in orbits. Comets also orbit the Sun.

A **comet** is like a giant, dirty snowball that is $\frac{1}{2}$ to 3 miles wide. It is made of frozen gases, dust, ice, and rocks.

As the comet gets closer to the Sun, the frozen gases melt and evaporate. Dust particles float in the air. The dust forms a cloud called a **coma**. The "wind" from the Sun blows the coma away from the Sun. The blowing coma forms the comet's tail.

There are more than 800 known comets. Halley's Comet is the most famous. It appears about every 76 years. The last scheduled appearance in this century was in 1985. When will it appear next?

Find the words from the Word Bank in the word search. When you are finished, write down the letters that are not circled. Start at the top of the puzzle and go from left to right.

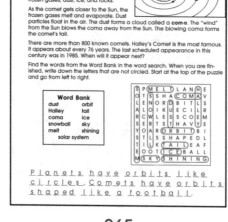

**Word Bank**
dust    orbit
Halley    tail
coma    ice
snowball    sky
melt    shining
solar system

Planets have orbits like circles. Comets have orbits shaped like a football.

265

## Comets

A comet has three main parts: a **nucleus**, or center; a **coma**, or head; and a **tail**. The nucleus is made up of dust, rock, and ice. The coma is a cloud of gases surrounding the nucleus. A nucleus a few miles wide can have a coma 50,000 miles across. The heat from the Sun boils away the outermost layer of ice on the nucleus to form the gas of the coma. Sunlight and the solar wind push the gas and dust particles of the coma back to form a long, filmy tail that can stretch millions of miles into space. The tail of a comet always points away from the Sun. A comet may spend most of its long orbit around the Sun where it is so cold that the nucleus is frozen solid and the comet has no coma or tail. Edmund Halley did not discover Halley's Comet but was the first to predict its return. It returns to Earth's vicinity about every 76 years. The last time it passed Earth was in 1986. Every time a comet visits the Sun, it loses a little more ice. After perhaps one thousand returns, there will be hardly anything left of the comet except rocks and dust.

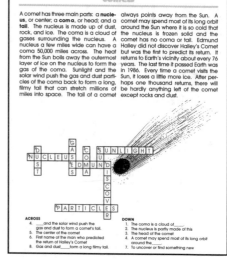

**ACROSS**
4. ____and the solar wind push the gas and dust to form a comet's tail.
5. The center of the comet
6. First name of the man who predicted the return of Halley's Comet
8. Gas and dust____form a long filmy tail.

**DOWN**
1. The coma is a cloud of____.
2. The nucleus is partly made of this
4. A comet may spend most of its long orbit around the____.
7. To uncover or find something new

266

## Asteroids

Asteroids are large chunks of metal and rock orbiting the Sun like tiny planets. Most are about the size of small mountains. There are thousands of asteroids in the space between Mars and Jupiter. This area is generally known as the **asteroid belt**.

It is more than 600 miles wide. Some asteroids, like Eros, Apollo, and Amor, travel close to the Earth as they orbit the Sun. Perhaps one day spacecraft will be able to mine the metal and important minerals of the asteroids.

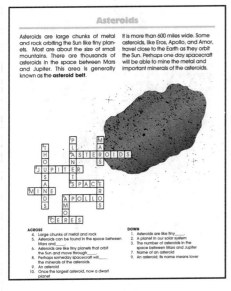

**ACROSS**
4. Large chunks of metal and rock
5. Asteroids can be found in the space between Mars and____.
6. Asteroids are tiny tiny planets that orbit the Sun and move through____.
8. Perhaps someday spacecraft will____ the minerals of the asteroids.
9. An asteroid
10. Once the largest asteroid, now a dwarf planet

**DOWN**
1. Asteroids are like tiny____.
2. A planet in our solar system
3. The number of asteroids in the space between Mars and Jupiter
7. Name of an asteroid
4. An asteroid; its name means lover

**270**

## Meteoroids, Meteors, and Meteorites

**Meteoroids** are small chunks of rock that travel through space orbiting the Sun and have entered the Earth's atmosphere. Some meteoroids have come from the Asteroid Belt and entered Earth's atmosphere. Some are pieces of leftover comets. When a meteoroid falls toward Earth, it travels very fast. The speed of the meteoroid through the air causes friction, which heats the meteoroid until it and the air around it glow white-hot. The streak of light is called a

**meteor**. From Earth you can sometimes see meteors shooting through the sky. Most meteoroids burn up before they hit Earth, but some large ones hit the ground. Once the meteoroid hits the ground, it is called a **meteorite**. Meteorites come in all sizes and shapes. If a giant meteoroid, as big as a building or bigger, hits the ground, it can land with enough force to blast out a hole, called a crater.

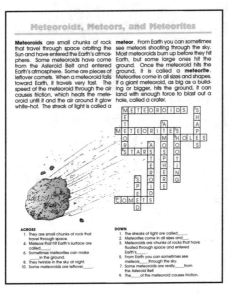

**ACROSS**
1. They are small chunks of rock that travel through space.
4. Meteors that hit Earth's surface are called____.
6. Sometimes meteorites can make ____ in the ground.
8. They twinkle in the sky at night.
10. Some meteoroids are leftover____.

**DOWN**
1. The streaks of light are called____.
2. Meteorites come in all sizes and____.
3. Meteoroids are chunks of rocks that have floated through space and entered Earth's____.
5. From Earth you can sometimes see meteors____ through the sky.
7. Some meteoroids are really____from the Asteroid Belt
9. The____of the meteoroid causes friction.

**273**

## An Interesting Word

In the old Greek language, *astro* meant "star" and *naut* meant "sailor." So, the modern word *astronaut* really means "sailor of the stars." Today's astronauts are men or women trained to explore outer space. Astronauts use rockets to fly around the Earth, to the Moon, and to other planets in space.

1. What kind of trip is a nautical voyage? Do you take a plane, a boat, a train, or a car? It is a trip on a boat.

2. What do you think scientists called *astronomers* study? The position, measurements, and appearances of the stars and planets.

3. What special clothing does an astronaut wear in outer space? A special spacesuit created to keep his or her body temperature normal and to protect the astronaut while in space.

4. When a rocket is launched into space, there is a countdown until blast-off. What does this mean? The hours, minutes, and seconds are counted down, or backward, until zero is reached and it is time for blast-off.

5. What kinds of food do astronauts eat while in their rocket ships? All kinds of freeze-dried, compressed food.

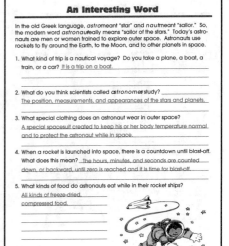

**277**

## Amazing Astronauts

Draw a line to match each astronaut on the left to the correct fact about his or her life on the right.

Laika — First living creature to go into outer space.

John H. Glenn, Jr. — At age 77, became the oldest space traveler.

Alan B. Shepard, Jr. — First American to go into outer space.

Neil A. Armstrong — Said, "That's one small step for man, one giant leap for mankind."

Edwin E. "Buzz" Aldrin, Jr. — Walked in space for 5¼ hours.

Judith Resnik — Second U.S. woman to fly in space.

Sally Ride — First U.S. woman astronaut.

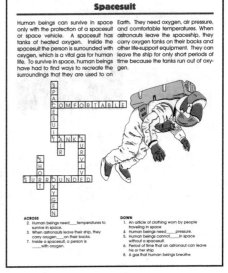

**279**

## Zero G

"Zero G" is an abbreviation for "zero gravity," which is sometimes called weightlessness. It means not being able to sense or feel the pull of gravity. The Earth's gravity pulls us toward the center of our planet. We do not fall to the center of the Earth because the structure of our planet resists our falling through it. We call this resistance to gravity weight. We feel weight because the ground supports us when we sit or a bed supports us when we lie down. When you fall, you feel weightless until you hit

something that resists gravity. A spacecraft in orbit is falling continually. It does not crash because its sideways velocity, or motion, keeps it from hitting the ground. The astronauts inside an orbiting spacecraft are also falling and so feel weightless. Some astronauts find that Zero G makes them feel sick, so they cannot work as well as they did on Earth. Others adjust to weightlessness very well, though they need to exercise a lot to stay healthy while in Zero G.

**ACROSS**
2. Resistance to gravity
3. Not weakly, but____.
6. The structure of our planet____ our falling through it.
7. The ground helps____us when we stand.
8. Velocity
9. Spaceship

**DOWN**
1. Zero G
4. A force that is constantly pulling on us
5. Sometimes astronauts feel____in Zero G.

**283**

## Spacesuit

Human beings can survive in space only with the protection of a spacesuit or space vehicle. A spacesuit has tanks of heated oxygen. Inside the spacesuit the person is surrounded with oxygen, which is a vital gas for human life. To survive in space, human beings have had to find ways to recreate the surroundings that they are used to on

Earth. They need oxygen, air pressure, and comfortable temperatures. When astronauts leave the spaceship, they carry oxygen tanks on their backs and other life-support equipment. They can leave the ship for only short periods of time because the tanks run out of oxygen.

**ACROSS**
2. Human beings need____temperatures to survive in space.
3. When astronauts leave their ship, they carry oxygen____on their backs.
7. Inside a spacesuit, a person is ____with oxygen.

**DOWN**
1. An article of clothing worn by people traveling in space
4. Human beings need____pressure.
5. Human beings cannot____in space without a spacesuit.
6. Period of time that an astronaut can leave his or her ship
8. A gas that human beings breathe

**286**

## Apollo Moon Mission

On July 20, 1969, Neil Armstrong became the first person to set foot on the Moon. Between 1969 and 1972, eleven other astronauts landed on the Moon. The astronauts set up science experiments on the Moon, and they brought back 843 pounds of moon rocks for scientists to study. Studying the moon rocks, scientists found out that they contained the same chemical elements that are found in Earth rocks. These chemical elements also make up living things. The proportions of the elements found in the Moon rocks were slightly different from those found in Earth rocks. The astronauts did not find life on the Moon.

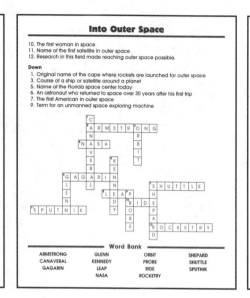

**ACROSS**
1. Name of the spacecraft that landed on the Moon in 1969
3. The Apollo astronauts brought these back for the scientists to study.
5. In what month in 1969 did Neil Armstrong set foot on the Moon?
7. Last name of first person to set foot on the Moon
8. Moon rocks contained chemical_____ similar to rocks found on Earth.

**DOWN**
1. People who manned the Apollo spacecraft
2. Earth's closest neighbor
4. Our planet
6. The astronauts did not find any _____ on the Moon.
9. Between 1969 and 1972, eleven other astronauts _____ on the Moon.

**289**

## Into Outer Space

10. The first woman in space
11. Name of the first satellite in outer space
12. Research in this field made reaching outer space possible.

**Down**
1. Original name of the cape where rockets are launched for outer space
3. Course of a ship or satellite around a planet
5. Name of the Florida space center today
6. An astronaut who returned to space over 30 years after his first trip
7. The first American in outer space
9. Term for an unmanned space exploring machine

### Word Bank

| | | | |
|---|---|---|---|
| ARMSTRONG | GLENN | ORBIT | SHEPARD |
| CANAVERAL | KENNEDY | PROBE | SHUTTLE |
| GAGARIN | LEAP | RIDE | SPUTNIK |
| | NASA | ROCKETRY | |

**291**

## Liftoff

"3-2-1, liftoff!" With a mighty roar, the Saturn V **rocket** leaves the **launch pad**.

Riding high on top of the Saturn V in the **Command Module** are the three Apollo astronauts. Below their Command Module is a Lunar Landing Module which will land two of the astronauts on the Moon's surface.

Below this, the Saturn V has three parts, or **stages**. It takes a lot of power to escape the Earth's pull, called **gravity**. The spacecraft must reach a speed of almost 25,000 miles per hour. The bottom, or first stage, is the largest. After each stage uses up its **fuel**, it drops off, and the next stage starts. Each stage has its own fuel and **oxygen**. The fuels need oxygen, otherwise they will not burn.

The astronauts are now on their 3-day journey to the Moon. Using the color key, color each Saturn V section a different color.

Apollo Mission
Saturn V

Color Key

■ Command Module
■ Lunar Landing Module
■ 3rd Stage
■ 2nd Stage
■ 1st Stage

Fill in the spaces with the highlighted words from above.

1. The Saturn V R o c k e t has three main parts, or s t a g e s.
2. Rocket engines burn f u e l and o x y g e n.
3. The Earth's pull is called g r a v i t y.
4. "Liftoff." The Saturn V leaves the l a u n c h  p a d.
5. The Apollo astronauts ride in the c o m m a n d  m o d u l e.

**294**

## The Space Shuttle

Read the short story below. Then answer the questions.

The space shuttle takes astronauts into space. Rockets launch the shuttle. The shuttle orbits the Earth. The astronauts work in space—they set up satellites or conduct experiments. When it is time to return to Earth, the shuttle lands on a runway like an airplane.

1. What takes astronauts into space?
   The space shuttle takes astronauts into space.

2. What launches the shuttle into space?
   Rockets launch the shuttle into space.

3. What kinds of work do astronauts do in space?
   The astronauts set up satellites and conduct experiments.

4. Where does the shuttle land when it returns to Earth?
   The shuttle lands on a runway like an airplane.

**295**

## BLAST OFF!

Add or subtract. Use the code to color the space rocket.

If the answer has:
9 hundreds, color it gray.
7 tens, color it blue.
5 ones, color it orange.
4 ones, color it red.

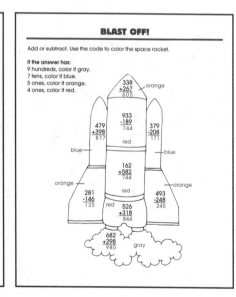

$338 + 267 = 605$  orange

$933 - 189 = 744$

$479 + 398 = 877$  red    $379 - 208 = 171$

blue — blue

$162 + 582 = 744$

red

$281 - 146 = 135$  orange    $493 - 248 = 245$  orange

red    $526 + 318 = 844$

$682 + 298 = 980$  gray

**300**

## Telescopes

The first telescope was invented in about 1600. In 1609, the Italian astronomer Galileo used his hand-made telescope to observe craters on the Moon, sunspots, the moons of Jupiter, and the stars of the Milky Way. The early telescopes were **refracting telescopes**. They collected light by refracting or bending it to produce an image. A different kind of telescope, called a **reflecting telescope**, uses a curved mirror to collect light and produce an image. An eyepiece lens allows scientists to magnify the image made by either type of telescope. The reflecting telescope was invented by Sir Isaac Newton in 1668. Because it gathers more light than the human eye, a telescope will make faint objects appear brighter. One of the largest telescopes is a six-meter reflector in the Soviet Union. Another large one is a reflector telescope at the Mt. Palomar Observatory in California. These giant telescopes allow us to see objects nearly a million times fainter than anything we can see with our eyes alone. New telescopes under construction will gather even more light and allow us to see even further into space.

**ACROSS**
3. Place were a large telescope was located
4. Early _____ collected light by bending it.
8. Scientist who observed sunspots in 1609
9. Building
10. Not made by machine

**DOWN**
1. One of the largest telescopes in the world is a six-meter _____ in the Soviet Union.
2. The opposite of dark
5. An _____ lens allows us to magnify an image.
6. Planet whose moons Galileo was able to see
7. Sir _____ Newton

**301**

# ANSWER KEY

## Live Via Satellite

"This program is brought to you live via satellite from halfway around the world." Satellites are very helpful in sending TV messages from the other side of the world. But this is only one of the special jobs that satellites can do.

Most satellites are placed into orbit around the Earth by riding on top of giant rockets. More recently some satellites have been carried into orbit by a space shuttle. While orbiting the Earth, the giant doors of the shuttle are opened, and the satellite is pushed into orbit.

This satellite relays TV signals from halfway around the world.

Satellites send information about many things. Use the code to find the different kinds of messages and information satellites send.

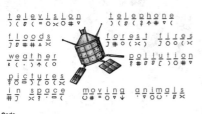

television   telephone
floods   forest fires
weather   pollution
pictures
in space   moving animals

**Code**

**302**

## Space Station Word Search

Below are hidden words that have something to do with a space station. Can you find them all? Use the Word Bank to help you, and circle the words as you find them.

**Word Bank**

| telerobotic | solar | battery |
| heat | modular | light |
| skylab | laboratory | |
| generator | astronauts | |

```
T E L E R O B O T I C   F
B S I K L J A P A N U R
O D G R D P U A C V N E
O V H E A T L S V U F E
M U T S H O K T I Y T D
T S K Y L A B R B T E O
G Q C R Q I A O N R L M
N E U O W U T N M A S D
C A N A D A T A Q R T S
A S A A E P Y W R E A T
S K R L R N R T E A T H
T R U S S A Y S T Y R M
R P T I E R T E R S S M
O N A U T S S O L A R L
K W M O D U L A R T J K
L B L A B O R A T O R Y
```

**304**

## Observatories

An observatory is a place with telescopes and other scientific instruments used for studying the sky. Most observatories are located far from cities and high up in the mountains. To get a clear view of the sky, it is important for telescopes to be far away from city lights with as dark and clear a sky as possible. Hundreds of years ago astronomers sat and looked through their telescopes to make their observations. Now most telescopes are used like giant cameras. Some observatories are used for special kinds of work. One of the telescopes at Kitt Peak National Observatory, near Tucson, Arizona, is designed only to study the Sun. The Lowell Observatory, near Flagstaff, Arizona, specializes in the study of the planets. There are observatories all over the world. There are some in Australia, South America and South Africa that are located in places with very good views of space.

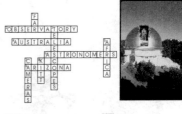

**ACROSS**
2. A place with telescopes and other scientific instruments
4. Kangaroos come from this nation.
6. Scientists who study the stars and outer space
9. Tucson is in this state

**DOWN**
1. The opposite of near
3. Instruments used to see objects in space
5. A continent
7. Observatory telescopes are used like giant____
8. ____ Peak is near Tucson.

**306**

## Space Friends

Look at the letters on the spaceships below. They spell out the word **space**. How many lines do you need to draw to connect each spaceship to all the other spaceships?

Try writing the letters **S, P, A, C,** and **E** on a sheet of paper to match the positions in the picture. Then draw lines to find the answer.

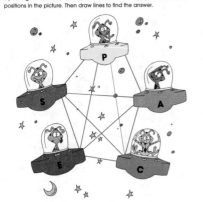

**309**

## Gorf's Word Game

Gorf is from a faraway planet. While traveling to Earth, he played a game to pass the time. He wrote the word **planet** on a piece of paper. Gorf erased the letter **e** from the word, and he was left with the word **plant**. Then he erased another letter, and he was left with a word again. Gorf kept erasing the letters one by one. Each time he was left with a word. Even the last letter that was left was a word! In what order did Gorf erase the letters? Use the area below Gorf's spaceship to work the problem out.

Two solutions are possible.
planet—plant—plan—pan—an—
planet—plant—pant—ant—an—

**311**

## Spaceship Search

Gus Galactic needs help in identifying these alien spaceships. Use the compass to write a ship's letter in each blank to solve these riddles.

1. I am **N** of Ship **H**.   I
2. I am **E** of Ship **Z**.   B
3. I am **SE** of Ship **Z**.   V
4. I am **S** of Ship **O**.   U
5. I am **NW** of Ship **Z**.   I

6. I am **SW** of Ship **B**.   V
7. I am **NE** of Ship **Z**.   T
8. I am **NE** of Ship **I**.   X
9. I am **SE** of Ship **U**.   H
10. I am **NW** of Ship **B**.   X or T

**Cosmic Challenge!**
Start at Ship **H**. Travel in the orbit given. Which ship will you dock with?

1. Go **NW** to Ship   U
2. Go **NE** to Ship   I
3. Go **NE** to Ship   X
4. Go **S** to Ship   Z

5. Go **SE** to Ship   V
6. Go **NE** to Ship   B
7. Go **NW** to Ship   X or T
This is your docking station. Congratulations!

**316**

### Googlies and Winkles

The Space Fantasy Theater invited aliens from all over the galaxy to the opening of a new movie. Some Googlies and Winkles waited in line to get into the movie theater. Googlies are creatures with two legs. Winkles are creatures with three legs. Read the clues below.

How many Googlies and Winkles waited in line?

Only Winkles and Googlies waited in line.

There were more Winkles than Googlies.

There were 18 legs in the line.

There are 4 Winkles and 3 Googlies waiting in line.

317

### Go, Team, Go!

Now look at the players. Draw a circle around the ones that are Zops. Draw a square around the ones that are Snarfs.

A    B    C    D

Each Zop has a matching number of antennae and legs.
Each Snarf has a different number of antennae and legs.
A and C are Zops; B and D are Snarfs.

319